PSYCHODRAMA WITH CHILDREN

In this book, Hanna Kende uses her wealth of experience to explain how psychodrama can allow psychotherapists to fundamentally change their relationships with children presenting with psychosocial, mental, or behavioral problems. Based on Kende's extensive and wide-ranging knowledge, *Psychodrama with Children* explores the origins and roots of psychodrama, and uses detailed case studies to show how psychodramatists can encourage groups of children to draw upon their natural creativity as a force for healing. The method draws on a rich theoretical base starting from the foundational work of Moreno and Adler.

The method is applicable to a wide range of children with varied symptoms (psychosomatic problems, distractibility, hyperactivity, inhibition, capable children performing poorly at school, etc.). By creating a warm climate of reciprocal tolerance and acceptance, psychodramatists allow children to express themselves freely in a group of their peers and to reshape their negative self-image. Psychodrama lets children use their natural language of play to mobilize their creative imagination, and to express their anxieties, conflicts and problems in a symbolic mode. This approach helps children heal through their own creativity.

Psychodrama with Children will be of interest to psychodramatists, dramatherapists and child psychotherapists, as well as psychologists, psychiatrists and other child and adolescent mental health professionals.

Hanna Kende is a clinical psychologist and Adlerian therapist. She is a Child Psychotherapy Lecturer (trained in specialized methodology) at the University of Budapest, and is Honorary President of the IAAP (Alfred Adler Institute of Paris) and MIPE (Hungarian Association of Individual Psychology). As a teacher and supervisor for the past thirty years, Kende has trained child psychodramatists in France, Italy, Hungary and a number of other Central European countries.

PSYCHODRAMA WITH CHILDREN

Healing Children Through Their Own Creativity

Hanna Kende

Routledge
Taylor & Francis Group
LONDON AND NEW YORK

First published 2017
by Routledge
2 Park Square, Milton Park, Abingdon, Oxon OX14 4RN

and by Routledge
605 Third Avenue, New York, NY 10017

Routledge is an imprint of the Taylor & Francis Group, an informa business

British Library Cataloguing in Publication Data
A catalogue record for this book is available from the British Library

Library of Congress Cataloging in Publication Data
Names: Kende, B. Hanna, author.
Title: Psychodrama with children: healing children through their own creativity/Hanna Kende.
Description: Milton Park, Abingdon, Oxon; New York, NY: Routledge, 2017. | Includes bibliographical references.
Identifiers: LCCN 2016025351| ISBN 9781138657663 (hbk) | ISBN 9781138657687 (pbk) | ISBN 9781315542935 (ebk)
Subjects: LCSH: Drama – Therapeutic use. | Child psychotherapy.
Classification: LCC RC489.P7 K46 2017 | DDC 616.89/1653 – dc23
LC record available at https://lccn.loc.gov/2016025351

ISBN: 978-1-138-65766-3 (hbk)
ISBN: 978-1-138-65768-7 (pbk)
ISBN: 978-1-315-54293-5 (ebk)

Typeset in Bembo and Stone Sans
by Florence Production Ltd, Stoodleigh, Devon, UK

Translated from the French by
Paul Hamburg
Assisted by Virginia Hamburg

Paul Hamburg was of great help to me because of the quality of his translation, his professionalism, and his valued collaboration. I consider him as the co-author of the English version of my book.

CONTENTS

PREFACE

It is a great honor for me to introduce Hanna Kende's book.

I first met Hanna in 2005, at the 23rd Congress of the IAIP in Turin.

Along with my colleagues from the A. Adler Institute of Turin, we were interested in meeting clinicians who worked as we did in the domain of childhood. We wanted to meet experts belonging to the Adlerian community and to learn about their methods of working with children and to exchange knowledge with them about the therapeutic methodology that we had developed and nurtured in Turin over the course of our many years of research and experience in this area.

At that time, there was no section in Child Psychotherapy Research in the organization of the International Association of Individual Psychology (IAIP), and we had not yet considered it possible to propose creating one, as happened later in Vilnius during the 24th Congress of the IAIP in 2008.

So this is how, among the participants at the 23rd Congress, we met Hanna Kende. From the outset, she drew our attention not only by her Lectio Magistralis, ("On the injustice against man from his compensation through culture") but because during the pre-Congress, several of our colleagues had become familiar with her method of psychodrama with children, this extraordinary treasure that was still hidden underground in the realm of Adlerian therapists working in the territories of childhood.

In Vilnius, besides discovering the guiding principle that we shared, the emotion generated by of our meeting Hanna went beyond our common passion for working with children; we were excited to discover her training method for psychologists wishing to lead such groups for children. This is how we came to discover the world of Adlerian psychodrama in the fullness of its complexity, its rich experience, its "good" therapists and its solid theoretical foundations. This was a world of a thousand colors and nuances, called upon for use in prevention as well as to treat children of different cultures and different ages, which made it possible for us to embrace them, to understand their secrets and to relieve the suffering entailed in the lives and histories of each of these children.

This was a fruitful encounter for us in Turin in a number of different ways. Completely consistent with the theory and methodology we had developed through our research and our experience in individual psychotherapy with children, we were now deeply enriched through a group dimension of particular interest because of its efficacy and its plasticity.

What was especially fascinating for us was the "discovery" of a theoretical approach in Adlerian methodology for the psychotherapy of children, articulated starting from the ideas of A. Adler, with valuable contributions from other relational psychoanalysts and specialists in developmental psychology, matured through time, practice in different countries and languages (especially Hungarian and French), which was entirely compatible with the analogous directions of research and practice that we had developed in Italy.

It was with this encounter that the opportunity took shape to create a section at the IAIP in research in child and adolescent psychotherapy. This section would now give "Cinderella" the chance[1] to attend the ball with her sisters, princes, kings, and queens, who had long been official protagonists in the scientific discourse at the heart of Adlerian thought around the world, and,[2] to make the first concrete steps in the direction of exchange and comparison between the Associations and our Adlerian colleagues from other nations.

And remarkably enough, the possibility came up in Turin for a training experience in psychodrama in Italy with Hanna Kende and Melinda Varga (Hungary), with the collaboration of Alessandra Zambelli (France). Thus began a trajectory that is still continuing today for a first group of psychotherapists and a second group assisted by the Turin psychotherapists who are in the process of being trained as trainers.

To read Hanna's book that I have the honor of introducing today gives one a taste of what "experiential" training in psychodrama according to Hanna Kende's method offers psychotherapists engaged in working with children. Considering the problems presented by our young patients and the specific challenges of working with them, we all know that it is essential for every psychotherapist and analyst to have undergone a personal analysis, but this is not all. An "experiential" pathway of training, focused on sensorimotor and symbolic play and on non-verbal relationships, enables us to explore aspects of pre-verbal communication, the "implicit memory" that is so fundamental for relating to children, and places us in touch with the personal functional register stemming from the realm of the physical body that is the repository of the earliest relational experiences.

To work with Hanna is to become immersed in a dimension of symbolic play, of self-narration in this register, and to become passionate about the infinite creativity in every individual, about the multiplicity of narratives, the recognition of self with the other, and it means reactivating a capacity for attention and listening that passes through personal, physical and emotional involvement and refines one's understanding of children's fundamental ways of being at different ages, lets us recover an experimental language and modality that we lived, loved and desired, recaptured from those times when we were children ourselves.

"I am passionate about play, says Hanna, but also about *understanding* play."

Immersing oneself in play and investigating its meaning, tolerating the anxiety of not knowing everything right away, entering into the "magical" realm and negotiating the relational space as a "transitional space" between reality and imagination, encountering emotions in the intensity and urgency of expression that must not overwhelm us, giving form to listening to oneself and the other in the possibility of shared communication permitting a new understanding of oneself and of relationships that does not neglect theory and the rational register, but relies above all on the capacity to "put oneself in the place of the child" and to back him up in the search for "good solutions" that will help him face his difficulties in growing up.

The possibility of "living" the group as a relational dimension implies discovering resources for verbal and non-verbal communication, emotional sharing and the complex interplay of transference and countertransference as amplified by the group, while at the same time, lends simplicity by staging one's own story and the story of the other. Along with these elements comes the pleasure of experiencing a "social sense" that emerges from the depths of a self-narrative that is shared and acknowledged, and mastery of how to recognize the other and offer him listening and aid, an indispensable skill when caring for children. One can experience together the pleasure of dialogue, of reciprocal comprehension and solidarity at its most deeply authentic level.

To work with Hanna is to learn the importance of the dimension of "being present" in body, emotion, and mind, to be with and for the child, in an understanding of our work that is open to profound listening and an essential faith in the resources that each of us possesses to confront the difficulties of life. For Hanna and for all of us, it is important that the troubled child encounter a therapist who is able to stay in touch with herself and with the other, to be passionate about the relationship and in the relationship, and committed to give voice form, and sense to what happens inside and outside us at every moment. We can become therapists capable of maintaining our presence within and outside the play, in the internal and external world of the child, trained to hear and to reflect, to speak and to live the imaginative language of the child, to allow ourselves to be involved and included, to hear the ensemble and the soloist in the way of a "good orchestral conductor," to accompany the child and allow him not only to express himself but also to develop, to understand, and to change.

In Hanna's book, I find the essence of this way of staying with children and with adults, her indefatigable desire to listen and to understand, her ineffable curiosity, her attention that is never superficial or faded, her capacity to involve everyone in keeping with his individuality, to be present for and with the others. I find in her book echoes of her clinical experience with children, her theoretical sources, and her intuitive capacity. I find an extraordinary concordance with current orientations in psychodynamic psychotherapy (starting from the insights of new neuroscientific discoveries and of developmental psychology), which emphasize relationship as the primary agent of change, in the specificity of its implicit emotional and physiological components. In a series of passages between the clinical realm and the realm of theory and methodology, Hanna introduces us to the complexity of psychodrama, allowing us to appreciate the richness and the possibilities of this powerful therapeutic instrument.

This text is so valuable for us. It is truly a precious gift, just like the gifts that Hanna is so brilliant at giving at those times when, in her role of the wise sorcerer in the magic shop, during only a brief moment of encountering an individual, she finds a way to collect desires, fear, developmental possibilities and concretize them in the form of a small object, a gift that is full of meaning, hope and the courage to live.

What is so valuable for the Adlerian scientific community is not only a biannual testimony to clinical experience, but also this methodology through which children of different ages from different cultures can recognize themselves as "good enough" to let them to grow and to overcome their suffering, a methodology so consistent with current perspectives in the psychodynamic domain.

Thank you Hanna!

Anna Maria Bastianini
Training Analyst in the Italian Society for Individual Psychology
President of the Section Child and Youth Clinic of the IAIP
(International Association for Individual Psychology)
Secretary of the Scola Adleriana di Psicoterapia di Torino (Italia)

Notes

1 This is how our colleague Bruno Vidotto characterized child psychotherapy in his 1998 Communication at the 7°Congresso SIPI de Turin, "Psychotherapy's inferiority complex."

2 The Section on Research in Child Psychotherapy was officially constituted on the occasion of the 25th IAIP Congress in Vienna in 2012.

1

IMPRESSIONISTIC INTRODUCTION

A recollection in three voices

At a distance of thirty years, we will call up a common melody. The first soloist is a former co-therapist, my partner in psychodrama, Claude Lepineux; the second is a young participant in those long-ago workshops, a girl who decided to call herself Shanti. The third soloist, as you must have surely guessed already, is none other than myself.

Together, the three of us have tried to evoke the memory of the Psychodrama Workshop that functioned for two decades as part of a Consultancy for the French Ministry of Justice, welcoming children from 7 to 12 years of age who were considered "at risk" because of their seriously underprivileged circumstances and who, in addition to their disadvantaged social milieu, presented with major individual psychological problems. Characterized by distrust, lack of self-confidence, and difficulties in connection, these children, as will be evident in Shanti's narrative, had no self-esteem, devalued themselves, and at times even suffered from self-destructive tendencies.

Over time, we developed the working methods of this workshop, in the light of our studies, our readings, our analytic and psychodramatic training, but above all based on our common experience of what the children gave us the opportunity to learn.

To the best of our ability, we listened to each child's secret melodies, and this made it possible for them to listen to them in each other. We gave them our attention and tried to resonate in unison with them in order to overcome their inhibitions and liberate themselves from their internal imprisonment, from their false selves, from their lack of identity.

To be able to hear both the melody of the ensemble and the magnificent voice of each soloist, the group therapist or facilitator of the psychodrama needed to have a kind of perfect pitch. This is how Shanti spoke about her participation some twenty years later:

> I, too, discovered to my surprise that young children had something to say, that they possessed an inner world.

So let us first hear from my psychodramatist colleague, Claude.

Claude

I would like to touch upon two different aspects of the workshop: that of ritual and that of individualization. The workshop is a ritualized space, and children's psychodrama is a particular space where rituals that have been developed over years take on a structuring quality for the group, for each child, and also for the therapists. Let us begin with the role of ritual.

Role of the ritual: alienating or liberating

It is hard to provide an unequivocal response to this question. Ritual may have a double aspect. It can alienate the individual or the group:

> Ritual is alienating if the rules do not carry intrinsic meaning, if they have lost their original signification. By contrast, in our workshop rituals had a triple meaning – they were carriers of signification, of questioning, and, ultimately they were called upon to resolve personal problems; they took on a globally liberating role.

I would not dare to claim that this liberation takes place every time, allowing us to surmount a painful or anxiety-ridden past, but such liberation certainly constitutes the preamble to our lived experiences, our freedom, and our subsequent development. The road taken, the evolution of an individual, is never entirely graspable . . . But what I do affirm as a guiding principle of the workshop – based on my internal conviction – can be summarized in a single sentence: What is important is not what has happened to us but the way that we succeed in making use of it.

From this perspective, the habits and rituals of the workshop were at once useful and encouraging, unlike obsessional rituals or the alienating rites of certain sects. When the ritual constitutes an end unto itself, it loses meaning and leads to depersonalization and alienation. In the potential space that constituted our workshop, rituals retained their meaning. It was in the spirit of Jean Cocteau's quotation, that we made use of different rituals:

a the welcoming ritual of drawing together around a table. This created an intermediate space for each of us between the everyday world and the psychodrama. These generally calm and collected moments facilitated the emergence of feelings and emotions.

b the ritual of conversation through the intermediary layer of the drawing. Beyond their creative accomplishment, children's creations had a double function, to calm their anxieties, fears, and aggression, while at the same time mobilizing their internal energies. I want to emphasize this, because I believe that anyone who limits himself to emphasizing difficulties and problems is not a good therapist.

c the ritual of elaborating the story. The group sits in a circle. The rule: don't repeat a story you saw on television, or that you know or have heard. Every child chooses his/her own role, the child who suggested the story selects first.

d the ritual of beginning the psychodramatic play. Three knocks signify the group's entry into the imaginary world and also its departure from that world. At the end of the play, each actor reaffirms his/her own identity and is applauded.

e the communal ritual of eating lunch together. The communal meal signifies the replenishment and fortification of each individual and concludes the morning (we might term this the chicken-French fries ritual).

The functions of the rituals listed above:

- they provide orientation in space and time;
- they allow for the modest and discreet expression of anxieties, fears, suffering and pleasure;
- they mobilize internal forces (the unconscious is not an exclusively chaotic or malicious domain, but is also rich in resources);
- they boost self confidence, encourage respect for others, facilitate listening to each other, and strengthen healthy narcissism or the sense of self worth.

The idea of the child recognized as carrying values and whose word inspires respect is a deep and essential one for these children in the throes of multiple difficulties.

Mimetic violence and individuation

I would also like to analyze the functioning of the workshop from an entirely different point of view, based on the conceptualization of René Girard, a psychologist who was considered to be a dissident and marginalized by Parisian psychoanalysts, and is now a University Professor at Stanford. In his interpretation, desire has a mimetic origin. He challenges the formula according to which the desire of a subject has to do with a given object. Human beings are capable of desiring anything whatsoever. Desire is, by nature, mimetic, that is, it is addressed to the object of its rival, in other words, the desire of its enemy. It is the mimetic origin of desire (I want what the other wishes to possess) that would explain the origin of violence.

According to René Girard, "to act positively, one has to reflect negatively" (René Girard, 1972, p. 82). Seen from the side of the individual or society, it is not difference that sets off conflict, sometimes followed by violence, but lack of differentiation. The less differentiated we are the more we share the same desire – like twins. And the subjects of twin desire oppose each other in all things because nothing distinguishes them. Why am I speaking of this twin violence? Because the children in the workshop are often the victims of real or symbolic violence and in this symbolic or potential space that we have been able to provide them, they have succeeded, or at least I hope they have, in going beyond the undifferentiated state of personal and familial confusion to become differentiated, individuated, so that they are able to separate off their personality from the fused familial entity.

To summarize:

> The basic unstated idea of the workshop is that every child is capable of solving his/her problems by virtue of his/her own sources of energy. Each person's individual task consists of creating and perfecting herself starting from her own history while battling against numerous difficulties that she will have to confront.

The workshop and the psychotherapists play the role of catalysts in promoting the differentiation of the children and the recreation of their self.

Shanti

> "Is Shanti your assumed name?"

A Brahmin told me one day that this is the name of my soul. For me, the Workshop was an area of freedom.

What appealed to me right away at the workshop is that you could create stories there without constraints, which you made up together (or alone). It was fun to listen to the others tell about the plays that we would go on to stage afterward, because I found it validating to play out stories that people had invented themselves. For myself, I learned to express myself more freely, for I can recall that at the beginning it was impossible for me to take the floor or to speak in my own name. I always had to ask for permission in order to know that what I was about to say made sense. In this way, you learned to listen to yourself and to the others.

I also discovered that we carry inside ourselves an imaginary world that we can let surge forth, thanks to speech. Playing made me aware that you can be creative and inventive.

In this workshop, I discovered attentive adults who were curious to learn what the children thought. They tried to understand them, but without asking them questions. In fact, because of my problems at school, they had recommended to my mother that a psychologist follow me. She was charming enough, but it was a real nightmare, because she absolutely wanted me to talk about my problems. After every session, I told her I didn't want to come back. She always insisted.

Then, after a year, I stopped. But since I had failed at school for a second time, I had to go back to the psychologist.

At the workshop I had the sense of being surrounded by people who only wanted to help us and wanted what was best for us. They respected us as individuals (they never asked us questions about our private, personal lives). They were there to listen to us and not to judge us, casting a different light on the children that we were, recognizing our intellectual and artistic qualities, even though we were all failing in school. Moreover, the sense of being recognized by intelligent adults who appreciated me and accepted me allowed me to reconcile myself with the social group, with humanity.

Even if I'm unable to explain today what happened, I know that this experience was fundamental to my self-realization. I was able to regain confidence in myself there and to blossom intellectually. I left the workshop with the certainty that I was a creative and imaginative individual.

In addition, the later choices I have made emerged from this experience. Thus, I spent time at Rudolf Steiner institutions because I wanted to have contact with children who are different, whom I could help in turn.

Shanti is currently working for the French educational system. She runs special classes, providing help for illiterate immigrant children of different ages to prepare them to attend "normal" classes.

H.K.

As the third voice, I will attest to what has already been evoked above, that these children who had failed at school, were poorly accepted in their families, and had no confidence in themselves, did not know the extent to which they were gifted. They suffered from a major sense of inferiority and even considered themselves, as Shanti expressed it, to be worthless.

The principal changes that took place in the workshop.

Resilience

In her own concise style, Shanti already told us that the experience she had at the workshop changed her self image and her sense of self worth. She discovered the richness of her psychological potentialities. There, she discovered qualities in herself that she had not even suspected. And she was not the only one . . .

The characteristics of Shanti's journey are as follows:

a Artistic blossoming. It isn't only at the workshop that her acting talents were manifested. Invited by a friend whose father was a theater director, Shanti joined the Bob Wilson troupe for a couple of weeks. The troupe was in the middle of a tour across France, but Shanti ended up rejecting the offer of a long tour for fear of jeopardizing her school grades and failing her baccalaureate examinations.

b Her intellectual capacities became unblocked. The poor student about whom we spoke, who had to repeat two primary grades, was admitted after her baccalaureate to a *hypokhâgne* level preparatory program for advanced studies. After completing her studies to become a literature professor (French, Japanese), she decided to teach special classes in the French national education system in order to help children of immigrants of various backgrounds and ages.

Taking her inspiration largely from her experiences at the workshop, she has developed a method for working with children who are behind in school or virtually illiterate, in which she takes into consideration each child's individual circumstances – country and environment of origin – and potential, his or her intellectual and imaginative capacities. She offers teaching that is individualized and adapted to the needs of each child. She has the deep conviction that all children have the desire to learn and that it is the teacher's responsibility to guide them along the path to knowledge and freedom.

Social sense or group solidarity

Social sense develops by way of the capacity to identify with others and share with them. In the group, children were able to share their socio-affective problems and discover the values of the other children. They were attentive to each other and shared their emotions. To come back to Shanti as the main character in this introduction (you will encounter many other cases in the course of this book), her relationship to the other children was one of acceptance, mutual assistance, and support (for example, see Bruno, Chapter 6). Over the years, she took on a special place. When she returned to the group as a lycée student, she was regarded as an assistant facilitator.

Claude mentioned the problem of aggression in the workshop. Shanti experienced the group as being non-aggressive. Her perception of the group as non-aggressive corresponds to her own capacity to fend off and appease conflicts and to cheerfully overcome tensions.

Basic trust, the primordial we (Ur-Wir)

According to Adler, the sense of unconditional trust originates in the primary dyadic relationship. For Shanti, the workshop (the positive regard of intelligent adults) was called upon to compensate for the original injury of an inadequate maternal relationship. In his writings, the psychoanalyst Michael Balint expressed the hope that psychoanalysis could overcome such deficits through a corrective relationship, but in the workshop, the correction was a common task shared by the psychodramatists and the group. (For development of this topic, see later).

I have wondered if Shanti experienced our relationship as a maternal transference, but she did not share this opinion. But then, she recalled a scene when she struck me in the head with a plate of fries, fortunately already empty. Why, I asked her? I was angry at my mother, she responded.

The social dimension

As Shanti puts it, the experience of the workshop made it possible to overcome her feeling of existential marginality:

> The sense of being recognized by intelligent adults who appreciated me and accepted me allowed me to reconcile myself with the social group, with humanity.

What's more, Shanti tried to give back what she had received to others, to those more indigent than herself. When she began her journey, she cared for the blind, the elderly, and the mentally handicapped. Wanting to work with autistic children, Shanti discovered the Rudolf Steiner communities abroad.

To paraphrase André Green, we could affirm with Shanti: psychodrama is an exploration where "the self takes off in search of itself" (André Green, 2011, p. 87).

2

JACOB MORENO, THE GOD SYNDROME, AND CHILDREN'S PSYCHODRAMA

Moreno's family myth: the legend of his birth

According to his own telling, Jacob Lévy Moreno was born on May 21, 1892 on a boat of unknown nationality crossing the Black Sea in the direction of Constanza.

> The ship left from Spain, crossed the Mediterranean, and reached the Black Sea via Turkey. It set its course toward Constanza. All of a sudden, it was caught in the middle of a storm. The storm was unbelievable. My mother delivered me under difficult circumstances before the boat reached the port of Constanza in Romania. It is for this reason that I am in some sense, by virtue of fortunate happenstance, stateless. The birth took place on the eve of the Sabbath, just before the first prayer. With me, a new day began. Anonymously. In the storm.

Laxenaire calls this description of Moreno's origins, which "gives a good idea of the difference between the facts the way they actually happened and the way they are reconstructed in psychodramatic fashion" a psychodramatic birth (Laxenaire, 1986, p. 21).

Moreno elaborated and projected into the past a kind of family romance, a miraculous birth. In this legend, Moreno forged an image for himself of someone who came from nowhere having a mission on the scale of humanity. A birth on a stormy night on a mysterious boat of unknown provenance – this predicts an exceptional destiny.

However, Moreno's birth certificate indicates that he was born on May 16, 1889 in Bucharest, at the home of his parents. His mother, Pauline Iencu, was 18 years old and his father, Moreno Nissim was 32. Moreno Nissim Levy, the father, was in the retail trade. Later, his son used his father's first name as his family name. His parents divorced in 1906.

For some of his biographers, this myth of origin recalls to some extent the history of the Spanish Maranos who were persecuted and expelled on account of their religion. By evoking a boat navigating from Spain toward the eastern coasts of the Mediterranean Sea, he tacitly refers to the journeys made by Sephardic Jews 400 years before his birth in 1892. This event still resonated in the traditions of the Jewish community living in Romania.

> Other students of Moreno's life evoke the discovery of America by Christopher Columbus as another antecedent. This reference to the great explorer may have been part of Moreno's motivation when he settled in the United States.
>
> (*Anzieu, 1994, p. 22*)

Little Moreno in the role of God

> It would appear that the only thing Moreno held onto from his childhood and adolescence spent in Vienna, was the need that to play the part of God, something that continued to haunt him. Through this autobiographical view – no doubt retrospective and idealized – Moreno wants to suggest that from that time on he never stopped playing the character of the Creator.
>
> (*Ibid.*)

Moreno discovered psychodrama when he was very young, from a game that is interesting to mention. It shows us his motivations, his sense of a mission that went on to determine his whole life, and his resistance to reality. He tells the story with a kind of self-irony.

> The unforgettable Event goes back to the age of three and a half. Little Jacob Moreno Levy was playing "God and the angels" with the neighborhood children. The event took place in his parents' house in Vienna. In the basement, on a table, the very excited children constructed an edifice made of chairs and cushions that almost touched the ceiling. At the very top there was God's seat, onto which little Moreno had raised himself and from where, in his entire divine splendor, he was directing the angels. The children who were playing the angels were fluttering all around him. One of them suddenly asked the question: And you, since you are the good Lord, why don't you fly? Moreno accepted the suggestion, stretched out his arms . . . and a few seconds later, he was lying on the floor with a broken wrist. This first "psychodrama" left a deep impression, and it was this event that underlay his future work with children's psychodrama.
>
> (*Ibid.*)

It led later to him proposing:

a that there is a certain warm-up period required before the capacity for role playing emerges;
b that every actor, superior beings included, depends on others;
c that the illusion of identification with the character that you are playing can be shattered to pieces by the test of reality. (One has to assume that the idea of a scene situated on several superimposed levels can also be traced back to this experience.)

For our purposes, this first psychodrama affects us just as much by virtue of the fact that the dramatic play described here expresses the primordial desire to compensate for the child's sense of inferiority through the illusion of omnipotence: Moreover, in this "primal scene" we can also locate the principal characteristics of children's psychodrama:

1 Spontaneous improvisation.
2 Overcoming the sense of inferiority (God stands above all subservience to everyday life).
3 The symbolic staging of one's desires.
4 As indicated by the position that Moreno assigns himself in the group – "I am God, and you can be the angels" – an infantile, ludic if excessive expression of the will to power.
5 The inevitable and painful intrusion of corrective reality upon the fantasies.
6 In an implicit way, it signals what the child's imagination has not yet acquired, that it is dangerous to confuse play with reality – the importance of "acting as if."

Awakening the child's imagination is the backdrop for all of Moreno's work. Wildlöcher interprets it as the mobilization of the child's affective world: "Isn't it the role of God that is the ultimate goal of the child's inventive desire? All of the child's imaginary activity consists of recreating the world through the illusion of his omnipotence" (Widlöcher, 1979, p. 13).

Moreno with the children in the land of the King

Later, Moreno played God with children in the public places of Vienna. This was an important choice, as it invoked the All-powerful and the extremely large to compensate for all the feelings of being little, of inferiority.

This second series of games inspired by children's play still dates from before the First World War. As a young medical student, Moreno enjoyed walking through the city parks and making up stories for children. This state of mind was even the inspiration for poetry – he published two volumes of poems under a pseudonym. In them, he contrasts the mercantile spirit of the age to his own style of life.

> My real beginnings date to 1910. In the gardens of Vienna, I started between 1910 and 1914 to form groups of children and to improvise with them, and in this way, to sow the seeds for group psychotherapy and germinate psychodrama.
>
> (*Moreno, 1956, p. 13*)

A gradually enlarging group of children would flock at the appointed hour under the oak tree in whose crown Moreno would be perched. From the hundred-year-old tree, you couldn't hear anything at first except Moreno's voice, but then he would climb down a little lower (still some twenty feet up) and finally, he would reveal himself. At the outset, the children would change names. In the stories they enacted about kings and queens, the great and the small would switch roles, the adults became children and the children became adults. The children took charge of educating their parents and told them what to eat, and how much time they were allowed to speak and when to go to bed.

The children could even invent imaginary parents for themselves, which would sometimes lead to conflict.

The children would turn the stories they told into plays, completing them and transforming them. Moreno played with them. These games were childish and evoked magical kingdoms. In their games, the children made choices and conquests; they prohibited, obeyed, and revolted. Marvelous and miraculous transformations took place; people turned into animals, devils into angels, poor people became rich, children turned into Gods. Moreno took pleasure in the children's plays, and felt free. It was during this period that he wrote *The Novel of the King (Königsroman)*, which takes place in the Kingdom of the children. The *Novel of the King* was published anonymously in 1923.

So these plays took place in the kingdom of the children. In his collection of expressionist poems, *The Testament of the Father (Das Testament des Vaters)*, Moreno underscored some important characteristics of children's play – the need to be all-powerful and to feel that they were the creators of the world. He published this volume anonymously, but in the English edition, he signed his own name.

Moreno's self healing

The psychoanalyst-psychodramatist Michel Laxenaire, President of the French Group Psychotherapy and Psychodrama Institute has published numerous articles, studies, and dissertations about Moreno, presenting an original and spiritual portrait in which the founder of psychodrama is presented, or rather analyzed, with irony and perspicacity. He shows how Moreno succeeded in placing his human and psychological problems in the service of developing a magnificent theory and practice.

> Psychodrama emerged from the sublimation of pathogenic temptations, which, under other circumstances, could have led to failures or psychiatric disturbances. Moreno was the first of his own patients that he treated and cured.
>
> (*Laxenaire, 1986*)

The first words of Moreno's *Testament of the Father*:

> I AM GOD
> THE FATHER
> THE CREATOR OF THE UNIVERSE

With a certain degree of irony, Moreno summarizes the meaning of his poems:

> I wanted to present a man who has all the signs of megalomania, exhibitionism and social maladaptation but who nevertheless behaves in a disciplined and normal way and reveals himself as being much more creative if he expresses all of his symptoms through play, rather than if he tried hard to repress them and resolve them . . . there is no other way to cure the God syndrome than to immerse oneself totally in play.
>
> (*Moreno, 1953, quoted by Anzieu, 1994, p. 24*)

Omnipotence

We have already alluded, apropos the role of God that Moreno played in early childhood and in his literary attempts, to the power of his identification with God. Later, seeking out and accepting the divine role was part of the driving force behind his work.

Concerning divine identification, Adler says:

> This tendency is sometimes manifested overtly and sometimes in a transposed way as the desire to understand everything or know everything, or the aspiration to eternal life, whether by the transmigration of the soul or in the hereafter, all of this in relation to the wish for identification with the divine.
>
> (*Adler, 1978, p. 163*)

The megalomaniacal tendency remains a controversial question to this day. Some respected authors maintain that the desire for omnipotence represents an obstacle to a child's development and that the task of psychotherapy would be precisely to help the child overcome his desire for greatness. They argue that this would be the necessary precondition for recognizing reality, power relationships, and one's own limits.

"Infantile megalomania is a part of (an) a phase of child development. In the adult, megalomania is considered as an element of psychotic pathology." (We will return to this question as part of the analysis of the imaginary world.)

For the moment, we will limit ourselves to pointing out that the personal example of Moreno and the beginnings of his psychodramatic activity offer a preview of the not-insignificant role of omnipotence (or according to his own formulation, the God syndrome), the creation of the world, in the therapeutic arsenal of psychodrama. With regard to Moreno, he explicitly assigned himself the job of creating the world: "The historical context led us from the outset to undertake the recreation of the world from its beginnings" (Moreno, 1943: 1987, p. 9).

Adler holds that working to improve the world constitutes an appealing and inspiring motivation (Adler, 1973, p. 191). Indeed, in relation to Moreno, Laxenaire points out that even while being megalomaniacal, he considered his vocation to be working for the good of all humanity, a vocation of quasi-Christian intensity, which allowed him to get beyond his megalomania.

Exhibitionism

Moreno fulfilled his exhibitionistic tendencies and his comedic talents in psychodrama, both as actor and director. In a dramatic play of improvisational theater (*Stegreiftheater – impromptu theater*), whose motto is: "Let us dare to become what we are," each person, in fact, has the right to spontaneously realize himself while performing.

From marginality to the development of a social sense

"Moreno," says Laxenaire, "changed his characterological shortcomings. He could have become a marginal person, but he invented a scientific method, sociometry, for evaluating an individual's degree of socialization." Moreno developed a body of scientific work that includes certain concepts that are original ideas, such as spontaneity and the catharsis of action. Laxenaire considers the combination of theater and psychotherapy to be one of the most innovative new elements that Moreno handed down to therapists. With respect to Moreno's death, he recalls the last hours of Socrates: he was able to drink the hemlock, not as a condemned person but at his own initiative, choosing death. As his final hour neared he accepted death, refusing further therapeutic intervention. He played his role with tranquillity and serenity in the play that proved to be his final psychodrama (Laxenaire, 1986).

Moreno's nostalgia for children's psychodrama

Thus, the origin of Morenian psychodrama goes back to the period when Moreno played with children. Paul Pörtner (1978) suggests that Moreno's choice of method should be seen in the context of a new historical period, that of the rediscovery of the child.

We might add that Moreno always considered spontaneity and creativity as intrinsic properties of childhood that recede as we become adults; his principal therapeutic intervention was the reanimation of spontaneity and creativity. In the Morenian conception of man, the attitude of the child is exemplary. The father of psychodrama emphasized the contrast between the flexibility and openness of the infantile psyche and the rigidity and tendency for schematization of the adult. Children's psychodrama was an element of Moreno's nostalgia for childhood.

Thus, Moreno considered that it was one of the most important aims of psychodrama to reanimate, remobilize, and renew the aptitudes that are characteristic of children: their spontaneity, their faculty of improvisation, their dramatic aptitude, their role-playing, their capacity for adapting to each other, and the wealth of their imagination.

> The child is endowed with a creative spontaneity; he is the child of the first universe . . .
>
> (*Moreno, 1953, p. 17*)

Moreno's theatrical experiments as well as his psychodrama work with adults were greatly influenced by the improvisational games that he conducted with children. These games provided the substantive foundation for all of his work. We can find this nostalgia for the experiences of childhood in a wide range of creative individuals. Matisse defined the artist as "the one who observes with the eyes of a child."

Moreno eventually left the practice of children's psychodrama, but despite this, the domain of childhood did not disappear from his thoughts or his nostalgias. He often referred to it, emphasizing his wish to stimulate adults so that they could recover the spontaneity, improvisational capacity, originality, and creativity of children.

The paradox of Moreno

Aichinger has already noted (with surprise) the fact that Moreno, despite his early and intense work with groups of children, elaborated his method of psychodrama only for adults (Aichinger & Holl, 1997).

Yet Moreno, despite drawing his ideal from the spontaneity and creativity of children, constructed his methods principally through a dramatic elaboration of familial and social conflicts. Although it is certainly nuanced, this method does not permit the bursting forth of the exceptionally diverse, poetic, and unique originality of the child's imagination. Some psychodramatists, including Anzieu and Mérei and his school in Hungary, as well as others, have sensed the need to integrate the imaginary dimension into their work with adult groups.

3

MODIFICATION OF MORENIAN TECHNIQUE IN ADLERIAN PSYCHODRAMA WITH CHILDREN

(In this chapter, we will confine ourselves to citing those elements in the history of psychodrama that seem useful to us for the elaboration of our Adlerian psychodrama with children. We utilized, among others, certain elements to which Moreno referred, but which he subsequently abandoned, as he no longer practiced psychodrama with children.)

The history of children's psychodrama in France

Analysts have often asked why it was that French psychoanalysts were the first to adapt Moreno's psychodrama to groups of children. The psychoanalyst-psychodramatist M. D. Matisson concluded, "The introduction and evolution of psychodrama in France followed a singular path (this is the only country where psychoanalysis had considerable influence on psychodrama)." The parallel and intersecting history of the techniques of psychodrama and psychoanalysis provide a sense of this process:

- non-psychoanalytic methods that use Moreno's psychodrama with certain modifications;
- psychoanalytic methods of psychodrama that retained from Morenian psychodrama only the notions of the group and of dramatic improvisation.

Two other child psychoanalyst-psychodramatists raised the same question in 1995: "We should define what attracted psychoanalysts to psychodrama, even though Morenian psychodrama had distanced itself from psychoanalysis, had replaced words with action, even going so far as to suggest that human action was a revolt against verbalization."

In fact, Moreno made a comment to Freud, whom he met at the University of Vienna in 1912 that has often been cited.

> Very well, Doctor Freud, I am starting out from where you end up. You encounter others in the artificial world of your office, and I encounter them on the street or in their homes, in their familiar milieu. You analyze their dreams, and I try to breathe into them the courage to keep dreaming. I teach people how to play God.
>
> (*Widlöcher, 1979, pp. 21–22*)

> At the theoretical level, there isn't a single psychoanalytic thesis that Moreno didn't take pains to contradict: lying on the couch, transference, the interpretation of dreams, the dynamics of the unconscious, he refutes them all, one step further, he deliberately sets himself against them.
>
> (*Widlöcher, 1979, p. 22*)

Widlöcher, himself a child psychoanalyst and psychodramatist, finds it surprising that the introduction of psychodrama in France was principally due to the efforts of child psychoanalysts.

The first attempts were launched in France by Doctor Fouquet and Mireille Monod at the Centre psychopédagogique de l'académie de Paris (Psychoeducational Center of the Paris Academy) after they returned from the United States, where they had attended sessions of the Moreno Therapeutic Theater in Beacon New York in 1945–46. Mireille Monod described her method in two articles published in 1947:

> We would meet once weekly in a classroom where we used as a stage the little podium located in front of the blackboard . . . The groups were mixed and we were able to maintain an approximate balance in the numbers of girls and boys.

She regarded the optimum number of participants as four to five children. "If you go beyond half a dozen, one or two of the participants will lose the benefit of the session."

In their practice, these pioneers considered the critical moment to be the beginning of the session.

> Each of the children is called upon to say what has happened during the past week, what he/she has found interesting or remarkable and what he/she would like to play. The children have an easy time telling the stories of what they have lived and commenting on their comrades' narratives. . . . The ensemble of the narratives appears highly varied and totally lacks unity. During the first sessions, we would help the children to compose a unique topic starting out from the different events that each of them brought to the session.

> Since April, the children have taken the initiative themselves to create a topic, adding on events one after the other to generate a story in which each child would choose the roles that they had initially assigned themselves . . . After the elaboration of the topic, we take the children into a corner of the room, and give them five minutes to distribute the roles and to choose as they wish the adults that they will need.
>
> (*Monod, 1947, pp. 51–53*)

Citing this text, Anzieu summarizes the ways that the first French psychoanalyst-psychodramatists modified the original technique as follows:

a The sessions are led by two psychodramatists, a man and a woman, and the number of secondary characters is limited to one.
b An increasing measure of freedom is left to the children in inventing the scenario and moving away from the events of their real lives.
c They have found that taking notes is incompatible with the game and therefore have concluded that the best way to understand the game is to take part in the action (one of Moreno's key principles).

(*Anzieu, 1979, p. 91*)

The principal innovations introduced in the groups led by Diakkine, Lebovici and Kestemberg on the neuropsychiatry service:

a Given the absence of an audience, the stage, considered useless, is eliminated, and the room becomes the play space.
b Within this space, nobody can stay outside the drama, and the adult in charge of the play is integrated into the action on the same terms as the secondary characters.
c Once the play begins, participants are not allowed to leave for the duration of the session.
d Interpretations rarely occur. "It's not about explaining to the child why he/she behaves in such a way, it's about allowing him/her to relive the different situations that created the conflict."

(*E. Kestemberg, 1949, as quoted by Anzieu, 1979, p. 91*)

At an early point, Lebovici became convinced that children older than ten find their best means of expression through psychodrama and that the best indications for collective psychotherapy are situations of abandonment and highly emotional states with inhibition; tics, stammering, enuresis, minor antisocial reactions, and debility also constitute positive indications; contraindications are major inhibitions, perverse or sadistic behaviors, and severe instability.

Early on, these pioneer psychodramatist-psychoanalysts translated the principle of *say everything* from the psychoanalytic method to permission to *do everything* in the psychodrama group. Free expression turned into free aggression in the group.

Slavson felt that he had to change the method, as the children were hurting themselves, destroying objects, and breaking everything, without any of this having the slightest therapeutic effect (Moreau-Dreyfus and Lebovici, 1947, pp. 18–21). Child psychodramatists then introduced the principle of *pretend*. We will cite several aspects of their method as it was described in 1947 by J. Moreau and S. Lebovici:

> By chance – a chance that we then perpetuated – we happened to combine two analysts, a man and a woman, for leading collective therapy. We soon realized that for the four to six children in the group, we were substitutes for a father and mother . . . By accepting the children as they were and showing them unconditional regard, the psychotherapists create the ideal family milieu. Collective psychotherapy becomes reeducation through a change of milieu. Moreover, the play is the "symbolic transposition of the child's real situation."
>
> (*Moreau-Dreyfus and Lebovici, 1947, pp. 18–21*)

> It appears to be similar to a collective fiction, in the shelter of which each child exposes his/her own situation in a symbolic world comprised of all the participants and which clearly requires no explication. As a consequence, the essential tool of psychoanalysis, interpretation, cannot be used in the group.
>
> (*Dreyfus-Moreau, 1955, p. 253*)

To avoid deviating dangerously from classical psychoanalysis, the principal concern, as formulated by Serge Lebovici and his collaborators was to "conform collective psychotherapy to individual psychoanalysis."

Transference plays an important part in their method and principally concerns the two dramatists, one of whom represents the positive pole, while the other is charged with negative sentiments. They regarded children's aggressive behavior among themselves as derivative, as a transposition of angry feelings they had toward the adults. Glossing over the dynamics of the group, they reduced it to multiple parallel individual transferences. They thereby neglected, as Anzieu emphasizes, the therapeutic specificity of dramatic play – its group dimension, its power of symbolic communication, its cathartic effect.

The question of transference grew in importance, beginning in the 1960s. It has continued to divide psychotherapists ever since. In the psychoanalytic psychodrama of the 1980s, the same tendencies were still evident, namely a tendency to use concepts from individual psychoanalysis to interpret the meaning hidden in the scenes imagined by the children and played out during the psychodrama sessions. (We will return later to the question of transference).

In analytic psychodrama for children, the end of the last century saw a return to the theoretical approach of the Lebovici-Diatkine school, namely applying the rules of individual psychoanalysis to children's psychodrama. In March 1999 the author of this book attended a conference held at the facilities of the Sainte-Anne Hospital in Paris where the principal topic was counter-transference. The question of the role of the group was completely neglected – as was the question of creativity. Privat and Sacco (1995) summed up this trend:

> We can affirm that the discussion is primarily concerned with two fundamental principles of the analytic frame: abstinence and free association. We cannot in any case neglect the primary rule, which means, among other things, that we do not give a positive response to the patient's desire, and even less to the desires of the analyst, for this would imply the risk of excluding us from the field of psychoanalysis. With respect to the second rule, some modifications may be necessary if we wish to maintain psychoanalytic practices.
>
> (*Excerpt from a collection of articles Children's groups and the psychoanalytic frame, Éres, 1999*)

The psychoanalyst Daniel Widlöcher's excellent book *Psychodrama by Children*, published in 1962, assigned only secondary significance to the question of transference. However, the polemical debate had already begun at the group therapy meeting in 1958. It was there that Lebovici, Diatkine and Kestenberg published their assessment of ten years of psychoanalytic psychodrama. The authors tried to formulate their conception within a psychoanalytic context: "Interpretation of transference resistance – countertransference." Catharsis and creativity play no part in it. The group becomes an arena where psychoanalytic treatment proceeds.

The majority of French psychoanalytic children's psychodramatists have tended to neglect the theories of D. W. Winnicott and have held to the principle of abstinence, free association, and the necessity of interpretation. They consider the manifest content of the dramatic scenes as an expression of unconscious material, and they verbalize and interpret the latent content. They support the idea that dramatists should do everything possible to participate in the play, but they are, above all, sensitive to the exploration of categories of depth psychology (the Oedipus complex) in the children's dramatic play. At the beginning of the twenty-first century, the polemic debates among French psychoanalysts were mostly centered on the question of the situation and the definition of the frame, a question we will revisit in the chapter on the group.

Allow me to recommend the excellent book by Didier Anzieu, *Analytic Psychodrama in the Child and the Adolescent*, which provides an intelligent synthesis of Morenian methods with a psychoanalytic sensibility, and to praise the training center he founded, CEFRAP, where I learned a great deal that helped me in developing my own method.

Ms. Anne Ancelin-Schützenberger, a disciple of Moreno whose theoretical and practical activity as a psychodramatist was influential in France, was the founder of another school of training for psychodrama. She developed the triadic theory of psychodrama, the originality of which was its synthesis of diagnosis, sociometry (Moreno's quantitative method for measuring social relationships) and psychodrama. She made use of certain psychoanalytic concepts such as transference, but her conception of small groups was also inspired by American psycho-sociological theories (Moreno, Kurt Lewin, and James Ennis). Perhaps it was because of this that she was considered a non-conformist by the school of psychoanalytic psychodrama of the period (cf. Chaurang). However, her method was applied in certain children's psychodrama groups in France, such as those of M. Lemay in Rennes.

The characteristics of children's psychodrama

1 In contrast to Morenian psychodrama (whether as practiced by CEFRAP, Diatkine, Anne Schutzenberger, or their disciples), Adlerian children's psychodrama expresses itself in the natural language of children – through play. Play guarantees highly varied means of expression, and "acting as if" reassures children who dare to express themselves in a more authentic way than they can in their daily lives.

2 In contrast to Morenian psychodrama, where the protagonist is called upon to enact in the group scenes from his life in order to understand them better, the child is not called upon to evoke events in their reality.

I will cite some words from a student of Moreno on this subject, who attempted to specify the reason it was important to avoid making children reproduce their family problems:

> In the majority of children suffering from psychological problems, the conflictual situations with their parents play an important role in the origin of their problems. Whether this is related to the parents' demands, exaggerated expectations regarding their offspring's scholastic achievement, or parental valorization, the child has a feeling of non-being, of not being sufficiently loved. This is not the sole reason, but it does constitute a frequent element of the parent-child problematic. To deserve the acceptance and love of the parents, children try to avoid anything that, in their experience, might upset the parents. For example, the children often repress the aggression that is provoked by frustrating events. They have a tendency to fantasize to fulfill their desires, or try to maintain the illusion that their relationship with their parents is perfect.
>
> (*Heika Straub, 1995, p. 205*)

During psychodramatic treatment with children who repress their aggression for fear of losing love and/or with children who have the tendency to compensate for a lack of acceptance through their fantasies, we insist on not evoking conflictual scenes. The evocation of traumatic events carries too high a burden of affective charge. Thus, the therapist should not confront the child with the origin of his lack of well being, but rather, provide him with the means to express his suffering and his reactive aggressiveness in a transposed manner, by symbolizing them. For example, through his identification with the father, the child may choose an authoritarian role as the one who rights wrongs. (Think of our little Bruno, who compensated for his aggressiveness when he first arrived, by systematically selecting the role of the policeman (see Chaper 6).)

3 We could summarize the principal method in Adlerian children's psychodrama as: "curing action by action." Children's psychodrama practices the catharsis of action, we do not explain, we do not make commentaries, we do not speak about the moral of the story. To the extent that is possible, we avoid all interpretation. One of the principles of play is thus that explanation and interpretation do not take place verbally but in the course of the drama – it is enacted interpretation.

4 Similarly, the role of the psychodramatists is different from that in classical psychodrama, where the therapist plays the role of a "director" who organizes the scene and directs the action as a spectator, without taking part. In Adlerian children's psychodrama, there is no director, and the psychodramatists, whether there are two or more (which sometimes happens), participate on an equal basis with the children. They might take on a part if the action demands it. In most of our groups, the two psychodramatists participate in the play. The psychodramatist accepts the role assigned to him/her, or it might be one that none of the children want to take on (these are, for the most part, the negative roles – the abused child, the monster to be put to death, the villain, etc.). At the beginning of the group, the psychodramatist often takes the role of the narrator in order to guarantee the fluidity and dynamism of the action.

5 In the psychodrama, the child finds himself in a fantastic world. Immersion in the sometimes miraculous, sometimes ludic, sometimes poetic world of fantasy, although always a source of creativity is not an end unto itself but serves as an instrument that allows for changing one's self image and transforming one's way of living in the world. We might cite as an example the case of the young girl who, after expressing and interpreting the reasons for her emotional blocks in *The Magic Pearl*, suddenly changes, in both her behavior and her school grades. The change in her life is not measurable in terms of what happens in the group (her change of mood, the wonderful feats of her creativity) but rather, in her improvement at home and in school, that is, in her real environment.

6 The sense of solidarity, reciprocity – the *Gemeinschaftsgefühl* – among these insufficiently loved, solitary children from marginalized families, takes root and flourishes through their shared experience. The valorizing role of the psychotherapists and the holding environment of the group contribute to the restoration of confidence in a child who has lost his sense of security and doubts himself and his own capacities, one who is suffering from a severe sense of inferiority. This is how, across the potential space of the psychodramatic territory, we are able to stimulate a transformation in the child's defective self-image.

7 The dynamics of the group have direct therapeutic effects. In psychodrama, the child can assign himself different roles, and this expansion of his repertoire enriches his personality. At first, obsessional children can only take on a single role, which apparently serves a compensatory function for them (the timid little girl plays the princess, the small child takes the role of the giant, the wimp plays the hero). One of the goals of the group activity is to permit children to take on varied roles in order to develop hidden aspects and dimensions of their individuality. The issue is to not confuse one's real life with the role just staged in the play. An unusual role may permit the child to understand his situation better. Psychodrama is a more effective method for developing a social sense than individual therapy. The feeling of belonging to the group makes it possible to go beyond the familial frame; it facilitates independence and the development of autonomy in the child. The shared group experience promotes the emergence of a sense of reciprocity and acceptance of the other. More than any other form of group treatment, psychodrama contributes to developing a social sense, because communal improvisation presupposes alliances, and joint action cannot be achieved without collaboration. Thus, in the dynamics of Adlerian psychodrama, diverse forms of cooperation develop that prove useful in the socialization of poorly integrated children.

4

BEFORE PSYCHODRAMA STARTS

Diagnosis

The majority of the children participating in our workshop were young delinquents or children considered "at risk." The diagnostic group working under the auspices of the Ministry of Justice was given the euphemistic title, "Consultancy for Educational Guidance." It was the decision of the Justice of the Children's Court that we examine these children "for the purpose of formulating a diagnosis." The social workers, educators, child psychiatrists, and the psychologist were tasked with assessing the child's psychosocial status. It was after examination of the family and the child that the so-called "synthesis" would take place. The specialists spoke together about the case as a whole, determined the diagnosis, and made a proposal as to the procedure to be followed to the Children's Court judge. This proposal attempted to address the question of how best to promote the child's recovery. In the case that a child would benefit from psychological assistance, individual or group therapy would be suggested. Therapy could take place within the Ministry of Justice system or in family therapy groups, specialized drug abuse treatment services, etc.

Thus, the diagnosis was determined within the framework of the system that was still called *Éducation Surveillée*, but later re-baptized as *Protection Judiciaire de la Jeunesse* to indicate a change in approach.

The selection of children for the workshop was preceded by a complex examination. The children were referred to us by their teachers, their specialists, or by the school. Our choices tended toward those children presenting with the greatest difficulties, who were the least accepted in their families and in school (the decision fell mainly to the psychologist). Directing them toward different groups was problematic if for no other reason than the familial marginality and the specific nature of the problems.

It seemed important to us to separate the workshop from the judicial context, where parents and children had not gone on their own initiative but by the injunction of the Children's Court judge. To promote this separation, we chose as the place to meet, rooms at a music school in a suburban commune and a Youth Center in another suburb (Antony and then Chatillon). Moreover, it was important to guarantee a spirit of voluntary participation, not only on the part of the children but also the parents, so that they would not feel obligated by external pressure.

In addition to these children who had been evaluated by various specialists in the Consultancy, some children selected for the workshop were not "court children" (something they were quite proud of). These were friends of group members and, when we first started out, their brothers and sisters as well. Later, we decided not to include siblings because their presence shifted the focus of the activities to the problems of a particular family. In addition, as in the case of individual therapy, the child has a need to feel that he is in a special situation. Since those children who joined the workshop were the most deprived, the most lost, they needed to think of their admission as a privilege. No need to share this with your brother – otherwise, what would become of the privilege? If the parents brought along a sibling in addition to the selected child, we would try to dissuade them, and in exceptional cases (if, for example, the parents had not made provisions for child care), the sibling could stay, but we explained to the parents why this could not happen again.

An initial contact might take place if a child arrived at the workshop in the company of a friend. We rarely sent away the intruder, and would ask him to spend this session with us, but afterwards, it would be up to him and the group to determine if he could continue. This temporary admission underscored the fact that one did not accept just anyone. The psychodramatist(s) would then undertake an interview with the child to get a general view of his situation, meet his parents, and set up a contract.

We could thus speak of the group as having a semi-open character.

With regard to the newcomer, the order of procedure would be reversed. Without a history, a diagnostic evaluation, and without prior discussion, the admission of the new member would take place solely with the consent of the children. This method does not seem to us to be any less effective than the classical admission procedure, but of course, presupposes the collaboration of the members, and assumes that group solidarity has already developed. Whether the selection takes place by the Ministry of Justice or without judicial intervention, our initial question would be addressed to the child as to whether he/she would like to participate, and we would only ask the parents in the case that the child has already given his/her consent, attempting to persuade them if they were not on board right away.

The meeting

In Hungary, as in most European nations, therapies take place most of the time in the context of Institutions, Consultancies, preschools, and social welfare establishments, and upon external request. Thus, it is not the parents who are worried or unhappy about their child, but rather the school who sends them, because they are poorly integrated, turbulent, aggressive, or undisciplined. The psychologists then ponder how to interpret the symptoms described by the parents, what to do about them, and whether it makes sense to take the parents' description into consideration.

Karl-Heinz Witte and Anne-Els Stadler, two Adlerian psychologist colleagues, noted that parents are, above all, preoccupied with behavioral problems or other symptoms that are disruptive to family life or to parental expectations concerning the child's health, goals, and plans. However, the therapist does not stop with the listing of problems, especially as they generally can be traced back to something else, and it also happens that they look at the positive aspects of the symptom, for "the symptom is a poorly understood and equivocal attempt at healing." Therefore, one has to "discover the causes that precipitate the child's troubles" (Anne-Els Stadler, Karl-Heinz Witte, 1995, p. 71).

Even though the child does not come to us at his/her own initiative or will, it is important that he learn at the time of the meeting that he is not an object but a subject. The decision to accept him does not preempt his choice, and only is valid to the extent that he recognizes the need. During the initial meeting that precedes any individual or group therapy, before setting up the contract, it is to the child that we address the question: Why have you come to see me?

Most children respond: my mom thinks that . . . or my parents are of the opinion that . . . clearly these are not acceptable answers, and the child has to discover his own motivations and say what is bothering him. Is there something he would like to change? "I have problems," a little six-year-old girl with enuresis told us one day. This is enough for a start and does not necessarily have to do with the symptom.

This first phase of the meeting generally takes place in the presence of one of the parents. It is only afterward that they leave us alone with the child, and it makes sense this way, for it is only at that moment that we learn what is causing the child pain. "I am ugly," is Viviane's response to the question, and then she adds, "I would like to be good in class." The children often let us know that they are dissatisfied with themselves.

We try to specify together what we can undertake in the group to overcome the difficulties the child has cited. With respect to her efforts at school, this sweet, intelligent girl complains that at school, she is working by obligation and not by motivation. (And yet, she would like to become a teacher, and maybe help children who are like her.) And in terms of beauty (a cute little girl but a bit curvy) it is hard to make predictions but it's possible that as she grows, she'll stretch out. Of course, we cannot set a contract for her beautification, but when she is happier with herself, she will also see herself as being more beautiful.

At this first meeting we propose to the child the possibility of psychodramatic play and invite him to participate in the workshop. If the response is equivocal, and if the child does not seem really motivated, we give him time to provide us with a definitive answer, either by suggesting a second meeting or by inviting him, as indicated earlier, to a trial session. The "trial" does not represent a requirement, all the more so since, in order to guarantee the child's freedom of choice, we specify that he does not have to come to the sessions if he doesn't want to, but only if he enjoys them. This freedom of choice certainly does not simplify our task, a child may say no simply to exercise his power, but nevertheless, it is important for these children who rarely have the chance to make their own decisions. It signals a fundamental difference from other places that the child must attend by obligation.

It is only in the event of a clear "yes" that we plan for the child's admission, and we then turn to the parents to ask their consent, or the consent of whoever is responsible, before setting up the contract (see below).

Preliminary meetings

Thus, before any recommendation for psychotherapy, whether in private practice, in consultancies or in other Institutions, we suggest a meeting with the parents and the child. This applies to both individual therapies and group therapy, because without a personal history and clinical consultation we cannot decide upon the form of treatment that is best suited for the child. Before the first meeting, we ask the parents to come without the child, since the child's participation does not facilitate free expression of the parental problematics and one should avoid having the parents overburden or humiliate the child. Before presenting the indication for therapy, we meet with the two parents separately or together, according to their choice. If they are a couple living together, we do not begin treating the child before meeting the father. Mothers sometimes object, saying that their husband is hostile to psychology, or that he mistrusts it, or that he is uninterested in questions of this nature. It has often happened that fathers who were said to be indifferent or hostile provided their consent, or that, in the presence of their child, they were able to speak about the changes that they expected from psychological treatment.

It is primarily the parents who inform us about the most important elements of the family history, their personal experiences, and their own expectations, real or fantastic, regarding the child. Next, as indicated, we meet with the child. To establish a diagnosis, some colleagues use intelligence tests and projective testing. Others suggest several preliminary meetings with one or both of the parents or with the child to facilitate understanding of family conflicts or for whatever other reasons that such meetings might be indicated. If this diagnostic phase takes place in an institutional setting, we might request consultations with other specialists (speech and language therapists, educational psychologists) or medical or psychiatric examinations.

Some French, German, and Austrian consultancies are of the opinion that one should begin by hearing from the family as a whole. Our Austrian colleagues regularly invite the entire family for the initial meeting and, in establishing their diagnoses, they make note of the presence or absence of any of the individuals involved.

When it is the school that asks us to treat the child, the schoolteacher often makes reference to behavioral problems, problems in school performance and sometimes to family difficulties, to explain the referral. It is important in the subsequent course of treatment to stay in contact with the teacher, since change in the child's attitude toward school is one of the criteria for evaluating the effectiveness of our intervention. Such contact is all the more important since acceptance at school can also promote transformation in the child's self-confidence and self-image.

To establish a diagnosis, we need information from others who are familiar with the child, information such as integration in the school, knowledge about the environment, history, and family structure. We also need subjective information from the child, which includes, in a certain sense, the child's history of his/her own case, the child's understanding of her psychological problems, of her anxieties and how they originate, and her own assessment of her personal qualities, expectations of herself and assessment of potential. From an understanding of all this data, we can evaluate the type of intervention that would best facilitate the child's development and, more specifically, if psychological treatment is indicated, whether individual or group. If psychodrama is the therapy of choice, we briefly explain how it works, its character and the rules of the workshop and only accept the child's decision if we have the impression that this activity truly interests him. If this is the case, after the parents have given their consent, we organize a joint meeting that includes the child, parents, and the psychotherapists to talk together about the child's problems. This occasion gives the child a chance to express his point of view and his expectations. The psychodramatist(s) offer their help in resolving the difficulties described by the child and the parents. If the child and the parents agree, we set up the contract.

The contract

We set up the contract for a renewable period of one year, and specify the frequency (usually once a week), the day, and the length of the sessions. We ask that the child, to the extent possible considering his age, come to the sessions alone and that his parents not ask questions about what happened during the session. We add that if the parents do contact us, we will let the child know. We specify that while the therapists' principal involvement is with the children, we also have the need to consult with the parents from time to time. We cite the rule mentioned earlier of free choice (the child is not compelled to come if he does not enjoy the group). We specify that physical violence is not permitted and ask the child to try to establish relationships of friendly cooperation with the others.

As with the child, the contract we set up with the parents is generally verbal. However, we specify in writing that the parent is committed to assuring their child's regular participation.

In addition to the parents' commitment, we initially had asked for payment of a minimal sum at the start of each session. Our conception was that this symbolic contribution could signify a kind of reciprocity. Later, we gave up on this idea, because the children would keep the money under the pretext that their mother had forgotten to give them the two francs, and indulged in all manner of blackmail and manipulation. At the end of the school year we organized a closing celebration to which we invited parents as well as siblings, teachers, and the social workers involved with the family. Part of the program was a video montage of the children's activities at the workshop. For some of the closing celebrations, the children made up and performed skits composed for the occasion. The skits sometimes took on the character of coded messages addressed to the parents. These meetings gave us the chance to speak about the general problems of the group and each child's difficulties, principally focusing on the child's evolution and the progress he/she had made.

Work with the parents

It is important to give parents the opportunity to raise, discuss, and elaborate the problems they face with their children. Therapists fulfill this need in different ways. Some work with groups of parents who meet at regular intervals. At the time the contract is set up, the parents commit to participating in over ten meetings devoted to the psychodramatic elaboration of family conflicts. Thus, the therapists organize psychodrama sessions that allow the parents to change roles and directly experience their children's problems. There are other psychotherapists who set up groups where parents and children play together, either occasionally or according to a set timetable. A couple of psychodramatists start out the work with an initial session where each parent plays with his own child in a twosome, and at a given moment in the play, parent and child switch roles. The Consultancy in the Hungarian town of Zalaegerszeg brings together hyperactive children with their parents in joint psychodramatic plays. In other groups, joint psychodrama is organized on an occasional basis with particular parents. Sometimes the other members of the group will be absent, and the therapist plays with a single mother-child couple, but it also may happen that a single parent is involved with the group, and the group's play then takes a special turn. Here is an illustration of what can happen.

The clown who was crying

This play was invented by Michel, a child referred to the Consultancy because of his slow development and poor grades in school. He asked his mother, the only parent participating in the play on this particular day, to take on the role of the director. He picked the role of the clown for himself.

The scene takes place in a circus. There are trapeze artists, a juggler, a fire swallower, the director, and the sad clown. One day, the clown, who plays the flute while perched on a ladder, messes up his song and falls. The director becomes angry and throws him outside. He fires him.

Now all of the circus folk – the juggler, the fire swallower, the trapeze artists, and the lion-tamer demand that the director take him back. He's a good clown, they tell him, he made a mess of things, but the next time, he'll be sure to pay attention. But the director won't listen to them, he doesn't want the clown any more. So the entire company – the trapeze artists, the fire swallower, etc. all go on strike. They declare that they will only go back to work if the director rehires the clown. The director is stuck and finally ends up yielding. The clown, who was crying in the corner, is rehired. End of the play.

During the staging, the actors spoke with one another; they said that the clown really tried hard, that he did his best, and that he had lost his balance because he was too stressed and was afraid of the audience and the director. The children who took on the roles of the circus performers were unanimous about the arguments they put forward to excuse the clumsiness of the clown and to restore his confidence. After the play, during the round of commentary, the mother asked the question: am I sometimes too hard on him?

Sometimes it happens that the parental problems require therapeutic intervention that clearly cannot be provided by the child's psychotherapist. He can only counsel and provide some direction. But such suggestions rarely produce results.

Whether we work with parents singly or in a parents' group, meet separately with parents, or insist that such work take place in the presence of the children, whether we label our work as accompaniment therapy or not, what is indispensable is to modify the parents' behavior and the parent-child relationship, because otherwise the psychotherapeutic effect cannot become stable. We regard the parents as our allies in this work. Without close collaboration, without comprehensive acceptance, no positive evolution of any kind can be envisaged.

A certain degree of rivalry may become manifest between the parents and the therapists. The parent may dispute the idea that the therapist can accomplish what the parent has proved unable to do. In addition, if the therapist's own unresolved conflicts are stirred up, this may become an obstacle to acceptance by the parents. This tension may manifest itself by aggressiveness on the part of the parents, something that requires support from the psychodramatists in order to help develop a different, non-hierarchical relationship. On the other hand, a parent may attribute extraordinary qualities to the therapist, and to ask for her advice. Sometimes the parent projects his/her expectations onto the therapist, regarding the therapist as a miracle worker to the point of detecting radical changes in the behavior of the child after only a few sessions. This illusion may be the sign of the beginnings of a re-evaluation of the child and attenuation of conflicts, but the parent–therapist relationship cannot be confined only to this. Every therapist needs to make efforts to achieve a more comprehensive relationship with the parent based on equality. The issue is not to know better, but to collaborate in order to eliminate the collection of obstacles that come up along the child's developmental path.

5

PHASES OF CHILDREN'S PSYCHODRAMA

1) Introductory phase (warm-up and cool-down techniques)

The techniques known as *warm-up* or *warming up* in psychodrama for adults take on a different form and serve a different function in children's psychodrama, as the need is more for a *cooling down* period. Whether they are at risk, abused, hyperactive, or disturbed, these children are most particularly in need of de-stimulation; their personal problems, often in connection with family relationships, make them restless or anxious. Entering the group, they may be hyperactive or withdrawn into themselves; at this point they are focused on themselves and cannot pay attention to the other children. They are not ready for the joint work of the group because they are not able to concentrate. In this kind of group, we are confronted more with their difficulties in expressing themselves than with their resistance. As a group begins to function it is hard for the beginning psychodramatist to create a relatively calm atmosphere, stop the turbulence, the ambient noise, the fooling around, and the disorganized impromptu movements. As Aichinger puts it, one has to put the brakes on the more dynamic and hyperactive children in order that they not race into combat or play immediately upon arrival.

As my psychodramatist colleague Claude Lépineux formulated it one has to create a protective airlock that eliminates the noises coming from outside and changes the atmospheric pressure.

Ferenc Mérei, the founder of the Hungarian school of psychodrama said:

> In the children's group, it is not adequate to regulate the surplus of tension generated by the group but also the overflow of affect, the behavioral lability, the childish exuberance of fantasy, and the doublethink so characteristic of childhood.
>
> (*Mérei & Erdélyi, 1987, p. 41*)

A number of experienced child psychodramatists draw attention to the danger of the routine use of techniques of warming up. Such prefabricated techniques can distract the children's attention from real problems and constitute an obstacle to focusing on the current situation of the group and the conflicts that preoccupy ts members. Aichinger says that in the course of his early meetings, the children found these prefabricated elements silly, and thought that these rewarmed dishes made from Morenian 'canned goods' were annoying and irritating.

What the children and facilitators working with the children's group need is not richly colored animation or reheated canned goods (even if this type of technique may be used by some, Shearon among others), but rather, the understanding achieved through sociometry and by the symbolic play of psychodrama regarding the problematics of the group and of each of the children. "In our experience, it is the proposed scene developed jointly in the group that is the best warm-up" suggests Anzieu (Anzieu, 1994, p. 103).

Journey to Wonderland

The children need to feel that they are "somewhere else." Some psychodramatists used to think or still think that to implement this principle, you simply need to tell the children that nothing is forbidden. Here, everything is possible, you can do whatever you want, whatever comes into your mind. In this way, they try to create a universe without proscriptions (in this regard, see the commentary of the very sensible and original progenitor, the "father of psychodrama," Slavson, 1950). Rogersian group therapists who insist on their child-centered non-directive technique also regard themselves as partisans for total permissiveness. In fact, some pioneers also promoted regression as well as real (rather than symbolic) externalization of aggression, including acting out. This could be taken to an extreme, with young people breaking windows, destroying objects, smashing the furniture to pieces, etc. The therapists counted on this overflow, hoping that the children would finally become saturated by their own misdeeds. During the 1940s, when members of the French school of psychoanalysis, Ms. Dreyfus-Monod and colleagues, introduced psychodrama to France, they were of the opinion, as we have already pointed out in the chapter on the evolution of psychodrama in France, that completely free activity in psychodrama was the equivalent of free association in the analytic cure. But over a rather short time, they found (unlike the Rogersians and Slavson) that the free exercise of aggression had no therapeutic value.

The psychodramatic space (the workshop, the club, the group) is certainly of a very different nature from any other familial, scholastic, or extra-scholastic milieu. But the difference hardly means that everything goes. For Slavson or for the child-centered therapists, the method consists of waiting for the children to come to the spontaneous realization that they are able to accomplish activities other than pure destruction.

These inevitably ineffective acts, as Pélicier defines faulty actions, cannot resolve anything, since, as the French psychoanalytic school especially emphasizes, every child, every adolescent, and every therapeutic activity of the group requires a frame. Without an atmosphere of safety, the structuring of the group has no chance of success.

But what to do with the aggression that is there? We will have to move it to a symbolic field. According to Kaës's formula (1999), "play is mourning for the thing and mourning for the act." By the "thing" he means instinct, or more precisely, the immediate achievement of drives. Psychodrama is called upon to transpose the aggressive drive into the ludic dimension, something that might even instruct us about its origins, not to speak of the conditions that set it off.

Appeasement of real aggression is the precondition for the child to be able to access another dimension. This accurately pinpoints the specificity of the therapeutic group for children: permitting the child to pass through the looking glass (see Alice's adventures) to arrive in Wonderland. This land of fairy tales, the magic country, is not necessarily identical to the one invented by Lewis Carroll, which includes, as has often been pointed out, a number of schizoid elements (for example, changes in size, dismemberment, numerous metamorphoses – from baby to pig, from food to insect, from inert to living, even the animation of the figures in playing cards, who come to life. The wonderland of children differs significantly from this. Perhaps the fantastical rubbing against the irrational and the disquieting atmosphere of disappearances and reappearances will occasionally occur here as well, but our wonderland is generally more humane and rarely lacking in affectivity. Still, in the magic world created by the group, everything is different, everything can be transformed into something else and there is no limit to the expression of a fantastic world.

The coordinates of the universe of fairy tales, of this magical world are:

a the magical dimension, where the rules of the outside world (partially) lose their validity,
b the creation of the world, where each child is equally capable of creating his own personal magical world, with the benevolent participation of the others (*sharing*),
c in relation to what we have just described, the infantile sense of omnipotence, which was an impetus for Moreno from the very beginning, is one of the important factors in the child's imaginary compensation for littleness, for the child's sense of impotence.

Once the magic atmosphere has been established, the child is transformed into a magician. He can turn himself into an animal, into diverse characters; he can be a plant or become an object, anything that can express his affective experience, elements of his personality, and his style of life. The creator of this magical world is the child; as strange as this might seem, it is not the therapist, it is the child who is the storyteller. The therapist is merely an initiator, accompanist, or actor, or is simply present.

Potential space

Whether as relates to psychotherapy or psychoanalysis, the specific nature of the potential space of play, according to Winnicott, is that it belongs neither to the unconscious nor to the conscious realm. It is a domain peculiar to itself where the therapist and the client come together. This notion is generally accepted, and in fact, there is no school of psychoanalysis or psychodrama that does not make reference to Winnicott. We would propose adding to this model an important corollary emanating from our clinical practice. This potential space, this very special milieu that does not exist anywhere else, opens up, beyond creativity, the patient's (in this case the child's) capacity for self-creation. I want to emphasize – even though this potential space is the joint creation of the therapist and the child, the adult and the child do not participate equally. The potential space mainly mobilizes the creative power of the child, that is to say, the child's power to create the world. The role of the dramatist is to assure a favorable ambience, and in addition, to participate in the imaginary work of the child in such a way as not to impede but to promote the child's progress along the path he has chosen for himself. It is important to emphasize this aspect, as certain dramatists think that their own unconscious world should be called upon to provide the framework for the potential space.

There are some child psychoanalysts who bring their own fantasy world to this space and privilege it as a source of content. Our point of view, and the trust we place in the children resembles what Mihály Babits, poet and Hungarian writer of the twentieth century, formulated in his novel *Halàlfiai* as, "The child knows what he needs."

The first meeting

The first meeting of the group is particularly important. It sets the style and the atmosphere for all of the activity of the group. It begins with the introduction of the child and gives him a chance to answer questions that may be asked, such as, what he would like to change in his life or what bothers him about his own behavior (for example, his shyness, solitude, impulsivity, or bad grades in school). However, one should avoid making this introduction too negative. It is possible to balance it with a positive question, such as – what is your best character trait, what are the qualities in you that you value the most?

We might also employ a mode of introduction that is more playful – it's your friend, your dog, or your cat that will introduce you.

Other questions may have to do with the child's expectations – why do you want to participate in the group? In the case of timid children who are very inhibited, we may use techniques of introduction that sensitize the children to the expectations of make-believe. We will cite several examples, the first of them is the magic shop.

The magic shop

The 'magic shop' that Moreno began using in 1943 is a multi-purpose technique that sets fantasy in motion by eliciting desire. It was Moreno's disciples, Weiner (1965) and others, who elaborated the magic shop, mainly in the sense of a warm-up and for diagnostic purposes. They emphasized its ludic character, and since it is far more interesting and enjoyable than the simple evocation of real events, they utilized it often, especially in groups that were difficult to get mobilized. The process is a simple one, and it can be dramatic if desired, composed of brief scenes that are appropriate for generating initial spontaneity. The magic shop is regarded as a useful technique in group play, not necessarily for therapy as such, but simply to stimulate the participants' spirit of playfulness. We tend to regard it as a technique that lets children give expression to their principal area of trauma (similar to the inquiry about earliest memories in Adlerian therapies) and to elaborate prospective plans that let them project themselves into the future. It can also serve as a ticket to allow entry into the magical world that we are called upon to construct together.

Staging

The children are seated in a half circle. A table is placed in front, where the psychodramatist will soon appear, disguised by a pointed hat and black garments as the Merchant, the Magician, or the Sorcerer.

The good news is announced – an unusual and marvelous event is about to take place. The Merchant, once he/she arrives, announces that the famous Magic Shop has just come to their community. There, you can find all sorts of miraculous merchandise: flying carpets, angel wings, playmates, hats that make you invisible, the elixir of immortality, etc. He invites the children to visit the shop and to state their request – the magical product, object, or aptitude that they need – and so long as the products are part of the magic shop's stock, the children can have them right away. This does not require cash payment, but they have to offer something in exchange: an object, a toy, a habit, or a feeling that may be of importance to them but that they would gladly share, or something they wish to get rid of. The Storekeeper greets the children one by one. The children cannot simply request something but have to explain why they need it. Thus begins an interesting conversation that lets the child tell his reason for choosing a commonplace object or a simple wish that usually refers back, however, to an important lack. The offerings can be quite diverse – it might be a watch or secret contents of a pocket, a piece of string, or a superfluous brother. The exchange takes place, an agreement is reached; if the object is too important, we return it at the end of the session.

This technique demands great dexterity and tact. Sometimes the children brush against their essential problems, asking, for example, to change parents or even suggesting sacrifice of body parts; the therapist rejects any objects that involve self-mutilation (an eye or a finger, for example).

In a children's group we make every effort to satisfy the request, regardless of its scale. This is not always easy to do and demands great imagination on the part of the Sorcerer-Merchant, but we try to offer a symbolic object that the child can take away with her.

Specialties of the magic shop for children

This method was elaborated upon by a colleague, Krisztina Janovszky, working with a group of troubled children at a rural primary school in Hungary. She made use of the magic shop during the group's second meeting after she already had some idea of each participant's expectations. She reasoned that, to temper their wishes, these frustrated children would have need of a concrete object that they could hold onto. In advance, she procured a varied assortment of the most suitable objects for introducing the children to the magical atmosphere of a very special play space. "I tried to imagine what each child would want, I looked for objects with multiple uses (a cream, a powder, that could help make the user courageous, strong, adroit, famous, get along with his parents, etc.)."

She imagined that the best means of involving the children in a magical universe was to provide them with concrete objects that conformed to or symbolized their expectations. The children's excitement seemed to indicate that a miracle had taken place, that a particularly important wish had been "fulfilled."

Subsequently, these objects took on an affective value that had nothing to do with their market value (one of the little girls in the workshop replaced her quartz wrist-watch with a plastic watch that the Magician had provided for her). The objects received became bearers of miraculous expectations, kinds of transitional objects that represented something that went beyond their materiality. During difficult moments, the possession consoled, encouraged, and strengthened its bearer. This technique of the magic shop no longer functioned simply as an introductory game but augmented the intensity of the affective value of the psychodramatic group process. The objects became fetishized and accompanied the children everywhere, reminding some of these rejected or abused children, who suffered from an intense sense of inferiority, of a different image of themselves, one that was positive. The objects they chose were quite diverse. Emese, who lived in the shadow of a favored older sister, asked for a jewel to make her beautiful, even though she was actually an especially pretty child. Agnès asked for a little sister; she got a little doll that she carried in her apron pocket. Adèle, whose parents often fought, was given a magical saltshaker. This object had the gift of reconciliation and of being able to calm the person whose food one secretly seasoned with it.

"From that moment on, the group had been formed. We had a common secret conveyed by the object. The children could not even have revealed it to others: nobody would have understood what a plastic horse or an empty bottle could signify," Krisztina says.

Over time, this technique has been adopted by the majority of child psychodramatists. Some use it at the start of the group, while others select the moment when they feel it fits well into the dynamics of the group.

The magical object has the function of a special transitional object. It represents the child and the child's double – a kind of double that is different, her rehabilitating double.

Drawing, painting, coloring

Among techniques that are calming, we often use drawing. At times when the children do not arrive at the same time, there is an opportunity for one-on-one meetings with the psychodramatist. It is helpful for the dramatists to arrive 15 minutes early. This presence of the therapist is integrated into the children's ritual, and the children know that if they have something to discuss or communicate, they can make the effort to arrive ahead of the others. If drawing is part of the initial phase of the session, it is necessary to have a shared table that permits the therapists and the children to draw together. This collective activity introduces moments of silence and recollection that take place during the drawing time. This is free drawing, and each child can fill his sheet, selecting the accessories placed at his disposal, according to his preference of the moment (pencils, chalk, felt pens, gouache, crayons, brushes, or finger paints). During this time of interiorization the children work contemplatively. They rarely bother each other or make derogatory comments. I have only run into teasing, criticism, or mockery regarding the drawings of others in training groups for future psychodramatists who simulate the activities of groups of children, where each member identifies with a particular child, a real or imagined young patient. Groups of children distinguish themselves from their adult imitators, as they refrain from deprecating the work of the others; they appreciate it, and sometimes even express admiration.

The psychodramatists typically draw with the children at the beginning of the session. In this way, they underscore their belonging to the group and show that they are not simply observers of its activities. However, I know many art therapists, psychotherapists, and dramatists who would rather observe the children's work, their behavior, and their state of mind. Once the drawings are completed, the dramatists go around the table asking each child to comment on their drawings. The children speak freely, and their comrades ask questions and make remarks that are generally admiring or at least empathetic. With the exception of those who are still absorbed in completing their work, the others signal their interest in the drawings that are presented. They understand that the issue is not formal perfection, that it isn't about academic criteria, that the only things that are important are the content and the affect communicated by the scenes that have been drawn. The contemplation and discreet interpretation formulated by the child help strengthen the *Gemeinschaftsgefühl*, the sense that he is not alone, and that the others empathize with his desires, his fate, and his preoccupations.

Children who are three years of age or younger are not able to control the pencil enough to plan an image ahead of time; this has nothing to do with the "amodal perception" of the infant. The very little child draws, then looks at his scribbles and sometimes says something. We encounter a similar mechanism in abused, borderline, and schizoidal children. They draw instinctively, sometimes feverishly, and then they say something. Their words may transmit something of importance, but as with the very young child, it may simply be onomatopoeic and difficult to decode. We might say in their defense that a modern abstract painting also lends itself to verbalization only with difficulty. If the child sometimes says something that seems random, this is not necessarily "resistance" and it is possible that he cannot do otherwise.

The importance of the drawing phase is not limited to the creation of an introductory inward-directed and calming atmosphere; it also allows for the emergence of content, feelings, and reminiscences that are not yet expressible through psychodrama. This is why it is also important that the psychodramatists perceive, feel, and share in the needs, the appeals, and the lived realities that children express in their drawings. The emotions, traumas, tensions, and preverbal, pre-conscious or unconscious content are expressed earlier in graphic activity rather than verbalization: see for example, the deformed and excremental image of a child watered down in a liquid milieu drawn by François.

Drawing communicates better than language the affective universe of the abused child and his terrible dilemma, which, in the absence of love and acceptance, drives him toward non-being, and makes intelligible the reasons for his incapacity to express himself in play. His depression and despair are even more poignant than that of the little boy who states as soon as he walks in, "My mother beat me again."

The question arises: how can one articulate, express, and put into play this escape into non-being that seems irreversible? The question arises all the more acutely given the fact that such a child views himself as being bad and unlovable and that it takes time for him to accept anybody's friendship and to believe that the group truly wishes to welcome him. François is an example of this: he refused to come to the workshop, saying that the other kids did not like him. The children sent him drawings and letters to assure him of the contrary and to ask him to come back. It was only after this that he became able to choose positive roles and even to play the part of the hero. According to the Jungian child therapist Christiane Lutz, "an important part of the therapeutic process becomes effective by means of drawing and painting. Painting is a more spontaneous and more direct form of expression of the child's unconscious than words" (Lutz, 1976). It allows for the child's emergence from the schizoidal experience of fragmentation and splitting that is difficult to approach through dramatic expression. A young girl considered to be borderline drew hybrid beings that were at the same time animal, vegetable, and human in nature, as well as fragmented images. These fantasies may be difficult to translate into psychodrama unless in the form of science fiction stories or mythical narratives.

It often happens that the contours of the play to be performed emerge from individual drawings or the joint discussion about them.

Other introductory techniques

Before proceeding to drawing, if there is a moment as the children are arriving or when the entire group is seated in the circle, we usually ask them about what has happened in their lives since the last meeting. Not rarely, the emotion-filled narrative (of an event that was experienced, heard about, or seen) will serve as the introduction for staging a play.

There are different introductory techniques, some of which are non-verbal (rhythmic exercises with musical accompaniment, psycho-dance, pantomime games, etc.).

One uses non-verbal techniques especially in the treatment of severely disturbed children (schizoidal, autistic, psychotic), who generally have a limited capacity for verbal expression. The games of pantomime on a topic, which Blatner (1973) transformed into improvised psychodrama, are also practiced. There are specialized techniques for psychotic and autistic children, such as those used by the child psychiatrist Lafforgue in a Bordeaux day hospital, which consisted of fragmenting fairy tales and playing them in performance (see a more detailed discussion later, in the chapter on fairy tales).

Since psychotherapist-psychodramatists are very inventive, there are a number of different introductory practices, such as throwing a ball of yarn to help children memorize each other's names, musical chairs, selection of pseudonyms to memorize, and many others that my colleagues could enumerate.

2) Choice of a topic, development of the story

At the first session of psychodrama, Anzieu describes the instructions as follows:

> We are going to put on a play. Do you enjoy doing this? Well, here's how we're going to do it. You are going to tell us a story, any story, a story that has happened to you or that someone told you, or that you heard; it might be a story you read or a dream you have had. The first story that comes to your mind is the right one. Next, you will tell us which character you would like to be in this story. You will also tell us what roles we will have, because we are also going to take part in your story. And afterwards, all together, we will enact the story, in make-believe of course.

If several children are playing together (for Anzieu and his colleagues often play with a single child), they invite them to invent a story together, but they may also each tell their own story and then agree upon performing one of them.

In addition, each child may select his own role, but they decide together which roles to assign to the psychodramatists (Anzieu, 1994, p. 110).

Although the children can invent scenarios quite easily, the psychodramatists may decide to help them out during the first session. Lutz thinks that inventiveness is stimulated by the atmosphere that is created. Anzieu asks them simple supplementary questions to help them specify the circumstances where the story could take place: is it at home or at school, in the city street or the countryside, etc.? (Anzieu, ibid.).

Widlöcher begins right in the midst of things: "The group of children and therapists having come together, the psychodramatic space is defined, then it's up to the dramatic action to be born. It's up to the group to select a topic (Widlöcher, 1979, p. 40).

Aichinger describes the start in a similar way:

> At the beginning of each session, we ask the children to sit in a circle (the Germans call this format Stuhlrunde). We open the session with the question: what do you want to play together today? The children can suggest a story that they would like to perform. They can choose, modify, or elaborate a topic or group fantasy.
>
> (*Aichinger & Holl, 1997, p. 93*)

The choice of the topic is entrusted to the adults only in exceptional cases (such as in the case of didactic or diagnostic psychodrama). In therapeutic psychodrama it is possible to propose a vague topic that allows for different variations in a very inhibited group, but this method carries the risk of creating a passive attitude. "As a general rule, children themselves should improvise the topic" (Widlöcher, 1979, p. 41).

Generally, it is one of the children who suggests the topic. Sometimes the proposal meets with general agreement – this is the case, for example, if the topic resonates with various problems and conflicts in the others (see, e.g. the story of the lion and the lion cub that signaled a young girl's difficulties controlling aggression, into which a number of children could project their own set of problems – Blaise, his oral aggression, Clovis and François their ambivalence toward their abusive fathers).

> Every child has the possibility of developing the topic differently in terms of his own personal history. The game of symbolic psychodrama can thus express each child's unconscious at the same time as that of the group as a whole.
>
> (*Aichinger & Holl, 1997, p. 104*)

Acceptance of a story proposal is also a function of the dynamics of the group. The group sometimes responds impassively to a proposal and sometimes even rejects it. This may signify that the topic is encountering major resistance, touching on unconscious layers that the group is not yet ready to approach, but it may also happen that the rejection is directly related to the person suggesting the topic.

Individual or group invention

The episode cited above (the lion and the lion cub) illustrates that in a coherent children's group structured in such a way that the resonance among the members is intense, it is difficult to determine who is the true author of the story. We do have some formal guidelines, of course, but the others are allowed to modify, transform, and modulate the topic in the course of its elaboration. As Lebovici aptly puts it, "The story to be elaborated needs to be sufficiently general to involve everybody and sufficiently specific so as not to lose its meaning" (Lebovici, Diatkine & Kestenberg, 1970).

3) Choice of role

The topic as proposed may already be developed or simply announced. The dramatic action is then improvised from the spontaneous impetus of the play. Sometimes it happens that the story is told in the course of preparing for the play without determining its ending. It may end in different ways, for better or worse. Once the warp of the story has been laid, the next step is to select roles. The child who has provided the topic chooses first. This may not necessarily be the principal role, even though the children are fond of playing the hero. Sometimes the child who has suggested the topic doesn't want to perform at all and prefers to remain a spectator, and he is entitled to do so. This is accepted even if the child rarely wants to actively participate and generally takes on a passive role, such as the role of an object (a wall, a shrub, a curtain, the wind, the lapping of the sea, etc.). Next, the other children choose their roles. Some child psychodramatists adopt a different procedure. Considering that the child whose story has been selected is the director, he gets to distribute the roles as long as the other children accept them, as they are free to refuse.

Some psychodramatists, including Aichinger, ask the actors to specify the characteristics of the characters before the play is staged: Are you a little wolf or a big wolf? Are your fangs powerful? If the character has magic powers, the dramatist asks the group to decide their scope, and the limits of his power. He insists on specifying these elements to prevent conflicts during the play. We prefer to wait and see how the child comes to develop his character in the course of the play and do not believe that safety measures undertaken in advance are able to stem the flow of the child's fantasy.

There can be obsessive choices, such as that of the little boy who always wanted to play the gendarme, even if the scene was taking place among a group of animals or in outer space.

The two psychodramatists (and this is another thing that distinguishes children's psychodrama from adult psychodrama) generally both perform in the play. There are situations when only one of them takes part. In children's psychodrama during the 1920s, the rule in France was that both participated in every play (see Sacco, 1995). Psychodramatists take on the roles assigned to them by the children. These are often the roles that nobody wants (the abused or impaired child), or sometimes, when no child wants to expose himself to a negative identification (the monster, the sorcerer, or the devil), the roles the children refuse to play. On the other hand, it may be a positive role, such as that of the veterinarian who heals the sick fawn or puppy, or alternatively it may have a transferential or corrective quality such as the role of the hologram (see the chapter devoted to this topic). In this capacity, without being called upon to do so, the dramatist takes on complementary supporting roles or acts as a double. Let us take the example of the psychodramatist supporting the gendarme, mentioned earlier, who is still unable to play unless one asks him the question: "What are we going to do, chief?" "Should we take the car?" If a previously withdrawn and mute little girl suddenly decides to play the king's daughter, we don't dissuade her but in the role of the governess, her maid, or her sister, we provide rejoinders for her so she can dare to approach Prince Charming.

There are techniques that guarantee a more important directive role to the inventor of the story and allow him to be the director during the performance, and in which it is also up to him to distribute the roles. This may seem analogous to the technique of the Morenian protagonists but the function is not the same. We do not suggest using this technique (not only because the children protest against the imposition of roles but also because it tends to restrict their freedom of projection) except when it is with a view to strengthen the self-confidence of a child who is particularly withdrawn into himself, timid, and suffering from a strong sense of inferiority.

Anzieu emphasizes how important it is to respect the spontaneity of the child in each phase of the play. During the dramatic action, the actors do not have to follow to the letter the adventures suggested by the story; they may take the same kind of playful liberties that they have in inventing their story and in their choices of role.

4) The disguise

Since Moreno, adult psychodrama developed a conception shared by the majority of child psychodramatists, to the effect that you should leave it up to the imagination of the patient to adopt the role and choose the character with whom to identify. At most, one provides them with a few chairs as accessories. Other psychologists offer a wider selection of props; Professor Mérei would mark off the stage with a red curtain, and others, such as Walter Holl, allow for set design for the bandit's cave using pillows, polyethylene sheets, blankets or light effects. As a matter of principle, Widlöcher opposes all physical scenery: "Too abundant or too realistic materials promote the child to use them in a purely playful way to the detriment of dramatic representation" (Widlöcher, 1979, p. 31).

However, our own experience has convinced us that in children (and not only in children), the availability of multiple props promotes, encourages, and accelerates identification with the role. If during a story the witch has transformed the hero into a bear, the transformation will be more convincing if the hero can also put on a chamois skin, a fur-lined coat turned inside out, or even a furry vest. Now he becomes the bear. We also understand the short boy who chose the role of a dwarf and who responded a bit sadly to the question: "What do you need for a disguise?" after a moment of reflection: "Nothing!" The use of visual or theatrical props – including painting the face – provides major help for the child to enter the magic world. Nobody is a king without a crown, and what happens to the little girl who wants to be a fairy without a magic wand? In addition, we believe that the playful is not in opposition to the psychodramatic. Quite the contrary, for all practice of child therapy (whether individual or group), play constitutes a very important element, even the most important, of the child's natural language.

5) The action phase: the play

In his book *Homo ludens* [Playing Man] Huizinga emphasizes the importance of the enclosure and boundaries of play: "play is a voluntary action or activity, completed within certain fixed limits of time and place, following rules that are freely agreed upon but completely imperious, with an end only unto itself, accompanied by a sense of tension or joy and the consciousness of being 'different' than in ordinary life" (Huizinga, 1951, p. 28).

Huizinga believes that all play proceeds in a material or ideal play space that is different from the ordinary world and, as Roger Caillois describes it, is a "separate occupation; carefully isolated from the rest of existence, circumscribed by precise spatial and temporal limits set in advance" (Caillois, 1958).

The magician begins by separating off sacred space . . . From a formal perspective it makes no significant difference whether the separation is made for the purpose of a sacred aim or simply for play. Moreno's psychodrama is arranged in space in a rather original manner. "The performance space constitutes a major enlargement of real life. The Morenian theater is located in three spaces: the elevated stage, the room and a balcony that assures the vertical division of space." The author considers that the essential instrument is the stage, which is called upon to assure the participants of a multi-dimensional space.

We do not adopt this particular arrangement in child psychodrama, especially as there are practically no spectators. We also abandon the idea of an elevated place. However, it is important – and this is part of the ritualizing process – to designate a separate play space.

The synthesis of the collaboration of the group and individual creativity is one of the important energy sources for the interior dynamics of children's psychodrama. The play you can read below, "The Lion and His Cub" illustrates the transformation that takes place between the declared topic and the scene that is played out.

The construction of the play is thus entrusted entirely to the children, and the dramatist needs to avoid moralizing the play that is performed, modifying the ending in the interest of some kind of positive outcome. He must not intervene unless he has the sense that the anxiety unleashed by the action would expose a child or the whole group to too much stress.

Mélinda, a little blonde girl with blue eyes, comes in one morning with a story inspired by a news piece she heard recently on the radio or television. The story involved a criminal who wanted to burglarize a peaceful family and who, much to his surprise, became aware of the presence of the mistress of the household.

He robbed the apartment, killed the woman, and fled. Children often suggest stories of this genre. But since this was the first time that this particular child had suggested a story, the group accepted it. It was Mélinda who took the role of the woman and my psychologist colleague was charged with that of the burglar. But when the dramatist found himself face to face with Mélinda, her eyes expressed such terror and anxiety that he felt incapable of using the murder weapon (symbolic, of course). The dramatist who did not have a role in the play then joined the action. She emitted siren-like sounds signaling the arrival of the police. Two boys then spontaneously took on the role of the policemen and arrested the infamous burglar. This scene also illustrates the difference between the affective charge of inventing a story and enacting it on stage; the little girl who was able to imagine herself in the role of murdered mother of the family had trouble playing out the scene of her being put to death on stage.

Mélinda had been a child at risk, and had a rather turbulent course during adolescence. However, when I met with her at age 18 she gave the impression that, despite the many twists and turns of her life, she was on the path toward affective and social healing. At our meeting she recalled how helpful her participation in the workshop had been for her.

Sometimes in the scenes where the hero must die, the other children regard this as only a make-believe death and they resuscitate him at the end. Moreover, death on stage may signify the solution to a dilemma, as we shall see in "The Devil and his Hologram."

6) Exiting from the role

At the conclusion of the play phase, the following question arises: how to signal the return to reality. There are diverse acoustic methods one can employ – the sound of a bell, a drum, a gong, a broom handle, or the commonest, three handclaps – to indicate both the beginning and the end of the play. After the final three claps the children line up, and each one indicates the name of the character just played followed by his real name, in the following style: I was the lion, I'm Martin. They then remove their disguises, and finally, the other group members and spectators, if any, applaud each actor.

Most children's psychodramatists have concluded that commentaries and reflections concerning their experience are not easy for the children, and they prefer to avoid asking the children to verbalize. Aichinger asks the children only for simple feedback at a very general level:

> They will only say: it was fun, wonderful, stupid, etc. We don't interpret the children's play during this discussion phase as is customary for psychoanalysts. It is not a question of affective or intellectual elaboration as in adult psychodrama . . . The purpose of the final conversation is closure of the action, calming the emotions of the active phase.
>
> (*Aichinger & Holl, 1979, p. 128*)

According to Anzieu, systematic interpretations formulated after every session provoke anxiety in the children, who may be given the impression that the psychodramatist has left the play space. Anzieu introduces the formula of a "statement" close to the Rogersian idea of empathy and a non-directive method that limits itself to reflecting and repeating the affective expressions of the interlocutor. The "statements" are limited to making reference to the ambience, the theme, and sometimes to behavior (that they were fidgety or spoke too softly). Aichinger notes that, compared with adult psychodrama, the verbal phase is much shorter.

In our practice, it is the communal meal that provides closure for the psychodrama session: the communal meal is a method for calming the emotions and creating an atmosphere of conviviality. It mobilizes a certain amount of regression, but also creates a familial ambience. Sometimes it provokes tensions; who is served first, who gets the best pieces (it is important that each child can take abundant amounts of food). Replenishment, in every sense of the word, makes it possible for the guests sitting around the table to make comments about the play.

The communal meal is a pleasant way to reintegrate reality, evoking ideas of family cohesion and providing a kind of oral compensation for the children's frustrations.

But the table that is set seemingly by itself at the end of the session (magically, so to speak) with all the good things one could wish for also is a presence that exudes the ambience of fairy tales.

A gifted colleague, a good actress who volunteered to join the facilitators after hearing our desperate SOS concerning the aggressiveness and horseplay that we could not find a way to stop, was deeply outraged when she heard about our unhealthy dietary habits. She demanded healthier foods, with vegetables, fruits, and more variety. We realized that she was right. But the children no longer recognized their "table set yourself." We were forced to go back to the old unhealthy menu, which my colleague Claude had dubbed "the chicken-and-French fries ritual."

In those groups where the sessions last less than 90 minutes, we use simplified versions of the communal meal: consuming fruit juice with cookies or a snack. One of my colleagues, Margot Tompa, who made up stories about the rabbit with young twins, served her little clients "sweets" made of shredded carrots, cabbage, and lettuce.

Other colleagues who play with marginalized children have adopted the rule of designating a little boy as a master of the house and a little girl as mistress of the house at each session to heighten their sense of responsibility. The boy is in charge of distributing drinks and the girl serves the snack.

We might add that beyond its symbolic significance, the communal meal, breakfast, or snack has another function, given the fact that a portion of our children, whether in France or Hungary, were actually malnourished and came to the sessions truly hungry.

6

PREVENTIVE AND THERAPEUTIC FUNCTIONS OF CHILDREN'S PSYCHODRAMA

Psycho-sociology of marginal families

Alfred Adler expresses a sense of dread about the odd and tragic course of development of the "difficult child."

> He has the worst opinion of his future. He feels oppressed by his social relationships: he believes he is the weakest and smallest, and has never felt what it means to have the affection of others . . . having little esteem for himself, he will have a very strong sense of inferiority . . . These children manifest permanent hostility and anxiety.
>
> (*Adler & Jahn, 1958, p. 164*)

Children called "at risk" come for the most part from marginal and sometimes abusive families who suffer from a pseudo-hereditary illness that is transmitted from generation to generation. We will touch upon their problematic in its psychosocial aspect to understand the specific experiences of marginal families presenting with the scars of cumulative deprivation.

What characterizes those that Winnicott calls *the badly off* is that they suffer from multiple deficits, both affective and social. Theirs is a multifactorial handicap, pseudo-hereditary and self-reproducing, and characterized by:

1 Poverty

- Lack of financial resources, lack of safe housing
- Limited cultural resources/environment lacking proper stimulation, low level of education.
- Delayed verbal and intellectual development, etc.

2 Distortion or deficiency of social sense (*Gemeinschaftsgefühl*)

Asocial tendencies "that we can trace back to the first years of a child's life . . . may be seen in the behavior of the whole family, and in the behavior of an entire nation," states Adler.

(*Adler, 1978, p. 114*)

What keeps these families from developing a social sense?

a The sense of family failure/discouragement, pessimism

One of the major obstacles to the social adaptation of the child is being raised in a family that has lost its courage and suffers from a pessimism that can be transmitted to their children.

(*Adler, 1958, p. 35*)

b Perception of the world as hostile

A certain kind of environment develops hostile feelings in the child to such a point that he assumes the world is malevolent.

c Auto-defensive reactions, aggressive reflexes

They experience the hostility of the world with a great intensity and even exaggerate it. They are always dressed for combat and expect the worst.

(*Ibid., p. 37*)

d A social inferiority complex that is sometimes compensated for by a sense of superiority.

We might cite a fifth factor that sums up the preceding ones, which is the *lack of reciprocity*. Since it is difficult for them to identify with others, they do not regard themselves as belonging to humanity.

3 Lack of continuity of lifestyle

a Frequent changes of domicile (moving, change of partners, repeated placements, rivalry between parents and grandparents).

The abusive family bears some resemblance to the incestuous family. This primarily involves its ambiguous structure, which one could even call a perversion of affectivity: the child ultimately doubts the possibility of being loved.

Bruno, hunger and lilies of the valley

(The transformation of self-image in a pseudo-stupid little boy)

Perhaps we chose Bruno to illustrate this chapter because of his truly implausible life circumstances, including such a concentration of unfavorable conditions that if we did not recognize the possibility of children's creativity to allow them to overcome the determinism of familial relationships, if we were not incurably optimistic Adlerian psychologists, we would surely not have accepted this boy into the workshop, for we would have considered any attempt at changing the course of his life as being hopeless.

At age six Bruno is a delicate and withdrawn little boy. He makes no eye contact and stares off elsewhere. His speech is scarcely comprehensible, his vocabulary impoverished, and he mumbles.

His first drawings are self-portraits of a kind – an enormous head with little puny legs emerging from the head. This is a tadpole of a man. The face is without expression and asymmetrical, one eye is looking to the right and the other to the left.

Bruno is silent and withdrawn into himself, but the children accept him from the start, because he is nice and evokes compassion. His mother is a woman with protruding teeth, a desultory way of speaking, who smiles continually in a benevolent sort of way. Her two older daughters, who are seventeen and eighteen years old, were raised in the state foster system from a very early age. Three children are still at home, an adolescent girl of fifteen, Bruno, and little David – each with a different father. David's father lives with them, a man of short stature, who suffers from epilepsy and enuresis. He used to be a street sweeper but was fired from his job because he did his work badly, stopping at every corner to have a glass of wine to cheer himself up.

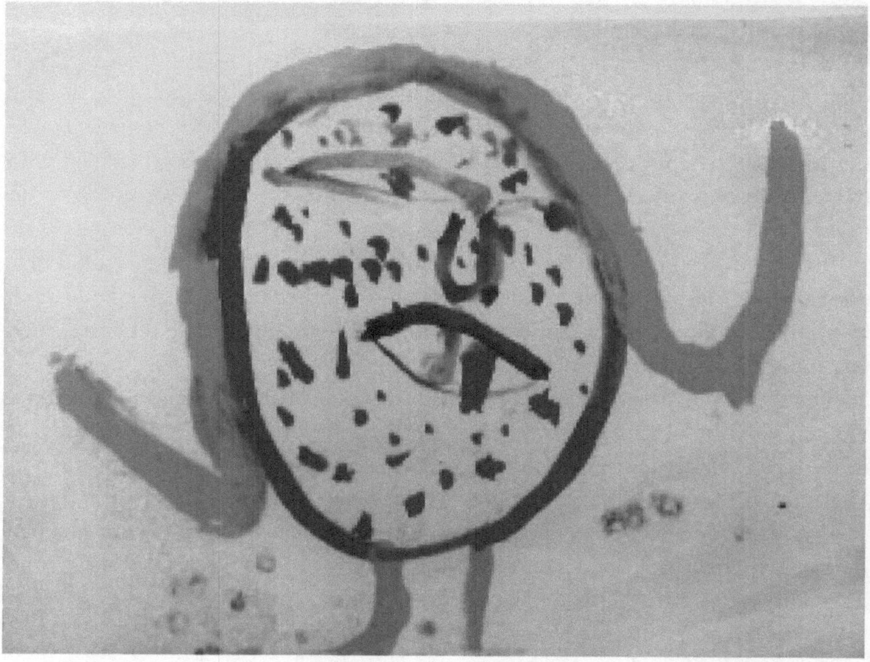

FIGURE 6.1 Bruno's self-portrait when he first came

Ms. Violaine had been a state fostered child herself. She spent her childhood – from the age of eight to fifteen – at the Valley Foundation, a psychiatric facility, admitted for reasons she does not know. After that, she was given a placement in a rural setting. She never learned to read or write. She was always kindly disposed to social workers and educators from the child protection service, including myself.

One day, an encyclopedia salesman came to her house with the *Universal Encyclopedia* and Ms. Violaine, who was ashamed to admit she was illiterate, subscribed to the twelve-volume series. It was with great difficulty that her educational worker was able to cancel the contract. The family lived in a three-storey apartment building in a Paris suburb. The house was built after the war, but for some incomprehensible reason, there was no bathroom – something very problematic, especially in view of Mr. Violaine's enuresis.

When we visited them, we encountered Mr. Violaine with Bruno in the stairwell. He had just purchased a May Day bouquet of lilies of the valley for the mistress of the house; Bruno was not Mr. Violaine's biological son but the son of, we'll call him, Mr. Dupont, who had been the mother's previous companion. The little boy was two years old when his father died, and he reacted to this death with great intensity. He became depressed, absent, anorexic, and for months he hardly spoke. At nursery school he was withdrawn and suffered from occasional attacks of rage. It was impossible to know if he was developmentally delayed or if he was mentally handicapped.

After only a short time he felt comfortable at the workshop. He would arrive in the morning having eaten nothing. There was always black coffee at home but rarely bread.

As the plays were being prepared, he would stand on tip-toe and, when it was time to choose a role, he would be the first volunteer: "*I'm* going to be the policeman" (whether the role fitted in with the play or not). Once he had claimed this role, my therapist colleague would take the part of an adjunct policeman who treated Bruno as his chief, and would ask, "So, chief, what are we going to do today?" etc.

Bruno was well liked by the group members. Shanti, an older girl, would play the part of a big sister with him, and he also had other friends. Later he learned to play roles other than the policeman, equipped with appropriate disguises, such as a cape, a cap, and assorted gloves.

The turning point happened when Shanti suggested a play in which an unfaithful woman took the street cleaner as her lover. My colleague, Claude, played the part of the lover, and Bruno joined him as a companion (Claude was unaware of Mr. Violaine's profession at that time).

Bruno was an affectionate, friendly, and sensitive little boy. I was very touched on the day when I returned after two weeks away from the workshop, and Bruno discreetly asked me: "Your mother died?" This was the first time that he began to tell me the story of his own father's death.

Bruno's intellectual progress was remarkable. He developed the capacity for a very rich symbolic expression of his experience.

One day, he invented the play, "Bottles in Love." The play was all the more interesting since, like him, the majority of the children in the group had alcoholic fathers. Bruno shouldered the role of a bottle in love. He also took part in many other dramatic plays. However, what I particularly would like to relate here has to do with his participation in a play that staged the affective experience of children abused by negligence and of children suffering from abandonment anxiety.

A play in which Bruno played one of the principal roles:

The parents are going out to eat in a restaurant. They waited until their sons were soundly asleep before leaving.

Bruno and Clovis are stretched out on top of two tables placed side by side. They are snoring and sucking their thumbs; each one pulls the cover to his side. As soon as their parents have left, Bruno uses the chamber pot, and the two boys are in a rage – there go the parents, off to banquet without them. The angry children make a horrible mess; they break anything they can get their hands on. Bruno smears the wall with his excrement and cuts his mother's dresses to shreds. When the parents return, the children resume their baby positions. They sleep rolled up in a ball while sucking their thumbs.

The parents are furious. First the boys deny everything – it wasn't them – but finally they admit the truth and blame the parents for being so self-centered, for thinking only about themselves and abandoning them. They went out for a banquet without them. (Once at the beginning of the month, we surprised the entire family, who were consuming take-out ice cream composed of a wide variety of flavors garnished with fruits and whipped cream.)

This is how Bruno staged the two possibilities for children who are deprived. Either, in regression, they pretend to be babies who have no awareness of the realities, who do not let themselves be conscious of injustice (this is what Bruno had done in reality – at the age of six he seemed like a baby), or else they express their discontent and revolt in a violent way. Bruno staged all of this in the play where the mode of aggression had anal resonances.

His precocious pre-adolescent revolt was also atypical.

When Bruno reached the age of eight, his mother considered him to be too independent and "unbearable," perhaps just because he had stopped playing the baby, was getting reasonable grades in school, and had moved from special classes to normal classes – that is to say, he had surpassed the level of the family. He learned to read and write (sometimes with mistakes) and had turned into an independent little boy.

The conflict was precocious – Bruno ran away. His mother decided to put him in state foster care, but ultimately, we managed to restore a peaceful atmosphere in their home. His older sister, who had likewise surpassed the level of the family, also supported him.

During this period, he was no longer drawing deformed babies, but instead, a young knight advancing along his way (Figure 6.2).

In subsequent years, I heard occasional news of the family. The older daughter married, and Ms. Violaine complained that she rarely let her take care of her baby. Bruno is working in a garage, and I don't know if he has started a family.

FIGURE 6.2 Drawing by Bruno two years later

I believe that in coming to realize that he was a creative child worthy of love, Bruno developed intellectually and affectively. He has ceased to adopt the style of marginal families – he will not transmit it. When he was immersed in the style of his family's life, given its impoverishment, he had no other option than to play the part of a mentally handicapped and incapable baby. But once he succeeded in going beyond the family symbolically, the pathway toward affective and mental development opened up for him.

Màday, one of Hungary's most brilliant leaders and theoreticians of individual psychology says: "Respect is more important than love." We think that one cannot recognize the child without loving him. What comes first is acceptance. When we met puny little Bruno for the first time, or François with his knife-edge profile, we probably did not feel respect for them but rather, the desire to take care of them so as to permit these children who barely existed to become.

7

GROUP THERAPY WITH ABUSED CHILDREN

Abused children constitute a special sub-group of children at risk. They experience a negative self-image that is especially intense, and they suffer from an acute sense of guilt and self-deprecation, which they are forced to take on in order to preserve family homeostasis. We could summarize this by: "If they mistreat me, it's surely because I deserve it."

One can distinguish three general categories of treatment of children that is regarded as abuse:

1 Abuse by omission, that is to say, neglect, poor care, leaving a child unattended, failure to provide adequate nutrition (this is the general case for children of marginal families).
2 Physical abuse.
3 Sexual abuse.

These three forms of abuse are frequently seen in combination.

One of the principal aims of all Adlerian group psychodrama for children is to restore their self-respect. In the framework of group therapy, we try to help them emerge from their painful sense of devaluation and strengthen their inadequate narcissism.

The drawing below illustrates the affective problems of such a child.

Family drawing by an abused child

Karine is the daughter of a mother – we'll call her Ms. P. – whose life was fragmented by ruptures and restarts, abandonments and foster placements, and returns home. Her parents were divorced and she fled her mother's home to live with her father. This did not go well. She made the circuit of many FLIC foster care

FIGURE 7.1 Drawing by Karine

institutions, which she left voluntarily. Finally, she ended up on the street, where, after different encounters with men, she became involved with a pimp. Little Karine was the daughter of this man, who was subsequently given a long prison sentence. Karine reminded her mother of her troubled past. This is how she became a scapegoat and an abused child. One day, Ms. P. took her daughter by the hand to bring her to the home of her own mother, from whom she had been estranged for a long time, and with whom she had always had a conflicted relationship. She was so afraid of the hostile feelings she felt toward her own daughter that she feared she would do something irreparable.

When we first met her, Karine's mother had embarked upon a new life with a very, very serious man who worked at a funeral parlor, with whom she had a second daughter, Roxanne. A few years later, after the couple's life had stabilized, she took back Karine.

Even though she strongly resembled her beautiful, dynamic, and intelligent mother, this little girl, as the bearer of the imprint of the past, represented the burdens of a past that had been left behind, which Ms. P. could no longer carry. She regarded Karine as a non-compliant child, the incarnation of a part of her own being, of the faults that (as is often the case with abusive parents) she could no longer accept. In addition, her mother complained particularly about the fact that, in her presence, her daughter became petrified and immobile, as if she were distraught.

We were pleasantly surprised when Ms. P. consented to her daughter's regular attendance at the workshop. Karine was a member for two years. At the time of our first interview, Karine was a pretty, blonde, seven-year-old girl with blue eyes and very pale skin. For incomprehensible reasons, her mother had put her on a diet (maybe so that there would be less of her). The drawing above (Figure 7.1) was sketched during her first year at the workshop.

In the drawing, one sees a mother who is quite tall, a somewhat shorter father (this proportion does not match reality at all, as her step-father is quite a bit taller than her mother), a little sister right next to the mother, and finally, in last place, herself. In the drawing, Karine is noticeably different from the other members of the family: she is the only one without either hair or feet; she is a very tall, bald baby. What is most striking is that the female members of the family don't have hands. The person who drew this picture has eliminated any chance of mistreatment, for how could a mother who doesn't even have any hands mistreat her child? Her own mutilation is the interdiction of her own aggression, the impossibility of becoming violent. On the family drawing – and this does correspond to the facts – the stepfather is the only character who is not aggressive.

We have presented Karine's drawing in order to illustrate the feelings of an abused child. In the second part of this chapter we will tell the story of her history, her evolution, and how she went from being the deformed being negatively different from the others – to become a magnificent young girl, conscious of her worthiness.

We will continue our analysis of the problems of abused children with a psychodrama invented by a young girl called Shanti (already presented in the introduction). Shanti's psychodrama speaks about physical abuse. It helps us understand the process through which a child becomes abused.

Shanti's psychodrama about the abused child

The topic of the story is related to an outside event. The previous evening on television, there was a news item about an abusive mother. Shanti was moved by the young mother's words: "I was beaten, I also beat. I can't stop myself."

> "It's awful," says Shanti.
>
> "But she got help, and she changed," I say.
>
> Shanti (angry): "Let's say she didn't hit ten times a day any more, but only five times a day. It's still terrible."
>
> "Come on!"
>
> "I hope," adds Shanti, "that when I have a child, I won't do the same."

She suggests we put on a psychodrama about this subject.

Preliminary discussion about the topic

Once there was a couple, and they had a good life. Then one day, they fought, and the man left the family. The woman noticed that their son resembled his father, and she started to hate him and hit him. After a few years, her husband came back.

Let's say he has a son by a different woman. This second son is beaten by his older brother.

"Why?"

"The parents mistreat the older brother, and he, in turn, mistreats his younger brother."

"So the father comes back: what does the son say?"

Alexandre: "He kills him, bang! With a knife!"

"And then?"

"Then," says Alexandre, "he will be killed, too!"

Choosing the roles

Shanti chose the role of the mother. The psychotherapist would have the role of the father. Since there was no candidate for the part of the abused child, it was up to me to play his part. Alexandre (who really has an older brother) would like to play the role of the little brother.

The psychodrama

Scene 1

The baby is lying down on two chairs placed side by side. The parents are speaking about their child, and they say he is a good boy who looks like his mother. The baby, sucking his thumb, looks first at one, then the other. Then they get angry, and the father declares that for his part, he's going to go to work.

Shanti: "Today? But it's Sunday!"
Father: "I have things to do."
Shanti: "But there's this child, you should pay attention to him."
Father: "He's your son."

The dispute gets more intense, and the baby cries.

Shanti (angry): "You shouldn't bawl for no reason. Just like his father!"

They scuffle. The father goes away. Before leaving, he says: "I want another son!"

Shanti turns to the child and yells at him. The baby cries louder and louder. Shanti grabs an object and hits him on the head. The little boy is quiet. He defends himself, placing his hands folded in front of his face.

Shanti: "Why are you doing that? To make me look bad in front of the neighbors? So they think I'm abusing you? It isn't true, you're lying!"

The child is silent; he hasn't said a single word up to this point.

Shanti: "You're the one who doesn't want to love me, it's not me!" (over the course of the monologue she becomes more and more aggressive toward the child).

For a moment, the child is silent, and then he starts to howl, shakes, twists, strikes his head against the wall, and writhes.

Scene 2

Several years later, the father arrives with his new son, played by Alexandre.

Shanti: "Where is his mother?"
Father: "She stayed downstairs in the car."
Shanti: "Is this your son? He doesn't really look like you."

The boy shrinks back into a corner, he is trembling.

The older son (H.K.): "Are you my father, mister?"

The parents argue. The older son attacks the father.

Shanti: "So many years have gone by and you haven't written. You never came to visit us."
Father: "But you're wrong, I often wrote, but you didn't give him my letters!"
Shanti: "That's not true."

Shanti calls upon her son to back her up. He doesn't listen to his father and takes his mother's side.

The father remarks that the big boy speaks slowly, articulates poorly and gets tangled up in his words.

Father: "What an odd child, he's not like my son!"
Shanti: "I raised him how I wanted to!"

They finally separate. The mother sends away her ex-husband as well as her son.

Comments

In this brief but rich scene, it is a child that stages the origin of the abusive situation. In it, we can recognize the relationship of the parents and the process through which the child becomes the scapegoat, and the conflict unfolds before our eyes in an interplay of alternating identifications.

When everything is functioning well at the beginning, the child is a marvelous being in which the mother recognizes herself. She perceives the child differently according to her different states of mind. In the desperate cries of the child, the mother believes she can recognize the husband's aggressiveness (the baby bawls like his father). As her anger mounts she moves to action, as if she were punishing the father through the child.

In the scene that was played, the child is the victim of a negative transference that is all the more absurd since the baby is behaving passively. He is quiet. The mother experiences his silence as resistance and attributes to the baby all the feelings and desires that are hostile. But well beyond this, the child confronts his mother with her own culpability.

It is in this way, via projection, that the child becomes the persecutor. One blames the child for wanting to humiliate the mother in front of the neighbors ("Why are you doing that?"), even though there is no neighbor present.

The mother's cry erupts with dramatic force: "It's you who doesn't want to love me!"

In this scene where she is abusing the child, the mother sees herself as someone who is unloved. The roles are reversed. The parent sometimes acts as if she were a frightened and unloved child, confronted through the child with an adult from whom she expects love and reassurance. The scenario illustrates that here it is an innocent person who is being maltreated.

As for the child, he is the character who is suffering, a prisoner of a relationship in which he is experienced as bad and is physically abused. This mistreatment has somatic consequences – the baby moves about convulsively, and bangs his head against the wall.

The second scene similarly shows that the child does not exist outside his relation to the mother. This is his sole referent, his unique connection. It is toward her that the child adapts and conforms himself.

We are witness to an odd set of instinctive transferences:

1 The child identifies with the aggressor (with his mother against his father).
2 He turns the reactive aggression he feels against the others (against his father, against his brother).

Shanti's identification in the play with an abusive mother made a deep impression on us (this role reversal would have been hard to imagine for a child who was still trapped in this kind of *double bind*). She lives the role so intensely that at a particular moment, she departs from the frame and becomes physically abusive – she actually hits the child's head – something that we regard less as a form of *acting out* than a result of the emotion evoked by the scene.

The question arises about the catharsis of action. The intensity of the psychodramatic experience produces a shock, a kind of affective shock, which may be considered as a factor that permits a rupture in the fateful path that connects the abused child to the abusive parent and reproduces the process from generation to generation. In the transitional space of psychodrama, the child can abreact, can liberate herself in a symbolic manner, but not without suffering, from the role of the violent mother.

Shanti presented with all the stigmata of marginal children – difficulty expressing herself, poor school performance, and withdrawal. Over the several years, course of her participation in the workshop, the extent of the human, intellectual, and affective capacities with which she was endowed became manifest. We consider ourselves fortunate to have had a chance to contribute to her self-realization.

With Shanti, we had the chance to witness, through psychodrama, the development of the abusive situation, the psychic structure of the abusive mother and the psychosocial conditions that are responsible for it. We saw the emergence of the mother's separation anxiety at the time of her break-up with her life companion, complemented by her negative self-image (starting from the question of her neighbor's opinions) and her incapacity to imagine that she could be loved. We are witness to her fragility, her affective hunger (she expects her child to nurture her), and on the other hand, her exaggerated and disproportionate reactions and her frustration. The bad mother who is abusive is impassioned, and her reactions are excessive.

François and the game of hide-and-(go-)seek (Freud's 'fort-da')

François was a physically abused child, who, together with his little brother, had been placed in a children's village but his violent father came and snatched him away. After his return, he enjoyed a moment of calm without abuse. It was at this time that he rejoined the play therapy group and painted this happy image (Figure 7.2) in which we see a boy who is a bit bloated, and with twisted feet, but in a good mood, swinging in a hammock. You see the sun just barely covered by clouds, and the hammock is floating between the sky and the ground, stretched between two trees.

François' drawings

The first drawing is an image of a rather passive little boy, but he is definitely present. Two weeks later, the same boy painted a picture with virtually the same structure, except that between the two images, he had disappeared; in the second drawing, we see the same two pillars (the two trees), and a few clouds, but there is no longer any sun. The warming sun had been a regenerative element for François, and this is why I would be inclined to consider this as a paternal symbol. Thus, the warming paternal symbol had disappeared, and at the same time, the little boy had disappeared as well! We see a brownish watery spot in the same position as

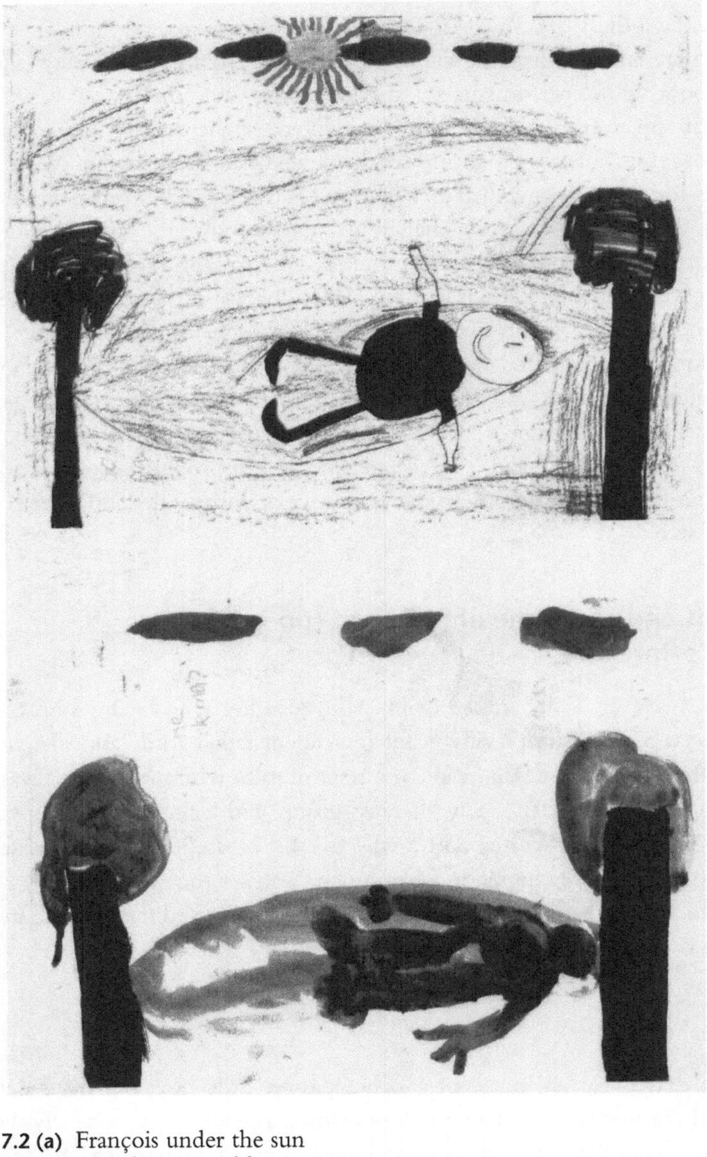

FIGURE 7.2 (a) François under the sun
(b) The disappeared boy

the happy kid from the previous drawing. Now however, he has no face or physical reality, and is only a formless mass with a wet appearance that makes us think of other things, we might say an intra-uterine shape, placed within the maternal uterus, a liquefied child who has ceased to exist.

However, we think that the abused child differs from the psychotic child, as he does not remain permanently outside of reality and the option of returning is not permanently closed. Sometimes he is present and at other times, he disappears.

François played games of appearing and disappearing continuously (let us recall Freud's 'fort-da'). When he arrived in the morning, he seemed to be elsewhere, looked out the window, walked right by us, without saying hello, of course, as if he were someone who was present without being there. François ran away if you called him, and could be found in places with symbolic significance, between the two casements of a double door, or in the armoire. However, his regressive behavior (unlike his second drawing where he is completely suppressed) had a double meaning. Beyond the regressive symbolism, it also contained a call: find me or make me be reborn, put me into the world. Sometimes, François would place himself high up – he climbed on the sideboard and became immobile like a statue. When we prepared for the play, he would climb to the top of the armoire and look at us from above (thereby signaling his independence, but also at the same time compensating for his sense of inferiority: I am elsewhere, but I am on top). What we had to avoid at all costs was to call him to order. We did not stigmatize his behavior as deviant, and did not indicate that he was disturbing the normal functioning of the group. What he expected was the call to order, which he would hear as a call to run away.

Alfred Adler expresses fear for the future potentially tragic development of this sort of child who finds himself in "enemy territory."

François would flee, run outside, and build himself a refuge in the garden.

But he was able to hear a friendly call. If we asked him to leave his perch and join the others, this might take some time, but finally he could sense something along the lines of "I would like you to be with us."

One could imagine that it is the dyadic relationship that made it possible for him to become integrated into the group, but it is not certain whether this dyad (as we shall see later on) consisted of an adult and a child, because most of these children have the tendency to recreate the sadomasochistic relationship to which they are accustomed with all adults.

Specifics of family relational systems in abusive families

What is oddest is that the abusive parent, who is often descended from a chain of abused children that goes back several generations,
does not merely abuse her child, but also adores him. This is not just the case with abusive mothers but also with fathers.

Anxiogenic love

As we have just noted, the mother who beats her child also adores him. Passionate and irascible, she has a tendency to be sentimentally demonstrative to excess. She cajoles her child, covers him with kisses – one can also see this sometimes out on the street.

Adler also noted this ambivalence: "I have encountered a large number of adults and children whose entire life was marked by the inadequacy of the mother-child relationship. Useless to point out that the mother loves her child very much, for this counterargument is never convincing" (Adler & Jahn, 1958, p. 162).

Absent presence

At meetings with the mother and child, one can see that the mother who adores her child pays scarce attention to the child who is present. She is only interested in herself. The little one behaves in an increasingly wild manner, and the mother pays no attention until – as if emerging from a dream – suddenly, she reacts in word and action, and she gives him a couple of slaps. She had been so self-preoccupied and had such a need that we pay attention to her that she almost forgot her child, who nevertheless was doing his best to get her attention. This absent presence provokes anxiety in the child, and he calls to his mother until the breaking point, when the mother is no longer able to stand the commotion he has made.

It was as if the only way to get his mother's attention was to tug too hard on the cord and make himself noticed as a child to punish.

Abuse is the price the child is ready to pay to obtain the mother's presence and her love. Over time, love and abuse become inseparable. But as time passes, it is the love that becomes anxiogenic. This anxiety is not entirely the same as that of the child who fears abandonment.

The child who fears abandonment constantly fears the loss of the one he loves. The child suffering from abandonment syndrome does not dare to make attachments because he is afraid – if he loses his mother, he won't be able to survive. For the abused child, it is love itself that is contaminated, made unnatural and deformed.

At this point, love and abuse merge; to be loved = to be abused. The *double bind* to which we alluded earlier is a sign of schizophrenia, but here, this object relation takes a different form.

The abused child is afraid of himself.

One says: I love you – but the child hears: I am going to kill you. What else can the child do other than what we have just observed in François? He flees or disappears.

The symbolic rehabilitation of a young abused girl: Karine and the ugly duckling

Shanti, who was not a physically abused child, but only an unwanted child who bore a multigenerational burden, was able to express the familial components of the process of abuse in a nuanced way. Karine, for her part, had suffered not only from profound rejection but also from physical abuse, as we have previously described. In her mother's affective life, she called up a rejected past. Her mother complained especially about Karine's acting fearful and rigid in her presence.

We recall three phases in Karine's history at the workshop. At the beginning, she presented as a very polite, cute, ambitious little girl; she appeared to have a well-adjusted personality, with a desire to meet all the demands of school. At school (in the preparatory course) she obtained good grades. This was the first manifestation of a *false self*. We might even have thought that she was a little girl without problems if we hadn't known about her history. During this period, she produced pretty drawings that were regular and conventional, and she did not initiate any psychodrama plays.

The second phase of her life at the workshop began when she brought in her little friend Venus, whom we placed in the group. Reassured by Venus's presence, Karine's style of behavior changed. She produced drawings that were much less elaborate; she took the initiative; she became wilder, undisciplined, and capricious. It was during this period that she made the drawing of the she-devils and the washcloth (Figure 7.3).

FIGURE 7.3 Like mother, like daughter

She painted two she-devils with horns, with their arms held tightly against their bodies (recalling the defense mechanisms cited earlier in relation to her family picture). The two horned beings, who appear to have a reduced capacity for movement, are arguing. Karine's commentary: it's the mother and her baby. The mother is pointing to the stained dress of her baby.

> "Look at that! Oh! How disgusting!"
>
> "It wasn't me," says the baby.
>
> Next, pointing to the mother's washcloth, she says: "And this? This isn't dirty?"
>
> And the baby starts to cry.

The two she-devils accuse each other back and forth, yet they are not alike. The drawing indicates a partial identification where the smaller devil represents the negative pole. Here an important recognition appears: the ability to both feel and reject cross-identification. Indeed, the situation of the two she-devils is asymmetrical (Karine accentuates the unequal nature of the smaller devil when she calls it baby). The level of responsibility of the two she-devils is not the same; it is the mother's washcloth that is dirty, while it is the little one's dress. However, we should not underestimate the fact that some critical elements of identification are evident in the drawing. Karine does not deny that she is a little devil (this is the way that the badness always emphasized in the family appears in the drawing), but it is as if she has added "you may think I'm dirty but I'm not the only one." Her system of defense mechanisms is not yet fully developed, does not stand up, and she defends herself against denigration with negation, "It's not me." And the scene ends in tears. (We should point out that on the two drawings, the child wrote not only her first name but also the family name she had been given by her adoptive father. This illustrates the way she integrates, beyond the conflict that is represented in the drawing, the Lacanian symbolic function represented by the name of the father.)

We might call the third period of Karine's participation in the workshop, which lasted a school year, the year of the duckling. This took place under the sign of her elaboration of the story of the ugly duckling.

There first appeared a drawing that depicts a mother hen and the little duckling (Figure 7.4). In the drawing we see a hen, and in the balloon that emerges from her beak, we can read the following text: "Oh, no, my egg broke! I won't have a chick." On the left side, we see a broken egg, and from it emerges the head of a chick that is complaining, "Why doesn't anyone want me?"

In speaking about her drawing, Karine refers to a story she read at school: the hen is looking at herself in the mirror. "Who is this ugly figure with ruffled feathers?" she asks.

Later, during the course of the morning, we learned from Karine what had actually happened: "My mother was taken to the hospital because she had a dead child in her belly and they had to take it out."

FIGURE 7.4 The broken egg

In the story of the hen, Karine refers to the image seen in the mirror. The hen was shocked when she saw herself in the glass, and she thought it must be somebody else. Couldn't we regard this as the paradigm of the mother's desire to project her negative image of herself onto the child? In the drawing, the chick (who looks more like a little duckling) senses the hen's desire that she be dead. ("Why doesn't anyone want me?")

Who is this chick? The aborted fetus? Karine?

In the speech balloons (Karine is one of the few children who add a written text to her drawings) there already appears a tendentious apperception, that is to say, a questionable interpretation of the situation. The hen expresses her sadness, she would have loved to have a chick born but alas, her egg broke. The chick (or duckling), by contrast, indicates that she has to disappear because nobody wants her. Did her mother lose her fetus or did she abort it? In this symbolic representation (we are not using the word symbolic in a Lacanian sense, but the one generally accepted in philosophical and aesthetic theory), we can already see the appearance of the fantasized image of a murderous mother.

Some three months later, during the first half of the year of the duckling, Karine found the need to tell us, to verbalize for the first time, the fact that she was abused. Once, under the pretext that Karine had lied about something, her mother had forbidden her from coming to the workshop. The following week, the three of us, my colleague Claude, Karine, and I spoke together, and Karine told us angrily, "I don't understand anything, I don't know why my mother is punishing me. She sometimes says white, and the next day, the same thing becomes black. She gives me chores as penance, for example, I have to write the same sentence a hundred times over. Sometimes she hits me. She is always afraid that I'll lose my identity card."

> "Do you lose things often?"
>
> "Yes, no, sometimes I can't find some things, but the next day they reappear. She doesn't give me time to find anything. She hits me. Sometimes I get punished on account of my sister. Her, they leave in peace."
>
> "Because she's little?"
>
> "No, because she's mother's little darling."
>
> "And what does your father say about it?"
>
> "She hits me when he's not at home. Mom annoys me sometimes, she is looking for me all the time."

Here, Karine is telling us in words about the physical and psychological abuse that she undergoes. And yet, it isn't the verbalization that helped her to resolve her problems. In the symbolic space of the workshop, she was able to elaborate the deeper reasons for her mother's murderous rejection of her: the mother's negative and divided self-image – see the hen in front of the mirror. Over time, beyond her symbolic understanding, Karine was able to take the path toward rehabilitation, toward re-creating her own self.

Over the course of the year of the duckling, different phases in the life of the little duck made this process of recreation. The little duck made numerous forays into the world, she traveled across the seas to meet her grandmother. (The real grandmother, who raised her when she was small, was an important maternal figure for Karine who was, by then, forbidden to her.) In other drawings, the ugly duckling is swimming between two banks and she is cast off from everywhere, until one day. . . . In her psychodramatic play, Karine re-enacted Anderson's story of the ugly duckling (as we well know, the author had lived a similar story himself). It took the passage of a year in the accepting and warm climate of the workshop before she was able to beautify the face of the chick/duckling once declared ugly, before the moment of symbolic transcendence could take place. Karine no longer was fighting against her imaginary with its partial alienating identification, as in the case of the she-devils washing up, where the little devil was the ugly reproduction of the bigger one. She overcame the identification of the rejected and murderous mother, by differentiating herself from her degrading mother and emphasizing her difference. This child recognized herself as other, but this was a compensating difference because the reason she had called herself ugly was none other than the promise of the ultimate development of an exceptional being. Thus, she could make herself beautiful and become a magnificent swan who could fly far away, equally at ease in the water and in the skies.

Karine's grades at school were remarkable, confounding the projected cloud of her mother's anxiety (who forecast that her superficial, absent-minded, and messy little one could only be a terrible student). Karine achieved a version of the swan, and was always among the best in her class. At the workshop, this young girl learned to play and rehabilitated herself through play. This is how the little girl who had retreated into her *false self*, whose superficial adaptation concealed an existential lack, became an individual with her own desires and her own character. She was able to fulfill herself as an original and unique young woman by reevaluating everything that others had designated as her ugliness.

We can confirm that her drawings and commentaries, as well as her play, included aesthetic references. The she-devils are ugly, the child is disgusting, the hen is repulsive. The turning point belongs to the duckling, who could only have been ugly by misunderstanding, and was only awaiting the moment to fly away. Karine recognized herself in Andersen's story of the transformation of the ugly duckling into a magnificent swan. We always had the sense of Karine as a child who was lovely, intelligent, sensitive, beautiful, and generous. The children easily accepted her in the workshop, but she did not form a friendship with just anybody. It was with Shanti, an older girl, that she became close friends.

Group therapy of Clovis, a sexually abused young boy

In this section, devoted to family dynamics, we will now direct our attention to Clovis. We chose Clovis to illustrate a certain moment of consciousness, a transformation and revaluation of self, and a profound realignment of a child's way of being and living, to which group dynamics, symbolic expression (drawing, play, psychodrama) and multiple affective transferences all contributed.

I met Clovis two years before he joined the group as part of personality testing ordered by the Juvenile Court Judge. It was on the occasion of his first visit that he painted a picture that was very dark, with a house and a transparent room (on the right) that let in the night (Figure 7.5). This picture, a devastating image, revealed an affective experience that was desperate, tragic, and depressed.

Doubling in the group situation

When we speak of the transferences that take place in the group, it is important not to neglect the role of the double – the alter ego. Children may discover this companion within the group. Sometimes relationship is found on the outside in the form of a brother, a friend, or a pal. For Clovis, it was François who became his double. Vénus had played the role of the disinhibitor for her friend, Karine, but François played a different role with Clovis. The Courts had removed each of the boys from their parental homes; they had each been abused by their fathers. Clovis's father had been sentenced to several months in prison, but at our request, he had been reprieved. In obtaining Clovis's history, it was revealed that his father was an abused person who became an abuser. When he was young he had been abused by his father (Clovis's paternal grandfather) and as an adolescent, he fled his parental home and enlisted in the French Foreign Legion. He underwent terrifying experiences during the Algerian War. He captured and tortured prisoners,

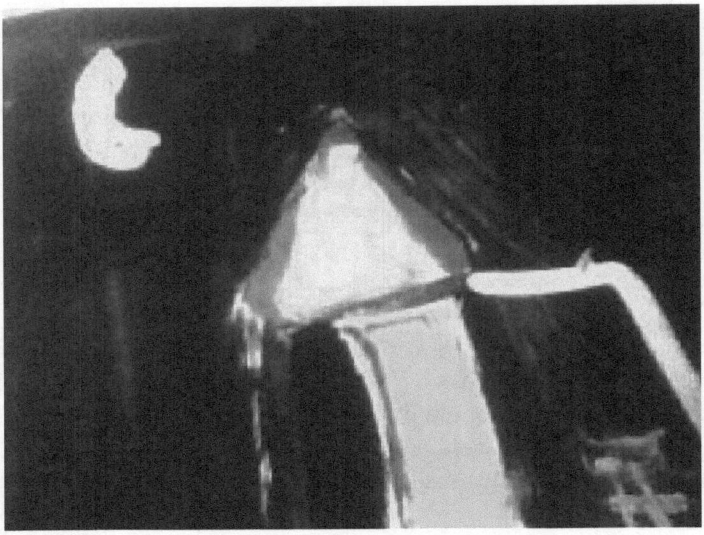

FIGURE 7.5 The house overrun by the night

and was tortured himself; he killed people and encountered death on a daily basis, all of which left a profound and indelible mark. Clovis was his elder son (he had a brother who was two years younger), his favorite and his scapegoat, doomed to abuse. In keeping with the habits of abusive parents, Clovis denied everything, but at one of our meetings, the father exclaimed, "at those moments, I want to cut off my hand." Clovis had been placed in a residential child psychiatry facility for two years and was then returned to the home. From that time on, the physical abuse stopped.

Clovis came to us after his return home, and he was a true wild child. He acted as if he were the only person in the world. He did not see the other children, and paid no attention to the adults. Although physically present, he made himself absent, lost in his own world. He certainly produced some beautiful drawings but would not comment on them, and would not speak about them with the other children.

His behavior was agitated and unstable. He would leave the workshop anytime the desire to do so struck him. Clovis preferred to leave by way of the window (we were lodged on the ground floor, but of course, entering and leaving by the window was forbidden). When he was called to order, he turned a deaf ear as if he truly hadn't heard a thing. His eating behavior was very odd: at noon he would eat amply, but he would then throw part of the food into the garbage only to take it back out and continue eating. Of all the children, he had the strongest suicidal impulses. One day he ran out into the street to lie down on the pavement in the position of a crucifix. Wherever he went, without his even paying attention, his mere presence evoked noise and furor. He perturbed the children's sense of safety.

People found him strange, and some children avoided him, perhaps those who had the most difficulty holding back their aggressive impulses. Clovis's behavior during this period made one think of an inaccessible psychotic child, insensitive to the world outside. If he participated at all in the preparation of the plays, it was only by calling up sketchy stories or terrifying images.

Then one day, for no apparent reason, Clovis moved into another phase. He would behave provocatively and, without waiting for a response from the adult, would then become aggressive, primarily by attacking the psychodramatist. During this period, he seemed to understand the rules of the workshop well enough, but sought to transgress them. From the moment anything was forbidden (like Eve and Adam in paradise) he desired the forbidden thing. Thus, he established a kind of communication, but a perverse kind, something like a call for punishment. This behavior inspired a negative counter-transference in the male dramatist that came close to rejection.

When my colleague came to understand the meaning of the provocations and began to refuse to participate in this game, a different kind of relationship was established between them. Although Clovis arrived in the morning full of fury, he would allow Claude to calm him down. Clovis often would speak to Claude and ask for his help. This supportive relationship allowed Clovis to express (through symbolic means in drawings) his aggression and his wish to kill the group one and all, including the psychodramatist. In this way, he succeeded in resisting the violent impulses that had led him to flee all contact.

Over time, Clovis's modes of communication changed, and he became able to approach the others with confidence. The person he most sought out was the psychodramatist, Claude, but he also communicated with the children. He tested our affective responses on multiple occasions, but I won't speak more about this now. I would rather move on to the turning point precipitated by the arrival of François to the group. This skinny little boy with a tormented face, his profile like a knife's edge, immediately provoked rejection from Clovis, who declared:

> "I don't like him."
> "But why?"
> "I don't like his face."

This dialogue took place at the table during the first meal that François ate with us. François had almost no reaction. He pretended he was deaf as if it wasn't about him at all. He responded with his typical technique, trying to disappear in order to ignore the abuse.

Clovis tried to engage in a test of power to humiliate the other boy and make him submit. He confiscated things that belonged to François, sometimes objects of no real importance, such as the wrappings of a package of cookies. He tried to make him change his place from a chair with a taller seat than the others. If we had let him, he would have taken over François's place. In François, Clovis recognized his double, the person he had been two years earlier, but a little smaller than him. He believed he had rediscovered his former self and at the same time, a supplemental personality.

This relationship reveals the family dynamics in abusive families. We were able to observe it not only in the symbolic creations (drawings, dramatic play) but also in reality, in the potential space for replacement created at the workshop. Clovis staged a number of elements of this complex situation in his play, "The lion and his cub."

The lion and his cub

The theme

The story line was the idea of a little girl, Heidi. The play takes place in a circus. A lion, not yet tamed, runs away. He is wild and he bites. Everyone panics. People no longer dare to leave their houses to buy their groceries. A lion-tamer tames the lion. He performs acts at the circus, and leaps through a ring of fire. He is trained and no longer a wild animal.

One of the boys, Bruno, comments:

> "He still gets very angry and when the tamer puts his head in his mouth, whammo, the lion swallows him up."
>
> Clovis says, "The lion was enraged because he lost his son. He'll get him back later on; the lion cub will come back. And afterwards, he won't get angry again."
>
> "And the lion-tamer?"
>
> Bruno: "They glue back his head with super-glue."

In this preparatory phase of the psychodrama, we discover how many individual motivations and personal symbolizations come together in a collective story. Heidi is an undisciplined girl of 6 – she is "not yet tamed." Bruno donates his aggressive, murderous impulses to the lion who bites off the lion-tamer's head. Clovis, for his part, projects his ambivalent relationship with his father onto the tamed lion – with a reversal in roles, since here, he is the lion-father.

Selecting roles, staging

Clovis takes on the role of the lion, and François the role of the lion cub. When the lion cub returns, there is violent friction between them, but there are also cuddles. We witness a scene where tenderness and battle exist side by side. The two lions do not seem especially tame. They join forces to mistreat the trainer who has recovered his head.

Commentary

For Clovis, the story of the lion recalled the abusive father and the family's explanation for the father's abusive behavior – he is wild because he has been deprived of his child. (See the father's comments when his sons were put in placement.) However, the play showed that the problem of the lion's aggression was not entirely resolved by the return of the cub.

Clovis thus addressed the frustration that the father experienced. But in the play, the lion does not appear appeased by his reunions, and instead, has chosen the lion cub as his partner in aggression. Against whom was this aggression directed? Against his alter ego or in alliance with him against the outside world?

Like the father lion, Clovis suffered from François's absence from the workshop, for at one point, François decided to stop coming, because the others did not like him. This was the way he transferred his lack of love onto the workshop. The children then decided to send him a letter to show him that he was mistaken. There were only two children who did not join in writing this letter, Heidi, a little girl who had been similarly abused and Clovis. He was unable to find the right words, but he did send something – a poem by François Villon.

When François returned to our midst, the two little boys frolicked together in the courtyard like little horses.

The reparative relationship established with the psychodramatist thus allowed Clovis to emerge from the vicious circle of rejection-provocation-punishment. The development of his relationship with François from mistreatment to reciprocity permitted him to take an important step in the direction of symbolization. This time, Clovis's new play was no longer about the symbolic representation of violence but the elaboration of true insight.

His relationship with François had already made it possible for us to understand:

a the nature of his family dynamics
b the not-unequivocal relationship with the abuser
c the efficacy of expression in symbolic form.

What he succeeded in expressing during his last creative piece of the year was the result of hard mental work. For two weeks Clovis seemed distracted. He kept separate from the others, not in his former aggressive style of keeping distance, but in a state that was pained and depressed. We tried to approach him but without much success.

The day of the last meeting, he sat down at a distance and started to draw, hiding his sheet of paper from curious eyes. He worked for about an hour, and then pinned his drawing up on the wall. It was "the ab-used man" (Figure 7.6).

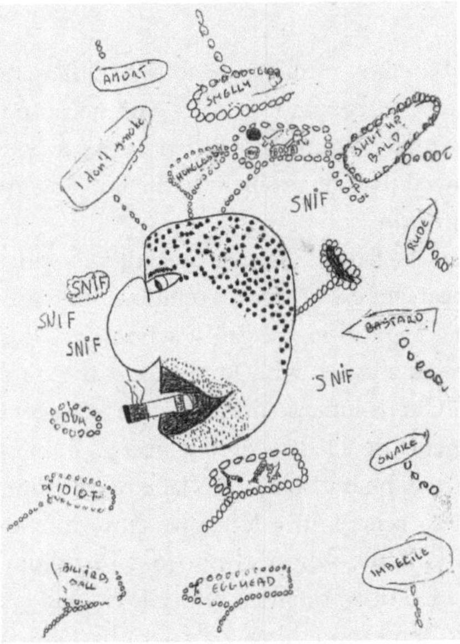

FIGURE 7.6 Drawing by Clovis

In the balloons that contained the words spoken by the character, there were texts that included ideas of destruction (war, explosion), devaluation (bum), and denial of what was visibly the case (I don't smoke). His fantasies reflect the treatment that he had received (explosion, gunshots), and the insults he bore regarding his physical appearance (billiard ball, egg head) and more generally, about his person (old imbecile, snake with glasses, garbage can). He verbally abused himself, he was abused. He deprecates himself, he is humiliated. This man has morbid thoughts. What haunts him is death.

This eleven-year-old boy understands the paternal problematic with a breathtaking intensity, and he understands and identifies in an exceptional way with the motifs and origins of his own abuse. He comes to an understanding of the pathological origins of his father's sense of culpability all the way back to the self-destructive suffering of the grandfather (the father's own father).

To review: it seems to us that in the potential space of the workshop, Clovis succeeded in liberating himself from a self-contained and self-destructive solitude that bordered on autism. This transformation includes creative elements: expression through drawing, including "the abused man," and the diverse roles played in different plays. The relational aspects of his rehabilitation were the special, re-equilibrating bond with the psychodramatist Claude (an ideal for the self and the positive father), the grounding relationship established with me, and the differentiated relationships he achieved with the members of the group. Besides the relationship described earlier with François, he also established a relationship of reciprocal gentle teasing with Heidi. Bruno was sometimes his partner in expressing their shared feelings of parental abandonment. Clovis ended up being accepted and respected by the whole group.

His return to affective life was accomplished with a backwards transference, something that a majority of abused men create with their sons and transmit to the next generation. Clovis managed to avoid following this path, and instead of following in his father's tracks, he understood and went beyond his father, although he paid for his transformation with a period of intense suffering.

8
BEHAVIORAL PROBLEMS

Aggression

Up until 1915, Freud considered aggression to be beyond the pleasure principle, an impulse whose character was not sexual, but rather tied to the instinct of self-preservation.

In his well-known work on aggression, Lorenz (1966) asserted that aggression is a real instinct that functions in the interests of preserving the species and is provoked in an automatic fashion by certain stimuli. Within the species, the principal manifestations of aggression are defense of territory, possessing the female and protection of one's progeny. Certain inhibitory mechanisms are manifested in the adult–child and male–female relationships and also for sparing the vanquished enemy. Such inhibition functions with a goal in mind, but unequally. It is determined according to the stage of life and is modified over time. For example, a female dog becomes sensitized to young animals around her once she begins to have puppies herself. But as soon as her puppies become bigger and venture from her, she may chase them away mercilessly when they return, as she no longer recognizes them as her own offspring. Management of aggression includes ritualized elements (a menacing posture, signals of submission, etc.), which serve to warn or placate the enemy or make him flee (Lorenz, 1995). Erich Fromm (1951) distinguishes two forms of aggression and hate. One form, which he calls rational, is manifested in the case of a reaction to attack. He attributes a biological function to such rational hatred, as it serves to defend life. Michael (Mihály) Bálint, one of the most illustrious members of the Budapest Psychoanalytic School believed that aggression is not an inherent trait, but rather, is induced by certain states – hunger, lack of love, lack of communication. Children who have experienced major trauma become aggressive. Aggression can also result from situations of lack that involve "basic" needs. The psychological development of such children creates the vicious cycle of abuse, victimization, and maltreatment. It is these abused children that Winnicott calls children with a hateful self image (1971). We have described the details of their affective life in the chapter devoted to them. The other possible origin of aggression is traumatization by acts of violence, or more precisely by the traumatic situation. There are some critical situations that provoke a breakdown of psychic structure (for example, experiencing tragic parental conflict, sexual violence, etc.), and following this, psychological development is arrested.

The consequence of aggression is that the lived relationship to others deteriorates. Violence transforms its victim into an object that can be manipulated at will and who has no possibility of responding effectively. The inter-human relationship is deformed into an objectified relationship. Fear, pain, anger, and humiliation are scotomized – they are banished from consciousness. The traumatic event is deprived of any possibility of symbolization or psychic elaboration.

According to E. Nacht, "the source of aggression is dissatisfaction, frustration, and suffering" (Nacht, 1968, p. 38). He adds, however, that the child who is raised without frustration will not have sufficient drive to obtain what he needs in life. The power of the self originates in the inclusion of aggression, but such aggression is not expressed in the form of destruction but in an assertive attitude toward life.

Widlöcher believes that aggression belongs to the defense mechanisms and emphasizes "The positive force of sublimated and socialized aggression contributes to the evolution of the power of the self and to creativity" (Widlöcher, 1979, p. 97). Adler thinks that hostile aggression increases in children who are deprived and is associated with the tendency to develop a sense of superiority. "The aggressive child tends to elaborate his sense of superiority, to pretend he is better than everybody. This need comes from a sense of insecurity, and the need to compensate becomes very strong" (Adler, 1978, p. 86).

Thus, aggression is an infantile form of resolving difficulties. It evolves from the need to counterbalance the feeling of insecurity in children who have no self-confidence and who do not have a positive self-image.

There is a very important relationship, essential for understanding aggressive children, and this is the inverse relationship of aggression and anxiety. Lebovici (1970, p. 92) describes it this way, "Aggression prevents the manifestation of anxiety."

Psychoanalysts and psychodramatists emphasize that aggression is often called upon to compensate for a lack of confidence in oneself. Christiane Lutz (1976) says that one often discovers a great deal of internal insecurity in children who are excessively aggressive. In such children, the dyad of fear and aggression has trapped them in a vicious circle and compromises their relationships with other children.

In general, aggression is not an isolated phenomenon but rather, as Bandura (1973) claims, sometimes it is nothing more than a repetition and reproduction of parental behavior and occurs in relation to the atmosphere in the family. The child exposed to continuous aggression may manifest his impulses within his family or in another setting. We could say that such a child is a victim of aggression. But this does not exhaust the question, for a child who is raised in an aggressive atmosphere develops a response according to his nature, that is, his own mode of behavior.

One interpretation of this phenomenon is provided by Ferenczi's (1933) by now familiar formula according to which the defense of the child raised in an abusive milieu is identification with the aggressor.

The child experiences intense fear and fears that the adult's aggression threatens to annihilate him. One of the most affecting aspects of aggression is aggression directed against the self, self-destruction, violence directed against oneself. In babies, this is the consequence of the absence of care (see Spitz-Wolf, 1946) and may become manifest at a very early age – the child systematically bangs his head against the wall, against the bars of his crib, against the radiator. He may inflict serious injuries to himself, biting his tongue, chewing his fist until it bleeds, plucking his hair, and biting his nails (alopecia, onycophagia). In time, this behavior may take on the quality of mutilation, from pulling off scabs to suicide. The child who is not protected, who is not loved, becomes auto-punitive (he bangs himself against objects, he has accidents and, overall, fails to protect himself). This is especially true for abused children.

Audiovisual experience as it is manipulated by movies, television, and the virtual world also contributes to the development and maintenance of aggression, because the media, whether in the form of public or private communication, is constantly competing for a larger audience. That goal is often reached by providing terrible aggressive scenes filled with blood and murder. There is a veritable bidding war among the media, where ordinary violence no longer suffices; and it must be enlarged to global dimensions. The range of sexual scenes has extended to include the most sophisticated practices and pedophilia. Children watch scenes of perversity, unspeakable atrocities, and collect images of each sexual act. The question comes up whether such activity reinforces or channels aggression as it turns the child into an impassive observer. It is beyond argument that, even though children might have a need for monsters and visions of superhuman dimension, their multiplicity sets off anxiety, feelings of fear, and insomnia. For a moment, it was dinosaurs that took the place of the traditional function of wolves and tigers – I had adolescents and young patients who recalled the scenes from *Jurassic Park*. It is the youngest children who are most sensitive to the mesmerizing effect of monsters. For one thing, this is because they are so infinitely small in the world of giants, and for another, it is because they witness these programs unattended. Since the imaginary and real worlds are not yet so well separated, this makes them particularly sensitive.

Monsters often appear in the imagination of children, pre-adolescents, and young people. They sometimes have a double character representing at the same time the child and the danger that threatens him (see the interpretation of the monsters drawn by "difficult" children).

In the Hungarian novel titled *The School on the Border* (Ottlik, 1953), the author depicts the verbal strategy of a child exposed to physical abuse. He disarms his attackers by bombarding them with curses and insults.

Demobilizing aggression

During the period that child psychodrama was just beginning in France, toward the end of the 1940s, the psychoanalyst Dreyfus-Moreau (1950, p. 247) thought that children should be given the chance for free expression of the aggression. "They could scream, fight with one another, overturn the furniture and even break the windows without any fear of being punished in any way." Such "acting out" had awful consequences – the children demolished everything and mistreated one another, without any of this having the slightest therapeutic effect. It was at this time that they introduced the rule of "act as if." Christiane Lutz (1976) came to the same conclusion. She realized that wild agitation given free rein might well bring temporary relief for a moment, but in the end, the children did not find it satisfying, and it was clear that the members of the group wanted something else.

Aichinger (1997) observed that people rarely organized groups for children because a chaotic atmosphere with destructive effects easily develops, in the face of which the therapists often find themselves impotent and weak. In some groups, the children begin to revolt against the established order of the sessions. This author believes that children are capable of provoking impotent rage in their therapists.

It is essential to avoid having a power struggle develop between the psychodramatists and the children. Their relationship must not come to resemble the children's habitual parent–child relationships.

Aichinger's group underscores the fact that tensions can be made useful in a group by transposing the conflict to a symbolic level. In symbolic dramatic play, the child's aggressive fantasies may go far beyond brawling, curses, and nasty words. On this plane, the child may sometimes manifest his need for murderous aggression, which may express a hidden fantasy (see on this subject, for example, the psychodrama about the pirate maid, or the incoercible instinct of the devil in the play "The Devil and his Hologram"). I have had the experience, on the occasion of the first meeting of a group, that the children who were incapable of playing would joyfully display terrible images of X-rated acts to the dramatists. In the absence of the desire to play, that is, before the dynamics of play had become established, I suggested to the children that we play-act murder. In the group of four children, the two little girls who were less passive agreed to play a part but the boys were incapable of acting out their murderous fantasy in psychodrama. We came to a compromise. The psychodramatist took the role of a robot directed by two boys and it was he who killed the real or imagined actors. All of this from the perspective that the simulation of murders committed within a double transference in which the boys did not take an active part could free up the children so they would themselves be capable of playing out their aggressive fantasies.

Aichinger tried to construct stories based on real conflicts so as to allow latent hostility to be expressed in ways other than fighting. He thus attempted to transpose the children's struggle for power and domination into play. In the case of aggression acted out in play, the therapists took on the role of observer and commented on the dramatic action in a reporter-like way. Thus, they tried to defuse aggression by reorienting the play and by appeasing or separating the fighting parties so as to calm them down. The advantage of this type of active intervention is to enclose the children inside a symbolic space without interrupting the action.

The Swiss couple of therapists Rodriguez and Siebenthal adopted a rather directive method. They often suggested themes or introduced their own solutions or interpretations into a psychodramatic play invented by the little girls with whom they were playing. If aggression showed up, their response was to stop the action by a verbal or gestural intervention. In the phase in which all of the children were sitting in a circle, they would, on occasion, even forcefully move a child from his place in order to reestablish discipline. It sometimes happens that a word or a gesture is insufficient to deactivate the child's emotion or aggression. To prevent the child from disrupting the group, they would eject the child from the play *manu militari*. The psychotherapist who has had to resort to this extreme measure leaves together with the child and stays with him until he has calmed down. We try to avoid all aggression if it is the children who initiate it toward other children or toward the therapist, but we do not consider that the therapist has the right to take on any kind of physical measure. With regard to aggression between the children, Anzieu suggests that one stop the play as soon as one of the children considers it to be an attack against his person. We believe that therapists have no recourse for responding to violence except to respond verbally, and the ultimate sanction they can apply is to send the child away or temporarily exclude him. It sometimes happened that a little boy would behave in a very destructive manner, and we felt obliged to remove him from the play while suggesting that he calm down. Jean, a little eight-year-old boy, left and went to a neighboring area. There was a kind of fire extinguisher foam that floated everywhere in the air. Then we decided to send him home. At the end of the session, little Jean was standing in the courtyard and greeted me with the words, "I really don't know what happened to your car, but your tire is completely flat." (He hadn't put a nail into the rubber but just removed it from the rim.) As a result, he was banned for a week, but in the interim, we visited him at home in order to talk with him. In my recollection, this was the only "serious" piece of aggression that took place in our whole time at the workshop.

In cases of other damages, we have prescribed reparative work, for example, to help the gardener in his work. In addition, we agree with Friedmann (1972), who noted, "We should never lose sight that during play therapy, the child may re-live (ausleben) but may not discharge (ausstoben) his anger" (A. Friedmann, 1978, p. 345).

We believe that we have to treat and defuse aggression and that the conditions of play are not assured until *acting out* has been eliminated and a tranquil atmosphere has been created. One of the possible means to this end is the technique described in the phrase *warm-up – cool-down*. Perhaps even more important are indirect means, which include the atmosphere of the group, or put otherwise, the creation of a magical world, the effects of "acting as if," the creation of potential space, all of which is complemented by the affective climate of the group and framed by ritual.

Getting beyond aggression may take place in a much less formal way. This consists of providing the children with other means of expression than active aggression. We will return to Fromm's definition, according to which destructiveness, aggression, and hate are associated with a narrowing of the possibility of spending one's energy positively. If the child discovers creative activity, this may channel his aggressive impulses and open the path to a different way of living. In view of this, we believe that children have the need to emerge from their hopeless self-devaluation and their expectation of failure – that is to say, to recognize their own capacities and to experience their many potentialities through the play. The function of the psychodrama workshops is to create frameworks for self-realization; these are the surest and most permanent means for overcoming aggression.

Surgery until half death

This is a breathtaking surrealist story rich in fantastic details invented by young pre-adolescents.

Therapist: "I'm glad that you are all here! I can see that you are already in your disguises. Did you find a story? Norbi and Viki, who just arrived, don't know what it's about, either. You seem to have an idea. Tell us what's happening."
Marc: "There are these doctors. People are having operations."
Tibor: "We are already back from the operating room and . . ."
Together: "There's blood everywhere."
Tibor: "We are taking care of everybody, and there arrives a . . ."
Marc: "We are even doing things to the people who aren't sick . . . we're taking out their heart and so on . . ."
Therapist: "So you are leaving the operating room . . ."
Balint: "Yes, but we've got to go back, because another patient arrives."
Therapist: "So what exactly are the three of you?"
The three together: "Doctors."
Balint: "Docs, surgeons."
Therapist: "But where are the patients if there's only the three of you?"
Balint: "Nowhere, over there."
Therapist: "Is the patient over there?"
Balint: "We agreed that Norbi will be the narrator who tells the whole story."
Therapist: "Wait. Has Norbi agreed?"
Norbert: "Yes."
Therapist: "So you are going to be the narrator for the whole story?"
Norbert: "Yes."
Therapist: "You're going to get it ready, or are you already all set?"
Marc: "We already know it!"
Therapist: "Who needs to know about it?"
Marc (pointing to Norbi): "Him."
Therapist: "Would you like them to summarize the story?"
Norbert: "Yes."
Balint: "The story tells about Norbi, he's the one who is the patient and tells his own story. He will say, 'they transported me to the hospital and three doctors started to operate on me,' and then they will operate on him, and at the end, he'll say, 'I'm all better.'"

Marc: "We'll make up some nonsense, and we'll play all sorts of tricks on him."
Therapist: "You're the ones who are going to do this?"
Ensemble: "Yes, it's us."
Therapist: "Is that OK with you, Norbi?"
Therapist: "What's going to be Viki's role?"
Ensemble: "Nurse, nurse."
Therapist: "Do you accept this role, Viki?"
Viki: "I accept."
Therapist: "What's she going to do?"
Marc: "She's going to make injections . . . these . . ."
Balint: "She's the one who'll put people to sleep."
Marc: "She'll hand out the toilet paper."
Therapist: "What's her job going to be? What do you expect to do in the role of the nurse?"
Viki: "Put people to sleep, help."
Therapist: "Good, we'll work out the details as we go along."
Balint: "I thought she would say, 'the coffee's ready' and when we take out his heart and he feels very, very bad, we'll drink a cup of coffee, and then a man is going to come and ask, 'Whose heart is this?' and then we'll put back the heart and it's going to be a brand new heart."
Therapist: "Do you agree, Viki? Would you like to make coffee in the meanwhile?"
Viki: "Yes."
Therapist: "Good, that's a nice story, but it doesn't have a title. What title are you going to give it?"
Marc: "It's *my* story."
Therapist: "Let's hear what Norbi has to say. What title do you suggest?"
Norbert: "All things considered . . ."
Therapist: "What title would you suggest, Tibi?"
Tibor: "Don't know . . ."
Marc: "I know! Operation till you're half dead."
Norbert: "Yes. Operation till you're half dead."
Therapist: "Does that mean he won't be completely killed, but only become half-dead?"
Together: "Yes."
Therapist: "Good, let's get started, and what about me, will I have a part?"
Balint: "Yes. You're the one who'll give back the heart and will ask, 'does this heart belong to you?' "

The children get ready, set the operating table, and dress up for their roles.

Norbert: "One day, they transported me to the hospital (a truck accident, what do you think of that?) I was driving a truck and I collided with another truck, and they transported me to the hospital and I saw that the docs were coming . . ."

Balint: "Well, things are getting hot."

Tibor: "Let's go see who it is."

Balint: "It's an old guy, he was here before, last year. I told him not to drink so much! He wouldn't stop drinking!"

Marc: "Hand him over to me. I'm going to take out his heart!"

Balint: "With a spoon. Ah, the heart is gone."

Therapist: "Look at him. You threw away the patient's heart."

Balint: "This is a sleeping pill. Should we give him a sleeping pill!?"

Viki: "I already put this guy to sleep. In his butt!"

Balint: "I'm giving him a suppository that will make him sleep!"

Marc: "Scalpel! scalpel!"

Balint: "He is still alive, I thought he was dead already, Darn! Look how big he is, the cow! He's still alive!"

Tibor: "He needs to be sewn up again."

Marc: "He's dead, go on, stitch him up."

Balint: "Where is the gun? Where is the gun?"

Tibor: "Where's the thread? Have to sew him up again!"

Balint: "Go ahead: wash out his stomach! get out of my face!"

Marc: "For bloody sake, his lungs are gone. He's really in bad shape!"

Balint: "You can sure see, Father Denis, you shouldn't do that."

Marc: "Bring on the other lungs!"

Balint: "Ooh la la, this can't be true, Dame Juliet, with the gauze mask, went on smoking. Oh, look! the hospital is on fire, Look!"

Marc: "We have to resuscitate her. Where did the other one go?"

Balint: "Resuscitate quickly. He left, I think, be careful, there's his ghost, Oh, no, there it is."

Viki: "Here's your coffee, good doctors."

Marc: "Thank you."

Therapist: "Hey you guys, you're drinking coffee while my husband is about to die."

Balint: "Why didn't you tell him to stop drinking?"

Therapist: "But my dear sir, that's not it, he was run over by a car."

Balint: "And still, he sure looked like it."

Therapist: "Oh my, oh my, what's going to become of him, what's going to become of him, good doctors? I saw just a little bit earlier that you threw away his heart, it's still on the ground."

Balint: "That's true, that's just what I was looking for. Thanks for finding it. Here's the glue."

Therapist: "May I stay here in the operating room?"

Balint: "No way. Nurse, make her leave."

Therapist: "Can you cure my husband?"

Tibor: "Yes."

Balint: "Don't worry. Rest assured, he's not going to die."

Therapist: "And you, nurse, do you think my husband is going to stay alive?"

Viki: "Yes."

Balint: "Total extraction of the heart! We also have to take out his eyes."

Therapist: "Tell me, nurse, are these doctors doing what they're supposed to?"

Viki: "Yes."

Marc: "Gently, he has a biliary testicle!"

Balint: "You're right. Wow. Wait, wait! don't go there yet!"

Marc: "Oh my, he's got an erection."

Balint: "Stop, wait! I've got to go look for something. Where's my gun? It's still gone. I could shoot him in the head, he'd go to sleep forever, you see?"

Tibor: "Oh yes; he's got an erection, look at his erection."

Marc: "I'm going to remove it right away. Attention: testicle to be removed!"

Balint: "Let me do it. Calm down!"

Marc: "Darn it, one of them was littler than the other!"

Balint: "We could exchange it."

Marc: "Yes, which one? We don't have any spare testicles."

Balint: "Wait a minute, I'll go look for one in the waiting room. Hey, mister, what were you thinking? (*He improvises the role of the castrated man in the waiting room*). We needed a new testicle. I only could find little ones."

Tibor: "He's already dead!"

Balint: "We'll do it now. Excuse me, sir (addressing Marc:) Would you like a bit of whiskey?"

Marc: "Sorry, I never drink during surgery."

Balint: "No problem!"

Norbert (in the role of the chief doctor): "Hurry up sirs, there's been a huge new traffic accident!"

Balint: "Well, well."

Marc: "The devil take him!"

Balint: "We'll leave him right here. Hey, wife! Come here!"

Therapist: "I wish you a good day, good doctors, I'm back. Is my husband all better?"

Balint: "But of course. He's dead. His body has become a bit of patchwork. He has a blue head with red patches. We exchanged his balls."

Marc: "He has one leg shorter than the other."

Balint: "Now, let's go see the other one."

Norbert: "I'm the chief doctor, and I'd like to attend the operation."

Together: "Sure, come along, OK let's go!"

Tibor: "Let's say it's a pregnant woman."

Balint: "A pregnant woman!"

Marc: "I'm going to be the one to get the baby out!"
Together: "Push, madame, push! His head is out already, a foot is out."
Balint: "Take him out, there, he's out, he came out!"
Marc: "It's a girl!"
Balint: "No way, it's a boy after all! It's a boy."
Tibor: "He's lost a foot. We'll have to re-amputate it."
Balint: "His heart isn't beating. Quick! Wait! We have to rinse him off! No, that's not it. Resuscitation. We'll re-amputate his leg later! (oua, oua)."
Tibor: "Let's amputate him! Put him to sleep."
Balint: "All right, let's put his leg back on."
Balint: "That was good, wasn't it?"
Norbert: "You're all fired."
Balint: "Hey. Why am I being struck down by fate like this? All right, we can leave, we've been fired."
Tibor: "We're being thrown out!"
Balint: "Would you like to smoke a pipe? a big pipe? Let's smoke."

End, it's over!

Commentary

Despite their efforts, these children's scholastic performance is unsatisfactory. Their ineptitude at school and their fragility go back to their disadvantaged socio-familial situations, and to early organic trauma. For Tibor, this goes back to intrauterine problems, and for Norbert, to the experience of perinatal anoxia. For Bálint, his difficulties are the result of an accident he had when he was two years old, which resulted in epileptic seizures. We do not know the somatic origins of Marc's psychological problems. The only female participant, Viki, was hospitalized on several occasions because of asthma attacks.

Psychological traumatization related to organic problems (an inferiority complex with organic antecedents, as Adler would put it) is difficult to characterize, because it has taken place at a preverbal age and, as a result, is difficult for the children to verbalize. Instead of verbal expression of their experiences, the children enacted them by staging their entire set of problems symbolically. Their play represents an attempt to be the ones who operate on a body that has been provided to them until it is half dead.

Elements of castration anxiety and fragmentation can be found in this play along with perverse elements, and finally, in the last scene, the desire for rebirth. The baby is not perfectly whole (so they need to "re-amputate" his leg), but is nonetheless viable.

The symbolic efficacy of psychodrama and the catharsis of action is manifest in this play as the expression and representation of a preverbal experience.

In terms of the group dynamic, we could distinguish three sub-groups. The first sub-group consists of the three little boys who invented the story, the three gynecologic surgeons, Balint, Marc, and Tibor. Their instinctual impulses are at once archaic and compensatory – to extract, operate, eject, and thus fragment and ultimately repair major organs (heart, lungs, eye, testicles) even if they are uninjured. "We even did things to those people who weren't sick . . . we took out their hearts and so on . . ."

The function of the second group is to defuse conflicts and to create frames. This sub-group consists of the psychodramatist and Norbert. Norbi was selected as the narrator, perhaps not by chance. He was interposed to make known his own hospital experiences (he was the one who had suffered the worst damage at a very early age). But in this role, Norbert was also excluded from the communal action.

In his narrative Norbert tried to rationalize, and then he retreated, in order to seize the principal role at the end. He announces that he is the chief doctor, and puts an end to the series of amputations with his cry, "You are all fired." He halts his three compatriots' awful surgical careers. And quite oddly, the surgeons accept his decision without protest.

From the outset the psychodramatist plays an important part in setting limits. She underscores that in the case of "surgery until you're half-dead" nobody should actually die, and she thus eliminates the free expression of murderous impulses. These limitations are all the more important as the symbolic victim of the psychodrama is not simply the adult, but in displaced ways, the child as well.

The third sub-group is composed of the female members of the group, to whom the directors assigned secondary roles. Viki can distribute scalpels and toilet paper, can serve coffee to the doctors who sip it next to the dying patient. Marianne, the psychodramatist, was charged with simply bringing back the heart that was thrown away (according to the play instruction: you will come back with the heart and say, "does this heart belong to you?"). However, her role is not a nominal one. In this heartless hospital universe, she symbolizes something essential. As a result, over the course of the affective evolution of the group, she takes on an important function. What I want to emphasize here is her position in the group, her possibilities of acceptance and tolerance for aggression that is not only taking place in the scenic universe (on the operating table under the "blood-stained" drape, there were only inanimate objects, no living beings) but in the no less terrifying universe of the rampant children. An example of inserting oneself in the imagination of children eager for compensation in order to bring a participating presence that interprets their words in terms of the boundaries that must be respected. (Does that mean he won't be completely killed, but only become half-dead?)

This psychodrama signaled a turning point in the history of the group, in that there was an intellectual liberation and the school grades achieved by the children.

Inhibition

The solitary girl

This symbolic psychodrama conducted by two girls is an expression of what might lie hidden behind the anxiety of inhibited, fearful, poorly adapted, and depressed children. What fantasies lurk in the soul of a young girl who is very modest and well behaved?

Génie is one of those troubled children that Adler includes in the category of passive individuals who are docile, dependent, and anxious, the opposite of the active, impatient, aggressive person who eagerly seeks power.

There are a number of psychologists since Adler who have recognized that these two excessive forms of behavior – that is, passive, fearful indifference and violent aggression – constitute the two poles of a range of flawed behaviors and are not independent of each other.

To what does the following spontaneous and symbolic play bear witness and what is its function?

The two actresses in the psychodrama come from an entirely different environment from that of the workshop, from comfortable families in the Paris suburbs. Génie's father was an engineer with a good job and her mother, Thalia, was a talented painter. Geneviève's father taught at the university and her mother was a mathematics teacher at the lycée. Each of the families had three children. Génie was the eldest child in her family, and Geneviève the youngest of hers, with two older brothers.

The two young girls were good friends, and from time to time, they would get noisily angry at each other. According to their mothers, each of them – but especially Geneviève – wanted to boss around her friend, which led to conflicts. Then they would make peace. These were two little girls with good posture, cute, with long hair, and at eleven years of age, just entering adolescence.

Geneviève had been coming to see me for therapy for some time, and we were on very good terms. By this time, the psychosomatic problems that she had previously suffered had ceased, but she was still a bit stressed, and at school, she had trouble concentrating and difficulty finding friends. Génie was referred by the family because of mild dyslexia, withdrawal, depression, and problems with closeness. Her mother was especially troubled about their mother–child relationship. She did not think that her eldest daughter was as close to her as the two younger children (her other daughter and her little boy). She complained about the lack of communication between them: "If I ask her questions when she comes home from school, she doesn't answer or says, 'I don't remember,' and if I ask her why she's in such a bad mood and to tell me what's the matter, there's complete silence!" "What's wrong with this child? Génie is a very sensitive little girl; if her piano teacher makes a comment she starts to cry. If I talk to her or ask her something, she looks at me as if she had to guess what she was supposed to answer, something that might please me, and then there's silence. She seems worried and some-times sad.

She sometimes forgets to do her homework, and sometimes, she can't remember anything." Génie doesn't even need any warming up, she has such a need to communicate that as soon as her mother has left the room, she immediately starts telling a story.

The pirate maid

This story takes place in olden days on a pirate ship. The captain is a woman, and everyone obeys her.

> "Why?"
>
> "She's got a whistle. All she has to do is blow in it," she smiles. "And a megaphone. If they don't obey, she decimates them. Every tenth person gets thrown in the sea. They attack a Spanish ship. They find treasure, silver, gold bars and jewels. They strip the boat, and then they tie up the crew. When they have transported their loot, they ask the crew if they want to join them and become pirates. Those who protest they throw into the water."
>
> "And the loot?"
>
> "I do give them a little bit, but the majority belongs to me. There were one hundred pirates before, and with the new ones, a hundred fifty. Spaniards."

(Here she is already speaking in the first person, she steps away from her role as narrator, which suggests the intensity and primacy of emotion, despite the fact that she is telling her story in a bit of a monotone and never raises her voice.)

Her habitual restraint has turned into its opposite here: she's the one who is the captain, master of life and death – all she has to do is to blow into her whistle. The chief has power and exercises her authority without mercy over the 150 men. Those who obey are tolerated, but anyone who revolts pays for it with his life and is thrown into the sea.

Her mother complains about this girl's excessive obedience, but here, it's all reversed. She has become rich and all-powerful, and reigns over the destiny of her subalterns. The story is reminiscent of Jenny, the pirate maid in the Three-Penny Opera. Brecht's Jenny, a lowly servant-girl who washes everyone's dishes and makes their beds, dreams that one day a pirate ship with eighty masts and fifty cannon would throw down its anchor nearby, destroy the city, and ask Jenny the question, "Whom should we kill?" Jenny responds, "Everyone" and as their heads fall, she says, "Hoopla." (This is what gave me the idea of calling the little girl Génie, even though she had no idea about Jenny.) The compensatory mechanisms of Jenny and Génie are remarkably similar. In Génie's imagination, there is only the pirate ship that has shown up and the mistress of the pirates. As regards the heads, see below.

The character of the psychodrama was just begging to be played. I asked Génie if she wanted to play with Geneviève and I asked Geneviève if she wanted to play with Génie. The idea seemed to delight the two little girls. I asked them if we should include their mothers in the game, "No way! We'll play just the three of us."

We agreed. The girls announced that at the next session, they would bring some paintings and that during the interim they would make up a story.

They came back with the following scenario.

A woman tells her new employee to bake a cake and to clean the house with Paic Citron (household cleanser). Instead, the employee cleans the floors with butter and mixes up the cake batter with the Paic Citron.

"I'm going to be the distracted employee, says Geneviève, and Génie will be the lady!"

Génie had put makeup on her face, her eyes painted blue. I put together the disguises, a silk dress, hats, a broom, a scoop, a man's coat and a pair of crutches.

Geneviève remarked, "You'll be the husband!" (On such occasions, she always addressed me with the familiar "tu.")

She played with great focus, spreading the wood floor with the imaginary butter, and putting the cake in the oven. However, it turned out that besides the Paic Citron, she had stuffed the cake dough with a telephone. She also added that the new employee had just escaped from a psychiatric ward and that her behavior was really crazy. As for the man, he had slipped on the buttered floor and was limping (walking around with the crutches). The employee was gesticulating and crying and trying to explain her actions. The woman, Génie, was behaving in a discreet and elegant manner.

In fact, they had already staged little scenes of this kind in school.

This is where the real psychodrama began and it became clear that the comedy at the beginning, which I had reluctantly accepted despite its banality, only served as an introduction, a warm-up.

The headhunter

Characters:

Inspector Dubouchon:	Geneviève
The Victim (sometimes called Inspector Blanchard):	H.K.
The Solitary Girl:	Génie

During the night, a woman slips into Inspector Blanchard's room. Her victim is very tired, which was convenient, since it gave her the opportunity to accomplish her project – to stick a needle in his arm. When Inspector Dubouchon arrives unexpectedly, the victim is stretched out in his room. After a few hours, however, he wakes up.

Inspector Dubouchon examines the premises (Geneviève inspects the floor with a magnifying glass) and discovers footprints. He thinks that he may have seen such footprints before somewhere. A woman arrives to visit. Inspector Dubouchon asks her the question:

> "What is your name, Miss?"
> "I am the solitary girl."

The Inspector identifies the footprints and finds out that she was the one who committed the crime and puts her in prison. The cunning malefactor escapes from prison and reappears at the scene of the inquest.

The inspector interrogates her and suspects that she is none other than the headhunter they have long been searching for.

> "I don't like men," says the solitary girl. "Inspector Blanchard is none other than the murderer of my poor brother!"

Dubouchon tries to find out more and learns that the brother of the woman died of a heart attack, and was not the victim of a murder.

The inspector asks his unexpected visitor how many men she has killed.

> "A good hundred."
> "What?"
> "Yes, I poisoned them with the syringe, and then I cut off their heads with an electric saw." And she points to the bookshelf. "On the bookshelf, you'll see some of them. One is three years old, the others are seven, twenty-one, forty-five and fifty years old."

Next, she opens the refrigerator, and takes out a frozen brain, reads the date, and as it is expired, she throws it away in disgust. She takes out another one, which she eats while the others are watching.

> "Before eating you need to inflate the head so that it grows back a bit of its volume."
> And then, with great gentility, she offers two bouquets of flowers to the inspectors. "Surprise!"

There is a bomb inside the bouquets. That is the surprise. The girl leaves. The two inspectors explode. The ghost of inspector Dubouchon comes back, however, and kills the murderer. Three cadavers are lying on the floor of the room.

Geneviève insists that the solitary girl was very intelligent, something that wasn't surprising given the fact that she had eaten so many brains.

It was Génie who had made up the story.

Here, cruelty presents in a symbolic form. It does not cut off heads before our very eyes but only makes reference to that act. Eating the brains is simply mimed.

She killed inspector Blanchard with a pencil that looked like a knife, the syringes she had only made up during her "confession."

She enumerates her crimes without emotion or excitement, gently, with her reedy voice of innocence.

Geneviève was more excited, and as the crazy servant, she had forcefully smeared her face with paint before entering the scene, and she accompanied the scenes with lively gestures and screams. Génie is more discreet. She plays the lady, puts on gloves and exudes charm.

The decapitation was Génie's idea, and eating the brain was Geneviève's. Génie joyfully accepted her suggestion and ate the brains with gusto in our presence.

We were witness to a morbid orality of cannibalism that appears to go beyond primary orality, a murderous desire, and a hatred of men. She cut off their heads and lined them up in a row, then showed us these heads of men and little boys.

All of this without the slightest sense of guilt, as if this was simply the way things were supposed to be, even though Dubouchon came back from the grave to render justice.

Inhibition, inability to express herself when asked a question. In that situation, Génie is incapable of saying anything at all. Whatever she might have been able to say would not change the basic problem, the obvious problem that her mother had articulated – the mother does not feel that this child, her oldest, is close to her. Perhaps it is because she projects onto this gentle and cute child her own devaluation (it is the mother who is displeased with herself, and is incapable of accepting Génie, although she can accept the two others, her son and her younger daughter). How do we explain the mother's devaluation of herself – she is a talented artist who is loved and appreciated by her husband? Génie's repressed aggressive impulse is too terrifying and excessive to be spoken. It is possible that its cannibal intensity is due to the fact that her parents had an oral type of fixation and regression.

In her psychodrama, terrible events take place. There appears the rejection of men characteristic of girls who are still in their latency period, and an explicit and pronounced hatred of the man. But the two little girls are not implicated to an equal extent. Even though it was Geneviève who proposed eating the brains, for her this gesture had a kind of inter-cannibalistic character committed within the family to appropriate the knowledge of men, perhaps the father (on this subject, see in the novel by Conchon (1964), the ritual of consumption by Black tribes when they eat the brain of a white man).

The tendency that these eleven-year-old girls are revealing here is different from sexual inhibition and the avoidance of the Oedipal situation. This is an over-compensated exhibition of omnipotence and the desire to annihilate the male gender.

Why is the enemy to be destroyed male, why is it against him that Génie's murderous instinct is directed and why does the primary Oedipal complex fail to appear at all?

In a transposed manner, the murderous scene played out here does have to do with the Oedipal world, as the designated victim is the woman psychodramatist (me) who at the time the story was being prepared, was named the victim and was not yet called Inspector Blanchard. Everyone who remained in the scene until the end, including the victims of the attack with the bouquet of flowers, was, in reality, female. The third victim was none other than herself, a third female in character as well as in reality. This psychodramatic dynamic is clearly not unequivocal, as the principal idea of the scene was still the extermination of men. They were the ones who were the chosen targets for terrible murderousness. What is troublesome is the withheld anger. The visible intensity of the catharsis of action is very modest.

Génie is incapable of representing the maternal refusal and the anxiety that stems from it, which goes beyond separation anxiety to become a truly existential anxiety. The neurotic traits of her way of functioning suggest the difficulty faced by children who are insufficiently loved to separate from their mothers – the compulsive need to hold on, and the refusal to recognize the maternal rejection.

The conflict that cannot be spoken and is unresolvable, the dilemma, or the "original defect," is the consequence of a poor dyadic relationship, charged with rejection and therefore unsatisfying.

Génie fears that any conflict or contradiction would jeopardize her relationship with her mother. She can only shake her head to all of her mother's desires and needs, whether expressed or secret, real, or imagined. She is polarized by fascination with the mother, as is the case for many little girls who are actually mistreated, who, filled with fear, watch to find how they might be able to satisfy their mother's expectations. The paradox: no matter what they do or say, it will be turned against them.

Karine, whose story we told in the chapter on the abused child, was another child who was poorly loved. It was after two years with us that she became able to stage her conflict with her mother, that she became aware of her mother's rejection. The confidence in her own worth having been strengthened, she was able to prepare for her detachment and get beyond her captive state.

Geneviève's situation is less troubled. Over the course of her psychotherapy she succeeded in putting her anxieties on the table so that they could be calmed and overcome. And her mother, although anxious, was affectively available.

Génie needed to go down a long road before getting to such a place. Perhaps out of feminine solidarity and by identifying with her mother, she transferred her reactive aggression onto the male gender, compensating for the pain of her personal frustrations by engaging in the war of the sexes.

She was only eleven years old, and had lots of time ahead of her, and the advantage of her exceptional creativity. After all, her first psychodramatic performance was a highly expressive exploit, shocking and breath taking. And her play allowed us to understand better than any theoretical analysis what is hidden in the heart of a well adjusted, passive, depressed, and inhibited child.

9

THE ROLE OF THE PSYCHODRAMATISTS

Theoreticians of children's psychodrama have defined the role of the psychodramatists in quite different ways. For a first approximation, we might say that the role of the psychodramatist is to heal the children. These children are suffering from a complex set of problems; they are often in an unfavorable psychosocial situation; they are children at risk, indulged or neglected, presenting with a wide range of psychosomatic symptoms, with behavioral problems (some of them aggressive, some inhibited, some psychoneurotic). These theorists suggest that we create an atmosphere in which the children's self-image can be transformed, their self-confidence increased, and their spontaneity and creativity freed up, and where they can find the means to ward off the obstacles that are in the way of the development of a harmonious lifestyle.

From a situational point of view, psychodramatists can intervene in the group on three different planes of action (Heigl-Evers, 1972):

> *Intervention in the alpha position*, in other words, in the position of the leader or model. The therapist assigns himself the task of assuring the fluidity of the play, especially during the first phase of the group's activity; through his own play, by his personal example, he sets the stage for the activation of the children.
>
> *Intervention in the beta position.* The psychodramatist takes part in the play, but takes the role of observer. For example, in a complex and fraught activity, the psychodramatists assign themselves the role of reporter (see Aichinger) – which also gives them the option of making positive comments about the children's actions. In a group play directed by my colleague, Julia Urbanics, the dramatists took the roles of two neighbors who criticized the family's way of living and its lack of cohesion, and commented, surprised and

delighted, about the sense of cooperation among the children freed up from their parents.

Intervention in the gamma position (the psychodramatist intervenes to resolve internal problems of the group). If the group is very divided in an acute conflictual situation, the therapist may feel the need to intervene from the outside to unite the players to battle together against a common enemy. For example, in an exacerbated situation of struggling for power, the psychodramatists may introduce an external danger. Anzieu thinks that the psychodramatist may choose to play the part of a kind of double for the child, with the idea of modulating and attenuating his emotions and representing the missing ego function, thereby assuring the continuity of the self (or the play).

There is a certain element of paradox in the definition of the psychodramatist – on the one hand, Moreno states that the role of the psychodramatist resembles the role of the members of the group, and he repeatedly affirms that in the psychodrama, the patient and the therapist are on equal footing." On the other hand, he attributes a directive role to the psychodramatist called "director," preferring that he participate either as an observer within the play (as a journalist covering the events, for example) or observing from the outside to better understand the meaning of the events.

The modified role of psychodramatists in psychodramas

Anzieu says,

> The concept of director is eliminated, two or more psychodramatists have the option of taking on roles if the action demands it, if they are invited to do so, and if they feel internally motivated to accept the role.
>
> One of the psychodramatists, with the approval of his colleague, may assume the function of signaling the start or the end of the play. In some established groups, this role alternates. The therapist who feels that it is time to end the play will take responsibility for it.
>
> (*Anzieu, 1979, p. 101*)

In his practice,

> The psychodramatist can accept the role that is assigned to him, but he may also refuse it and later, if he feels the need, he may also enter the scene so long as he does not break the dynamics of the play; should this happen, the play needs to start over.
>
> (*Anzieu, 1979, p. 138*)

Most children's psychodramatists – as we have already alluded to with regard to the French psychoanalysts – consider it as a fundamental rule that the two psychodramatists regularly participate in the plays. They explain their choice by the claim that it is from the inside that the psychodramatist can be best situated for orienting, structuring, or even interpreting the events of the drama.

The role of the dramatist in children's psychodrama is all the more nuanced by the fact that on account of the "act as if," the double aspect of the play and reality, he has to be comfortable with these double dimensions of the psychodramatic group.

The first challenge could be defined as the need to differentiate between two simultaneously present stages of psycho-affective development. The psychodramatist is present at once in the position of a child and in the position of an adult. He shares the affective life of the child, and thus finds himself in a regressed position, sometimes in the capacity of a baby or a very young child. At other moments, with young adolescents, he may be inflated with heroic or conquering ambitions. He is in the same place as the child – that is, in his play he is sharing the child's wealth of imagination. This capacity for doubling both facilitates and complicates the situation. The therapist is present in two dimensions, in a position where not only the child has permission to regress, but the therapist is also invited to do so, something that is not the exclusive province of group play but applies equally to all child therapy. Moreover, the therapist adopts a different mode of pretending than do the children, in the sense that he is pretending to be a child, but alongside his evocation of his childish being, he can never forget his status as an adult. Once, a very intelligent child noticed this, and told me that he regarded me at the same time as a child and an adult – a relation that in my view does not completely take care of the problem pointed out by Anna Freud (1965), of how difficult it is to get beyond being considered by the child as representing a kind of superego. We think more of the permanent state of the double nature of being a child therapist or psychodramatist.

The psychodramatist participates in the play with full affective involvement. He shares the intensity of the children's feelings. But at the same time, he stays on the outside, to respect the boundaries and avoid an overflow of the dramatic action that goes beyond the capacities of the frustrated child. An example: one day, an eight-year-old participant at the workshop, Mélinda, suggested a psychodrama. Criminals break into an apartment that is supposed to be vacant and are surprised by the presence of the mistress of the house. They decide to kill her. During the play, it turned out that the role of the victim, even though she had chosen it voluntarily, provoked total panic and existential anxiety in this little girl. So we had to end the scene before the murder. To find out the solution that the psychodramatist chose, Chapter 5.

The psychodramatist needs to be spontaneous while remaining respectful of what the child has imagined. It is a balance between spontaneity and adaptation, as at any moment he has to join the play of the children, since they were the ones who set up the scenario: "The golden rule of the psychodramatist is that he has to play actively even while complying with the child's imagination" (Widlöcher, 1979, p. 137).

We could express this doubling by underscoring the following: the psychologist needs to feel what the child wants to express beyond words, that is, he needs to accept his role in an intuitive mode. At the same time, in order to understand what the child wants to express in the story, he needs to demonstrate an active presence of mind. The simultaneous presence of intuition and cognition represents another exigency of the psychodramatic attitude.

This double vision or bilateral presence is the source of other conditions: the psychodramatist needs to be flexible. He must be capable of changing his play in midstream to conform to the child's expectations. Moreno underscores the importance of the dramatist-therapist's flexibility, which allows him to change his position, his bearing, and his movements to the unpredictable requirements of the action. Some theoreticians insist on following certain formal criteria or require that one should keep the action from deviating from what was anticipated at the outset. In our opinion, exaggeration of the role of the frame (as it is the psychodramatist's unconscious that is called upon to define it) is nothing more than the restriction and appropriation of the psychodramatic terrain, an attempt to strengthen the narcissism of the psychodramatists and to overemphasize their role.

Intrusion upon the unfolding of the story – modification of the succession of events imagined by the child – is incompatible with the spirit of psychodrama. It should be regarded as resistance on the part of the psychodramatist.

Another effect of doubling also deserves mention, which has to do with the psychodramatist's deep sensitivity, a capacity to capture multiple resonances that can only be compared to the activity of an orchestra conductor – to which we have made reference earlier in the introduction. He must be able to distinguish the melodic fragments carried by the children in the ensemble and beyond this, he must simultaneously perceive individual motifs and the beauty of the melody produced by the dynamics of the group. He has to understand what each child is expressing but the overall melody, the story, and the dynamic of the group as well.

These complicated and nuanced points of view are not necessarily achieved by the psychodramatists in the course of the play, and this is why it is necessary and indispensable that they set aside some time for talking together after each session, as sometimes the profound meaning of the events can only be clarified once the emotions have settled down. "The conversation between the psychodramatists which follows the sessions reinforces the double situation of the psychodramatist, who is at once actor and spectator" (De Neuter, 1978). For Matisson, these post-session discussions can take rather a long time, perhaps even longer than the duration of the session itself.

In French practice, two psychodramatists, ideally of different genders, conduct the work. If the group is directed by a single psychologist (or psychiatrist), it develops in a very different way, especially in the intensity of the dyadic relationship between the group and the dramatist. The intensity of regression is heightened, detachment of the children is more difficult, and the nature of fraternal jealousy seems more intense. Finally, there is also a different manifestation of the subjective phenomenon known as the "illusion of the group" in the fantasy of the dramatists. Some of my male dramatist colleagues have noted that the "matriarchal" relationship develops even if the solo dramatist running the group is a man. One finds discussion of this phenomenon in otherwise widely divergent texts by male psychodramatists. They postulate that, in a cohesive group, there develops a group psychology that favors group identity over personal identity (Pierre Privat, 1997).

Matisson (1978) advises "the psychodramatist should not share in the group illusion with the others but must always keep a clear head," and adds a harsh warning that we ourselves do not accept without reservation, in fact, something that seems to us detrimental to profess: "The psychodramatist is not there to take pleasure in the action nor to help others experience pleasure but to understand the process." On the other hand, his summary of the task of the psychodramatist is quite poetic: "The psychodramatist observes the actor in the drama who goes beyond himself in order to create himself freely."

Up to this point, we have spoken of the role of the psychodramatists in the context of the play, and have left aside another aspect, the relationships created outside the world of play, in reality.

The child experiences the group, the psychodramatists, and beyond their encounter in the symbolic world, he also experiences the psychodramatists' presence in the dimension of the real world.

In the imagination of some psychodramatists, the group amalgamates to become a veritable living being sewn together by the skin of the group. Certain psychodramatists project themselves onto the imago of an archaic mother-goddess surrounded by the children, the members of the group. We have heard a lecture by a psychodramatist who, in her sleep, dreamt about the participants (while it is unclear whether she shared this experience with the members of the group, it is something she shared with the people attending her lecture) as being the fruits of her entrails. We would tend to believe that perhaps it is more important to mobilize children's fantasies than to integrate them into the psychodramatist's unconscious.

This confusion follows from the projection of the psychoanalyst's unconscious as an exclusive measure and the ultimate source of truth about the group. At the same time, this confusion has another element that is less hermetic. It results from the confusion of the roles of the psychodramatist in the potential space (the magic world, or if you like, the world of "act as if") and his role in the real life of the group.

However, all children, even the youngest, are capable of making this distinction. I was playing one on one with Celine, my youngest patient, who was three and a half years old – (I should add, in the presence of her father, unfortunately). When we left the psychodramatic scene in which she had assigned me the role of a baby fed aggressively from an imaginary bottle despite the baby's protestations, I asked her, "But who am I?" and she looked at me incredulously and said, "You're Madame Kendé, the lady who plays." Even though she did not say "the psychologist" her statement corresponds perfectly with reality, that is to say, she showed no confusion between the present and the regressive world, between illusion and reality.

Transference and/or corrective relationship

Laplanche and Pontalis's *The Language of Psychoanalysis* (1967) defines transference as "the process in which unconscious desires that are transferred to objects are principally realized in the analytic relationship" (p. 492).

This encyclopedia of psychoanalytic terms describes the way that the concept has evolved and changed over the course of the evolution of Freudian theory. Originally, it referred particularly to the infantile relationship that the patient relives as his current experience. Over time, the concept has taken on a larger meaning and signifies the terrain on which the problematic of psychoanalysis takes place: "It determines the modalities and the interpretive solutions." In other words, in classical psychoanalysis, it is the analysis of the transference neurosis that permits the interpretation of the malady.

Kestemberg and Jeammet (1987) indicate, apropos of analytic psychodrama, the difficulties raised by classical transference. "Transference transposes old imagos, principally infantile and mostly unconscious, onto new persons (the therapists) responsible for its birth and its being, and who represent the source and the aim of the psychological flux situated between love and hate."

Because the affective charge of the original imago is very strong, a particular situation develops, which Kestemberg and Jeammet describe in the following way: "A paradoxical situation is constructed in which nothing is possible without transference, but the patients prove to be incapable of deciding to relive their transferential feelings." The authors thus propose: "The aim of the rules of psychoanalytic psychodrama is to promote the development of a transferential relationship that is analyzable and interpretable, that is, to attenuate the intensity of transference and its associated mechanisms of defense." The utilization of transference is an essential element that distinguishes psychoanalysis from all experimentation and even from all psychotherapies (Kestemberg & Jeammet 1987).

Our approach differs significantly – as we shall have the opportunity to explain in what follows. It does not have to do with deliberately evoking or reliving alienating situations, but rather, with rendering the children capable of establishing different affective relationships. We let the child know – we do not want to make you relive what you have been through or recreate it. This is true for all of our patients who have suffered from early trauma, but especially for children who have been abused. Even more, we try to keep the child from recreating, in the form of transference, his need to be mistreated (which may be expressed in provocative behavior and a chain reaction of abnormal psychophysiological reactions).

In his paper on transference and introjection, Ferenczi reveals himself as the precursor of Melanie Klein when he proposes the existence of archaic (primitive) projection and introjection, saying, "loving and hating the object is the model for all subsequent affective transference" (Ferenczi, 1982, p. 131). He refers to a process that is much more archaic, that precedes all relationship, a corollary of the initial awareness of the object. Ferenczi considers that from the very beginning, the affective world of the child may be regarded as an original transference. This primordial transference, the expression of good and evil that precedes all parental relationships, brings us a step closer to the ways that comparative individual psychology interprets this phenomenon.

Winnicott situates this original and unique relationship in the realm of potential space. He believes that in the case of the child without a good enough mother, it is necessary, over the course of the analysis, to realize with him a primary relationship that is different.

Imre Hermann (1984) speaks of transference, but he understands it in an entirely different way from classical psychoanalysts. In his view, what takes place in transference is none other than the realization of lost potentialities, of unfulfilled possibilities. The patient "has to reconstruct something begun earlier but never completed" (p. 186). This real transference does not reproduce old character traits, but instead, traits with which one has lost touch. Balint (1968) regards this new relationship as the primary precondition for a new beginning.

The theory of comparative individual psychology does not consider that the child transfers a relationship with an absent person onto the therapist. Their relationship is based upon the therapist's acceptance and his empathy. The German Adlerian psychologist, Karl König (1991), sums up this relationship as, "here is a person who, despite his own weakness, never stops trying to recognize me" (p. 142).

This attitude corresponds to Adler's general philosophical approach. He puts the emphasis on the subjective experience of life, in which the internal and external worlds are difficult to differentiate. One could express this in Emmanuel Kant's terms in *The World as Will and Representation* as the subjectivity of the perception of the world. French theorists of individual psychology have asked the question, "transference or a new kind of relationship?" Their answer to classical psychoanalytic theory is "the psychoanalyst does not reflect earlier experience, but on the contrary, he presents a personality who is ready to share the feelings of the individual in order to promote the transformation of the patient's vital functions. He must also be ready to change the roles adopted by the child, such as 'the good student' or 'the class clown' who makes others laugh" (Mormin & Viguier, 1993).

Heisterkamp interprets the corrective relationship as the transformation of an inadequate maternal relationship. As he states sadly, "in an intransigent relationship without empathy, the situation of the child is hopeless"(Heisterkamp, 1985).

It is not a matter of reliving but of correcting the inadequate affective ties. Or as Ringel (1983) formulates it: "the child will tend to correct a relationship, a need that was not met" (p. 24).

The Adlerian view generally disapproves of the functionalization of people. Adler believed it was important to emphasize that the therapist does not replace something else, does not occupy someone else's place, but rather, is present as his own person to create the relationship that will help the child to correct his negative self-image and to overcome his crushing sense of inferiority. In therapy, the need for acceptance and love is primordial, and if I know analysts who speak about abstinence, who try to lock their own feelings in a box with the inscription "transference and countertransference," it is a rare occurrence for psychologists or psychiatrists to deny their feelings toward the children. They feel pleasure in playing together that is not limited by professional motivations. In this sense, today's German and French Adlerians have modified the Freudian theory of transference.

Moreno often touched upon the question of transference, which he contrasted with the encounter (*Einladung zu einer Begegnung, Invitation to an Encounter*, 1914) and "tele." Psychoanalytic transference, he said, is just one pathological version of "tele," and he thought that a group based on transference was a pathological group.

An example – in an experimental workshop, we suggested a story whose implicit content is the experience and acceptance of difference: "The Guenon" (see above). In the play, the story is completely transformed, becoming an expression of the Oedipus complex of one of the actors. The crucial moment of the story is when the ex-monkey's little one arrives in the world. Will the newborn be a human baby or a little hairy being, a monkey? Different child and adult groups worked out this dilemma in very different ways. Sometimes the mother would reject the newborn, "get that monkey away from me." In another version, the parents and the grandparents asserted, "You are what you are, but we love you." There were versions in which the newborn was perfectly human. In the version of the play to which we alluded earlier, the question took the form of a primary Oedipal relationship: "if the little one is a boy, he'll be yours, and if it's a little girl, it will be mine," – says the father.

It is interesting that a group of classical Freudian psychoanalysts modified the concept of transference when they were treating children, especially very troubled children.

Anna Freud, for example, had already emphasized the corrective nature of the relationship that was established between the therapist and the child. "The therapist is not uniquely a transferential object but, with regard to the healthy part of the child's personality, he is a real object that allows for the development of new forms of relationship"(A. Freud, 1965, p. 182).

The question comes up quite differently in group therapy, not to speak of children's psychodrama.

Widlöcher (1979) considers the dilution of transference as a particular feature of the kind of transference that develops in the group, in the setting of these meetings, which he believes is very different from the psychoanalytic setting. In groups, transference evolves not so much in time but rather in space. In other words, in individual psychoanalysis, transference changes over the course of the treatment whereas in a group situation, transference develops at the same time toward the facilitators and the members of the group. This fact diminishes the intensity of the transference because a part of each child's expectations "instead of being referred to one of the adults, is directed toward another participant."

It is in this way that the phenomenon of transference rejoins the dynamics of the group. Lagache (1952) proposed that the internal relations in the group did not follow along the lines of past experience but developed as a function of the positions taken in the group. He thus recognized the possibility of relations of a new type. "It is not a question of transforming the transferential effect but replacing it" (p. 104). He thought that the diminution in the intensity of the transference is positive, especially in adolescents, for whom the therapeutic relationship evokes very strong anxiety, camouflaged by intense aggressive reactions. This is one of the reasons that they have such difficulty tolerating any kind of therapeutic relationship. Younger children, especially those with major behavioral problems, may also be similarly vulnerable.

In psychodramatic plays, one encounters remarkable *fantasies of twinship*, for example, between two little girls of different ages and sizes, one of them a girl said to be "crazy" and the other psychotic, or between a French boy and a young Serbian immigrant who spoke hardly any French, the two of them between nine and eleven years of age. Such twinship fantasies create dyadic units different from the mother–child relationship, and are called upon to replace it. This type of dyadic relationship may serve as a crutch for solitary children who are without friends and feel isolated, and even for those who are threatened by a disintegration of their ego.

We have encountered a variety of different examples of *cross-identification*. A former group member thought he had discovered, in a new arrival, his former self that he had already gone beyond. What should he do about it? Should he protect or persecute him? We have cited the example of an abused child who finds a person to abuse (The lion and his cub).

A young girl who suffered from an early breakdown of the maternal bond took under her protection an indigent and very isolated little boy as a way of compensating, through a kind of cross-identification (taking the role of mother to the little one), for the fact of having been deprived of love.

The change of role in the group allows the child to modify the traumatic relationships of childhood, to create fraternal relations, sometimes complementary, sometimes charged with rivalry and fraternal jealousy.

In the relation of the group to the individual we can observe phenomena of exclusion or integration, for example, when the solitary child who has difficulties establishing bonds is affectively integrated into the group (regarding this subject, see the story by François or the play *Gaspard* that was performed by the psychodrama group in a Rogersian school).

In response to the question, "transference or new relationship," the classical theorist of Frenchanalytic psychodrama and author of the first book on child psychodrama, Didier Anzieu, already put forward the following response in 1994: "Psychotherapists encourage the participants in the game to develop, in place of the pathogenic relationships that they developed within their original entourage, a relationship of another type" (p. 95).

In children's group therapy we have set ourselves the goal of creating a new kind of relational system that makes it possible, for one thing, to work through the inadequate primary relationship and for another, to develop a new pseudo-familial structure, by which we mean a pseudo-family whose way of functioning is completely different from the child's original family and in the framework of which he can consider himself to be an accepted and valued being.

I want to tell you the story of the rebirth of a child whose life had been marked by rejection since the moment of her conception and throughout her intra-uterine life on the part of two parents who went as far as to want to annihilate their unborn and developing baby.

Rebirth in a bubble

This is the story of an extraordinary encounter between a young pregnant intern and a ten-year-old child suffering from severe psychopathology caused by what one generally calls, after Michael Bálint, a "basic fault," that is, the consequences when a pregnant woman totally rejects the fruit of her loins, and utterly fails to accept her still unborn child. This encounter took place in a children's psychodrama group. The unusual feature of the method was combining a "3-person individual monodrama" with the gradual integration of a rebellious child into the group, a child who had taken on a particular role in relation to the other members of the group. These turned out to be remarkable relationships that reawakened the resilience of a child suffering from severe problems of prenatal origin.

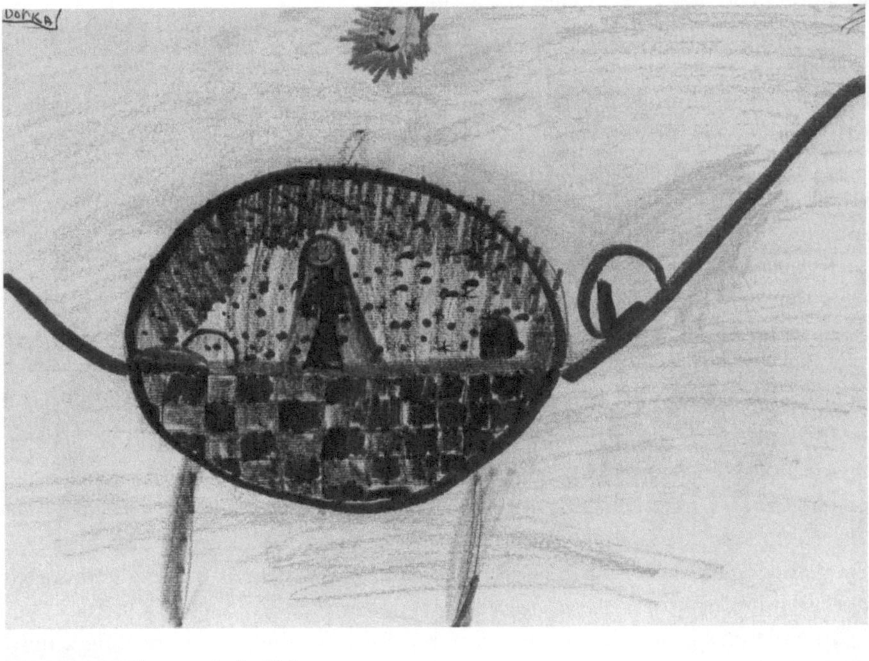

FIGURE 9.1 The magic bubble

The story as told by Anna Szendrei Klokniczer[1]

My most marvelous experience during my training as an assistant to the psychodrama group was that little by little, as the inhabitant of my womb gradually grew, Clara also let me come closer to her and together, we overcame obstacles that were considered insurmountable. I experienced the intra-uterine state together with Clara; the play took place in an unusual mode, a state of plural consciousness. The play had to do with Clara, but we were there as a threesome. This was an extraordinary experience, and what was particularly gratifying for me was that we were able to successfully conclude an effective therapy for Clara.

I would like to present Clara's "rebirth," how she succeeded inside the frame of psychodrama, in a space she constructed herself, to elaborate her core problems that dated back to earlier but were also related to her adoption, so she could begin to climb the steps toward the reconstruction of her personality.

The group of preadolescents in which I participated started in November 2008, met on twenty-five occasions and continued until the end of May 2009. The therapists, Timea and Sandor, had accepted me as an intern in their group. I attended the first four sessions as an observer, and then starting from the fifth meeting, I could take part in the plays.

Frames and the course of the sessions

Each session lasted an hour and a half, and was initiated by the question, "What happened to you during the past week?" Then, once the latecomers had all arrived and after a warm-up game, we would begin to develop the story, construct the space for the play, put on disguises, and stage the dramatic play – then the session would end with a time for drawing.

Often, one of the children would arrive with a character already developed in her mind and would immediately run to the costume closet. Sometimes, it would happen that at the end of a meeting, the story for next week's session would already be sketched out.

In the course of the session, we constructed clay masks over a cardboard template, molded and designed by the children themselves. The first and the last session of psychodrama included the participation of the parents.

The group

Six children, among them five boys. Facilitators: two psychotherapists, Timea and Sandor, and myself as intern.

Starting with the fourth meeting, two of the children, André and Clara, assigned me roles, but ultimately, I became Clara's auxiliary self, as she had monopolized me to such an extent and was so immersed in her universe that this limited my availability to the other children.

Clara was adopted when she was only five days old. Now, she was a girl of ten with medium length chestnut colored hair, big brown eyes, and she was cute, something that we did not discover until the end of her participation in the group. Her style was rough, her way of communicating brutal and aggressive. One could not easily speak to her because her responses were so off-putting. However, of all the children in the group, it was the change in her behavior that was the most spectacular.

The period of intrauterine life

Clara was the product of an unwanted pregnancy and her mother had rejected her from the moment of conception. According to her adoptive parents, Clara's birth mother "was a misshapen and mentally deficient dwarf who smoked throughout her pregnancy." Her father abused the pregnant mother in an attempt to prevent the birth of the child.

Thus, Clara never had the primordial experience of a protective maternal uterus, or the sense of well-being and symbiotic connection that is the foundation for all intimacy and the precursor of all confidence. During her embryonic period, she had lived in a milieu of anxious flux that permeated her being. She was born amidst uncertainties, like a small creature unworthy of interest without the slightest value. This is why she began her life full of mistrust for herself and others.

At school, she often felt that nobody wanted to play with her, that her comrades rejected her. She was the one who provoked rejection with her behavior; lacking confidence, she did not feel she was lovable. To use Michael Bálint's terminology, she was born with a "basic fault" resulting from very early disruption in the primary mother–child relationship. This earliest period of life shapes the organization of object relations, primary self-confidence, and the possibility of making connections. A deficient primary relationship creates vulnerabilities in the personality. Subsequent losses tend to reactivate this basic trauma. The affected individual has the tendency to respond destructively to emotional disappointment and object loss.

Comparative studies on children who were wanted and unwanted show that wanted babies have significantly better cognitive and relational outcomes (Roe & Drivas, 1993).

The rate of deaths, cerebral deficits, mental retardation, and severe socialization problems is significantly greater in unwanted children (Blomberg, 1980, Matejchek & Dytrych, 1988). The infant interiorizes the impulses, traumas, and rejecting mental representations of its mother.

Sandor Ferenczi discovered that unwanted children are born with a deficient will to live (Vajda, 1999). Making reference to Haeckel – according to whom, ontogeny is to some degree a recapitulation of phylogeny – Ferenczi believed that "perigenesis" still imparted phylogenetic traits, such as the desire for security, tranquility, and the comfort of the maternal breast.

Other researchers have demonstrated that the mortality rate for unwanted children during the first months of life is double that for wanted children (Bustan & Coker, 1994).

Other researchers have identified the occurrence of Kipp's syndrome during the first 48 hours after birth (alternating periods of apathy and spasmodic crying) in babies of mothers who rejected their babies during their pregnancies, either consciously or unconsciously (Rottmann, 1974). This group experienced the highest rate of birth complications and an increased frequency of premature births. Additional research has confirmed that an extremely negative attitude on the part of mothers was the source of spontaneous miscarriages, more frequent prematurity, and prolonged and complicated births.

Brezinka's studies showed that a portion of those children born after the *negation of pregnancy* by their mothers and who found themselves in a vacuum intrauterine relationship went on to develop growth retardation, premature death, or were severely handicapped.

In other situations, if the baby only represents an abstraction for the mother, that is, the baby is not experienced as a developing personality within a matrix of reciprocal relationships, and particularly as a simple surface for projection, the baby's development is negatively effected in a similar way.

Some researchers believe that only 34 percent of the IQ level is genetically determined, while the remaining 66 percent is contingent upon the uterine environment (Matt McGue, 1997). The intrauterine environment and the prenatal relationship are thus major determining factors.

Data from the research studies cited above inform us about the existence of a relational space inside the uterus that is full of events with potential positive and negative connotations. The more one neglects this space, the more tragic the consequences, and the more one makes use of it, the better one promotes the post-natal development of the mother–child relationship and the child's personality development.

Fonagy regards one function of aggression as being to defend against the emerging representations of the child's self – this is also the position taken when there are major personality disorders in order to defend a fragmented and threatened self (Fonagy, Target, 1999).

Clara's history and her present state as a function of her intrauterine experience

As described, Clara was adopted at the age of five days. This was never kept secret, and Clara has known about the fact of her adoption. The adopting couple had been unable to have a child of their own, and this was the reason for the adoption. After Clara, who was their first child, the family was further enlarged by the adoption of two boys, and then, four years later, the mother became pregnant and delivered a healthy little girl. Clara's symptoms intensified around the birth of her little sister.

Thus, there are now four siblings, Clara, who is ten years old, and her brothers ages nine and five, while the youngest girl is only fourteen months of age.

Clara has been described as demanding and stubborn ever since she was born, and this has been her way of fighting to survive. When she was hungry, she cried so loudly that no conversation was possible. She did not crawl very much, walked at eleven months, and was covered with black-and-blue marks, since she was unable to avoid bumping into things! She knew no fear, and often put herself into dangerous situations. At the age of one year, she had learned a number of words, and at two years she could form sentences and tell stories. At three years of age, she had repeated episodes of otitis, which medical interventions could not control, so the parents turned to a homeopathic physician and following his interventions, the symptoms went away. Currently, she has allergies to ragweed (*ambrosia artemisiae folia*), a plant reputed to be very allergenic in Hungary. When she started school, Clara was in special classes because she had difficulties with attention and concentration. She has a hard time reading unfamiliar texts and mixes up her letters. Once a week she goes to Delcato-type physical therapy.

It is hard to establish contact with Clara because she reacts so brusquely to any approach. Her behavior is tomboyish, and the boys in the group have difficulty tolerating her reactions and can't understand why a girl should be so crude. As an example, she hit Thomas so hard in the head that it left the boy in tears. She confronted the most dominant boy in the group; and her behavior was often provocative. There were complaints from the family as well as the school regarding her performance and her behavior.

When I approached her for the first time, I was concerned, and was careful to do so gently and discreetly, but I could sense that she was pushing me away and systematically rejecting me. Not knowing what to make of me, my initiatives had frightened her. The malicious and murderous image of her mother was transferred onto everything in her environment, leaving her anxious, unsure of herself in any milieu, and this motivated her aggressive behavior. For Clara, to be aggressive meant to survive. As an important ego function, aggression served a continuous defensive role to fend off intrusions from her environment. It is in this context that Clara's behavior makes sense – her anxieties and fears kept her from making attachments; she attacked to defend herself.

The outward manifestations of this child's difficulties concealed an anxiety with deep roots and a crisis of identity. She was coming to an age when she was meant to begin embarking on the rough road of searching for her identity. However, this proved all the more difficult now that her parents had a "real" and "authentic" child of their own. Other components of Clara's self-questioning included questions about belonging, such as, Who am I? Where did I come from, and Why?

Clara in the magic shop

This was the group's first magic shop experience. Clara did not want to participate in the play. When solicited by Timea, the therapist disguised as the Magician, she stiffened and categorically refused. Next, the co-therapist, Sandor, sat down beside Clara to speak with her. Timea was just about to close the magic shop, but after getting a signal from Sandor, she extended the time it was open and waited. Clara started walking and as she arrived next to Timea, she indicated that it was actually Sandor to whom she wanted to talk.

She asked him for a fairy dress in exchange for her malevolence.

This is the way that she formulated her wish, and it was a marvelous way to express what we considered to be the goal of her therapy.

In the warm-up games, Clara behaved in a rough and aggressive way, stayed in permanent opposition, and refused all contact.

However, she seized upon this opportunity to put into play her affinity "the Oedipal aspects of her behavior" for Sandor.

Clara's first plays

Over the first three sessions, Clara built herself a shelter in the far corner of the room. When someone passed by looking for a brick, she kicked at him to ward off the intrusion. She was very wild during the construction of her den, but once she had completed it, she isolated herself inside, not daring to come out again. Tucked into her cave, she observed what was going on. Making certain to stay invisible, she would not speak to anyone, and did not participate in the other children's play. Curled up in a fetal position, she protected her shelter and allowed nobody to enter.

She was symbolically communicating the ambivalence that characterized her being; wild on the outside, she trembled inside.

During the second phase, Clara began to accept diverse roles. In this narrative, we would like to touch upon the third phase of her participation, during the time I became integrated in the group as a facilitator and Clara made a new discovery.

I adopted the habit of sitting on the floor next to her. This felt like my place. I tried to approach her with more or less success, but a turning point took place when Clara looked at my enlarging belly and asked me the question, Are you expecting a baby? Starting from this moment, she opened up to me, sought out my company, and actually monopolized me as she drew me into her universe.

In the plays that followed, we fabricated bubbles for ourselves from which we would contemplate the events taking place outside. Inside the first bubble, she walked about like a leopard playing with a ball. Later, separating off a portion of the playground with chairs, we constructed bubbles by covering the chairs with silk cloths. The envelope we used to cover it became more and more refined, more colorful, more delicate, and we spread out ever more beautiful fabrics above our heads.

I made efforts to get her to participate in the play of the others, suggesting to her, for example, Come give us a hand, because the Bad Guy (played by Sandor, the facilitator) is too powerful and we ought to help them. But she shook her head no. Then I understood that she did not want to participate; she did not feel strong enough, all she could do was to contemplate, and she wasn't sufficiently mature to dare to venture outside.

Ultimately, it was she who sensed when the moment had arrived.

With Clara we had completely retreated into this interior world; sometimes I was surprised that I didn't even know what was happening outside, because we were so involved in the construction of the bubble.

Hearing the noise from battles outside, she pushed herself close to me, saying, "I'M AFRAID!" I held her, I reassured her, I cradled her. I always had something or other in the way of "food" that I would offer to her and she would accept it gracefully.

The group members took notice of our resplendent, reassuring and attractive place, and more and more of them wanted to come join us in the balloon. Clara let Alex and Tim come in – and they were the ones who needed it the most. Alex wanted to join us from the very beginning, but this was not yet a part of the framework of Clara's play. During one of the last plays, however, she let Alex come in. He behaved so well that he was rewarded with *capsules of goodness* that were capable of transforming the *bad guys*.

The two boys kept coming back to our place, staying for a little while, *pretended* to eat some food, and then left feeling comforted. Like a good mother, Clara took care of them. This is the way that she finally joined the play with her *capsules of goodness* born in *the bubble*, which were capable of defusing all violence.

On the last day of group play, Clara summoned the courage to venture out.

She chose the most beautiful silk from the roof of the bubble, put it over her head and her shoulders, emerged, joined the others, and walked among them. Her face lit up with a smile and she walked with assured and calm steps without worrying about the Velociraptors that were battling all around her.

She had matured sufficiently to share her life with the others and to face the meanness of the outside world.

This is how the wild leopard (a role that she assigned herself at the start of the group) was tamed and a fairy was born.

Transference or potential family

Given that it is impossible to change familial structures and dynamics that have been present for several generations, we find ourselves obliged to find or invent for the child a substitute family or surrogate family. This counter-family is not necessarily a real family (we have often encountered – without suggesting that this is inevitable – caring families, foster families, and even adoptive families who were unable to resist being impregnated by the negative force carried by the child and who ended up recreating a climate in which the child could not affirm his existence otherwise than by becoming the bad child or the rascal).

Thus we offer him a different kind of "counter-family," a family that is analogous to Winnicott's transitional object or potential space in that it is neither a totally real family nor a totally fantasized family – it is a transferential family, not in the Freudian sense where transference principally means projection onto the therapist (analyst) of past relationships, but in the Adlerian sense, that is, the creation of bonds of a different nature, of a new type of relationship in which the child can recognize himself as a creative, original, and lovable being. It is this counter-family that we made efforts to create in the psychotherapeutic space that the children called the workshop. Inside this potential space of acceptance, attention, and the affection of real people, both adults and children, provided the poorly loved child with a corrective experience. Horizontal and vertical connections were formed with the group and with the psychotherapists.

Thus, the transferential family is composed of a psychotherapist duo, preferably a man and a woman, who are at once substitute parents, sometimes conflictual, sometimes ideals, sometimes super-ego figures, but above all, validating pseudo-parental figures. Some abused children try to provoke us, in an attempt to induce responses of rejection and punishment, the responses to which they are accustomed. One has to be able to resist these efforts.

As for the others – the group of children who are also part of this substitute family – at the beginning they, too, are deprived, abused, poorly loved, and frustrated. And yet . . . all sorts of compensatory and fraternal bonds full of identification and empathy are created in the group, even though when the children first arrived, they could scarcely listen to each other.

It should be emphasized, however, that this counter-family does not function in opposition to the real family. It is essential to assure that the parents are involved, for once the child's self-image changes, this change needs to stabilize. Therefore, we tend to try to change the parents' image of the child even if this requires more extensive remodeling of the family dynamic. This is all the more true because, in addition to the psychotherapeutic work with the child, the word of the Judge also intervenes, prohibiting any mistreatment of the child. So we also have to work with the parents to modify their sense of what their child is capable of becoming. This work is not always easy. Sometimes, one has to become the target of the parents' aggression when, in a context of rivalry, they challenge any possibility of rehabilitation (cf. the mother who, after her son had been at the workshop for only a few weeks, reproached me in his presence, "Nothing has changed, he's just the same." She was alluding to her child's encopresis). In the longer run, though, one manages to create a special connection with the family, especially with the mothers, starting from the idea that all families, and all mothers, regardless of the relationship with the child, want to assure the well being and happiness of their child. We have to give them a chance to put this into practice. This is true despite all dysfunctionality, even if it seems perverse, and despite all conflict (on this subject, also see Work with the Parents, p. 30).

Joint activities in this affective environment of change make it possible to strengthen the social sense of children regarded as incapable of creating contacts or becoming integrated in groups.

Of course, the time spent in this "substitute family" is limited. In the days of the pioneers, the groups met for a half-day every week. The sessions would begin in the morning with a period of silent drawing, followed by the preparation time and staging of the psychodrama, based upon the invention of a single child or the whole group, and we concluded with a meal eaten together, a time of relaxation and communion. Since this form of children's therapy has spread (numbers are in the range of hundreds), the time available has been set according to the settings where it is practiced. It varies from a half-day (one morning), every day (summer camps), a morning per week (delinquent adolescents in detention), one or two hours a week in consultancies, hospitals, schools, institutions, etc.

In the potential space of these workshops, we have witnessed the awakening of extraordinary creativity – even in some pre-psychotic children and in other children considered to be mentally deficient, and in children at risk who are often designated as psychopathic. This creativity made it possible for them to express their aggression, undeniably existent, in a symbolic mode that proved to be self-reparative.

The dynamic psychological activity of the child at risk is the passage to the act, in other words, delinquency. This is his privileged mode of expression, and if it is not redirected, risks becoming his principal and unique language.

Dynamic psychodrama with children, while an enactment that involves the body and gesture, allows the child to acquire an intermediary language in the pseudo-family of the group; the act is transposed, symbolized, and thus not enacted in the real world. In this way, whether in the form of fairy tales or stories invented by the child, the child can express everything that stands in the way of his development: his family conflicts, the tendentious apperception of his family that degrades the baby swan into an ugly duckling (as in the self-revalorizing story staged by Karine, a magnificent little girl who was abused), and also her desire to change her projection into the future (cf. Bruno's drawing of the knight, Figure 6.2). The psychodrama in the workshop becomes a vehicle for self-realization and changing one's self image. For these children suffering from a devaluation complex, we suggest that they project themselves into relationships that they have chosen themselves; we give them the opportunity to experiment with the most diverse roles – an astronaut, an Indian chief, a punk, or an animal – not only selecting a character to identify with, but actually putting themselves into that character's skin. In this way, they can also realize their heroic aspirations. The transitional space, the space of transformation and multiple disguises that are also self-presentations is thus available to all the children. However, they each make a different use of that space depending on their personality and their particular nature, with a view of developing, completing, and enlarging their way of living.

The potential space of the psychodrama, taking place in the safeguarding presence of the pseudo-family, allows the child to experience even his reactive aggression and his sense of being a bad object in a cathartic manner that comforts him without harming others. After all, the victims of the plays, if any, come back to life at the end of the play even when they have been killed.

In this workshop, we make efforts to provide the children, if not with a real family, a replacement milieu. We bring the child our listening and our participation in order to allow him to overcome his blockages, his entrapment in non-communication, his non-existence. Winnicott's conclusion is also our own, "If creativity is reflected in the mirror, but only if it is reflected, it becomes integrated in the personality . . . and in the last analysis, it is this creativity that allows the individual to become"(Winnicott, 1971a).

Without intervention, the child will remain a prisoner of his compulsive relationships, forced to forever replay and reproduce in reality the type of family relationships in which he is entangled, prisoner of a scenario in which he must replay the only role that has been assigned to him, in which he alternately stages the child he once was and the parent who alienated him.

Note

1 Excerpt of the text presented by Ann Klokniczer in her examination of Adlerian children's psychodrama.

10

THE ROLE OF THE GROUP IN THE SOCIALIZATION OF THE CHILDREN

General comments regarding the group

The area of microsociology that studies the theory of small groups determined that historically, the group preceded the individual. Whether we place the origins of emerging individualization at the time of the Renaissance or the dawn of modernity, it is certain that the development of individual consciousness was the result of a later historical process.

The family is obviously an example of a small group, but in the research literature, both theoretical and empirical, the emphasis is placed on the formation of extra-familial groups in which criteria for belonging are established and the moral dimensions of the individual develop.

The group is a concomitant factor in the evolution of human psychology – without a relational system, the human phenomenon could never have been born (see the socialization of "feral children," Itard's *Victor* (1962 [1801, 1806]), by way of Kaspar Hauser, and those children who, for experimental or pathological reasons, have been deprived of their social entourage).

Developmental psychology, especially in England and Hungary, shifted theoretical attention to the primary maternal–child relationship, which theorists had the temerity to call the "object relation." While I do not want to make an inventory, there is copious literature in the field of analytic child development beginning with the brilliant Melanie Klein (whose theories have been refuted), through Margaret Mahler, the founder of the object relations school, and especially Winnicott.

The most significant change in theoretical focus has taken place as a result of modern research on infants. It is in this regard that the title of Daniel M. Stern's book, *The Interpersonal World of the Infant* (Stern, 1985), is significant. Much earlier, Adler had also situated the model of humanization in the maternal–child relationship, and beyond that, the model for all social relationships and, by extension, the bases for all socialization.

In child therapy, the treatment of children with problems – with the exception of approaches like family therapy – individual treatment is still the principal method. Although everyone acknowledges the familial factors at the root of personality disorders (abandonment, abuse, marital disharmony, separation, etc.), it is rarely recognized that the most efficacious way to rectify or even replace the function of the family is through small groups.

We will not delve into all the theoretical aspects of the creation and characteristics of small groups except to the extent that this contributes to the understanding of the primordial importance of the child's belonging to a group, a fact that especially pertains to children who are poorly adjusted, unstable, dislocated, or at risk.

Microsociological research and the study of small groups is a relatively recent area of scientific research. The socio-psychological study of groups and philosophical theories related to groups began with the work of American sociologists George Herbert Mead and Charles H. Cooley during the first third of the twentieth century.

Cooley's important discovery was that human value systems develop within the context of the small group; here also models and norms of behavior are formed. In *Mind, Self and Society*, George Herbert Mead concludes that the personality of the child develops through the child's contact with the people who are close to him, that is, with family and playmates. "The child not only learns the rules of the game but also interiorizes the behavior of the others. According to his natural gifts, the child is capable of adopting their roles, and in this way he is able to become conscious of himself as being different from others" (p. 83).

Other theorists have written about the relationship between the individual and the group.

In one of his earlier writings, Cooley delineated the relation between individual ambitions and the group:

> A given individual may have ambitions but the object of his ambition is something that figures in the value system of others as a desirable object, and he has the tendency to accept these common norms and respect the rules of the game.
>
> *(1909)*

> The group forms the natural milieu for the individual, and no normal personality chooses to be psychologically isolated from others. The study of relations with others constitutes an indispensable chapter of individual psychology.
>
> *(Anzieu & Martin, 1976, p. 134)*

"There is a domain in the study of human behavior that concerns the amalgam of the individual and the social," states Mérei ([1970], 1996, p. 92) referring to Zazzo. "This domain is the field of microsociology, at once different from individual psychology or general sociology. It is on this basis that all social relations are woven and that the network of human bonds is built" (p. 92).

Shared experience

The group, as Mérei reminds us, is not identical with the ensemble of its members but also comprises something more; the nature of the group determines the members' joint action and their productions.

Muzafert Sherif (1953), who is considered one of the pioneers in experimentation with groups, defined four criteria for the evolution of the group: they are a common goal, the effect of the affective echo exercised by each member on the others, the rules that structure the group, and the development of common norms. Mérei says about these four elements that they are not so much a system of criteria but rather designate the four stages in the evolution of the group, and he adds, "With regard to the periodization of developmental psychology, these periods are not chronologically determined, and it is more a question of their succession" (Merei, 1996).

Moreno (1969) also emphasizes that the solidarity of the group takes shape during a process that is quite long. "In the course of their shared experience, certain common habits and values develop. It is the members of the group who carry the group surplus. It is this surplus that emerges in the individuals that we explain by the fact that the shared experience evokes a greater level of intensity, and for this reason, it assures more pleasure and greater efficacy" (see Moreno, 1970).

Isolation or participation – Narcissism or positive identification (Gaspard)

> Group cohesion, the sense of solidarity of the group, is weak at the beginning; the goal of therapy is to help the group move forward from a weak state of cohesion to an advanced level of good communication and cohesion.
>
> (*Ibid.*)

Samuel R. Slavson (1953) is widely regarded as the father of group therapy. The idea that underlay its theoretical foundation was relatively new to psychology and psychiatry – "Man is determined essentially by life in common." It is a sign of illness if the development of a connection with the community does not flourish.

Sociometric evaluations indicate that the number of isolated individuals in pathological groups is greater than normal. The most important contribution of the group event for individual development is the modification or suppression of egocentrism or psychological solitude. This change increases the individual's ability to resonate to other people's feelings and to develop a positive identification. This change is illustrated by Valentin's paintings of the magnificent horse alone and untamed, before the period that he discovered his compatriots and began to be attached to the group.

FIGURE 10.1 Gaspard, the solitary child

For Moreno, the group signifies being together. Similar to Slavson, he sees therapy's first goal as overcoming solitude.

> The original theme of the experimental research that preoccupied me before and after the First World War in Vienna was: how do we help people who live in a group but remain isolated? The question that I originally posed is not of an abstract or scientific nature – it is therapeutic
>
> (*Moreno, 1970, p. 126*)

The question of integrating solitary children arose spontaneously in a number of children's groups. We would like to tell the story invented by a little girl with a sensitive heart, which was put together by a group in a Rogersian school in Budapest. The group gave the drama the title *Gaspard*, but we would be tempted to rename it *Adoption*. Viktoria Drinoczky, the psychodramatist for the group tells the story of its origins and staging as follows:

Let me introduce you to three participants in the group:

Andy, the inventor of the story, is a good soul, and she suffers if someone is left out of the group. She is an attentive child, always ready to help. She exercises this role in her school class as well, and she was the one who took charge of *Charlotte*, a handicapped child. Charlotte has suffered from a severe handicap and she is of short stature. She joined us at the beginning of the school year; she has difficulty walking and can barely stand upright. Her short stature, her handicap, her status as last-born leave her feeling that everyone should cater to her, and she even demands that people serve her. She regards those who don't meet her requests as being wicked and insensitive. Charlotte changes her way of being in the world, to show her that she is capable of offering something to others, as her handicap does not totally define her. It is in this play that she accepted, for the first time, in place of the little animal or the baby that she would habitually play, the part of an adult. Reversing their respective roles, she had chosen to be Andy's mother, and she was quite happy with this, for at the end of the play, she declared, "It was nice being Andy's mother."

Mischi is an anxious and contained boy, overprotected by his mother. He has difficulty making contact and stays solitary, even though the others like him on account of his docility and intelligence. The girls, especially, seek out his friendship. He is rejected by the wilder boys, and he does not take the initiative. Mischi never invented any stories, and he has a hard time taking a role because all choices are difficult for him.

Viktoria continued. To stay isolated or become a part of the group? Mischi, who chose to play Gaspard, asked himself this question. Upon leaving the play, he seemed to question the role he had played, saying that he did not like the idea of becoming established in the village: "I enjoyed being Gaspard and chasing people." However, his enthusiastic choice of the role and his performance expressed something different – his desire to be adopted. Given the uncertainty that Mischi expressed, (Viki explains), I suggested that we replay the story of Gaspard the following week so that Mischi could pick the outcome he preferred. But Mischi was not ready to take up the role so as to change the outcome. Yet the other participants insisted on replaying the piece, and this is what was finally done, except with a different distribution of parts.

As for Andy, the story also evoked a question: should we try to influence people who isolate themselves? Should we engage with them to help them overcome their fear and their fright?

Andy ended up giving a positive response even while recognizing that this was not an easy task, for the solidarity of the others could awaken the need to belong, the rejection of which, according to Adler was "the greatest misfortune."

For Charlotte, the maternal role that she played constituted a first step in overcoming her style of being childish or a "little thing that needs to be protected," she was able to take on responsibilities, and to establish relationships based on reciprocity.

The three children affirmed, each of them in keeping with his/her own personal history, the importance of the feeling of belonging to the community, something that, for Adler is of supreme importance. In *The Meaning of Life*, he wrote, "As for me, I am in agreement with all human efforts whose purpose is to create a sense of community" (*Gemeinschaftsgefühl*) (1973, p. 189).

So the children staged the story of Gaspard for a second time, but the distribution of roles was different. Three little girls participated in the play, and this time, it was Charlotte who wanted to be Gaspard. They remembered the story, having seen it the first time, and were free to develop it as they wished. The second version of the story of Gaspard went as follows:

The king solemnly declares that he will give his son (since all the players were girls) to the one who can persuade Gaspard to settle in the village. The girls begin to make efforts to convince Gaspard, they gather flowers for him, but he morosely refuses and pulls down his hat. The two little girls sadly turn back down the path, but along the way, they decide to write a letter in which they will describe the advantages of a life in the company of others: "Dear Gaspard, it would be so good if you returned to the village where all the houses have red and blue roofs. You could have a turtle and a dog."

Gaspard reads the letter but it doesn't shake him out of his decision. One night, wolves are circling in the forest and want to devour the solitary man, who doesn't know how to get away from them and takes refuge in the village.

"You came after all?" the girls ask as he knocks at their door.

"No," answers Gaspard, "it was the wolves that made me do it."

The girls are very happy about his arrival; he'll have his own house and the turtle. They let the king know, in hopes that he will reward them. The king welcomes the good news and reveals that Gaspard is actually his little brother.

In this second version, Charlotte played the role of the solitary and cranky Gaspard. This role intrigued her just as much as her previous one. If Charlotte avoids contact with other people, it's because she is afraid; they constitute a danger in her eyes because any movement whatsoever could destabilize her and she might fall down. According to her parents, this is the reason that she prefers the calm and safety of her refuge over the outside world, full of danger.

The two children playing the principal role in the different versions of the same play understand by personal experience the problem of being accepted by the group. But whereas with Mischi one can speak of an option, a defense mechanism more or less voluntarily chosen, for Charlotte, it signifies a hope, the hope for her integration in the group as an equal, despite her otherness.

During the unfolding of the play Gaspard vividly illustrates the fact that the therapist is not the sole owner of the therapeutic role. This phenomenon of group reciprocity Moreno calls "therapeutic interaction." He is convinced that every patient (here, every child) plays the part of a therapeutic aide. This is the role chosen by the little girl who made up the story of Gaspard, but it applies just as well to the other children for their listening and their spirit of mutual help that so characterizes children's psychodrama groups, in other words: to the climate of empathy.

Social hunger

We call the individual's desire to be accepted by the community "social hunger." According to Slavson, this is "the most important human motivation." In the therapy group, it is an important factor that stimulates children's development. The child seeks to obtain the love and friendship of adults. This primary desire impels the child to satisfy his parents' wishes, to adopt their models of behavior: later, it is social hunger that obliges the individual to accept the system of values and the habits of the group. The desire to be accepted has the same role in the group as transference in individual therapy. In group therapy, it is thus one of the engines of change: the child modifies his behavior in order to earn the acceptance of the group. Slavson believes that social hunger plays an important role in healthy ego development. Negative reactions on the part of the child's comrades are the likeliest motivation for overcoming isolation and restraining outbursts of anger. "The child wants to be loved and accepted, or at least, not to be excluded, and this motivates him to change his egotistical behavior." Moreover, children have to become used to the fact that in the group, and in all collective life, there opens up the possibility of developing modalities of behavior and new life experience. This kind of therapy, "treatment through the event" is based upon the effect of immediate experience.

The role of the group in structuring the self

The atmosphere of the group

In group therapy, we work primarily with children who are not accepted by their parents, family, school, and groups of children. Such rejection may be manifest in different ways. Slavson distinguishes between two forms:

> "Direct rejection" (real rejection) means that the parents, siblings, teachers don't love him, neglect him or fail to recognize him. "Indirect rejection" means that even though people love and support the child, the motivation of the entourage is rather egotistical: they are the ones who need to have a dependent being, or even a baby. The best example is the spoiled child who seems to be loved, but whose overprotective parents prevent him from developing his capacities to blossom and block the possibility of living as an independent individual.
>
> (*Slavson, 1958*)

> This type of parent, who pampers and spoils the child, does not respect his personality. These children have trouble getting along with their peers and with adults. "These children adopt a hostile and destructive attitude or they avoid the outside world and turn their back on it. They are excessively aggressive or excessively withdrawn and compensate for their anxiety or excessive sense of guilt with asocial or antisocial behavior."
>
> (*Ibid.*)

Children who are raised in such conditions become excluded from all community. They need a defense that protects them from this unfriendly pressure, this sense of ever-present danger. Alfred Adler also considered that the course of development of the spoiled child is damaged by the difficulty of becoming autonomous, and that they risked remaining permanently dependent.

But let us come back to the primary rejection, to the lack of love or withholding of love. It is in this climate that the child feels impotent and incapable – a feeling that is very difficult for him to shake off.

Does this kind of child who is discredited by his immediate environment have the slightest chance of valuing himself elsewhere? Adler doubts whether this is possible, and states, "After only a short time, his grades become unsatisfactory, proving that the child is no better at school than at home" (Adler-Jahn, 1958, p. 165).

Cure is only possible if the child is given the opportunity to change his life and become the active crafter of his own life. We must use psychotherapy to help change the negative attitude of the child toward people and toward life. One of the main tasks of treatment is to melt the child's affective isolation. The instrument for accomplishing this is the therapist's cooperative effort with the child to defuse his defiant and hostile attitude. In order to do this, there must be, first and foremost, an atmosphere of acceptance. In our view, the attitude of acceptance toward the child does not mean that we abandon the child to his impulses; once there is a relationship of trust established, he has to accept a certain frame.

In the case of the spoiled child who behaves like a baby, temporary acceptance of the regression may be necessary, but the moment comes when the psychotherapists and the group need to help him step beyond it. Slavson expresses the following opinion: "Infantile behavior has to encounter a solid guide in order to evolve." In the absence of a loving environment at home, we must provide a reassuring atmosphere for the child, which includes respect for his personality, recognition of his efforts, and meeting some of his needs.

Children whose neurotic behavior and symptoms are the result of premature rejection need compensation.

In Slavson's conception and treatment model, one point is crucial – as we have already suggested apropos of treating aggression – the acceptance of all activity, even including violence. Slavson created conditions in his workshop where the children had the right to do anything they wanted, anything that entered their minds. They could destroy the furniture, fight with one another, or use clay to throw balls, and at the end of the session, it was the therapist who took care of the mess and put things back in place, unless the children did it on their own initiative.

As these children encounter rejection everywhere due to their aggression, the therapist must accept them without thwarting them, – or so Slavson thinks. The therapist should not impose rules or interdictions or rein in their destructive urges. But this isn't all. Slavson goes even further in asserting,

> Hostile and aggressive actions have no therapeutic value unless they are permitted, and not simply by the fact of being committed. Destructive activity

> as such does not satisfy the child's need for love. It does not soothe his tension, and it cannot prepare the terrain for emotional change unless the adult accepts the destructive activities with understanding.

The vast majority of child therapists consider this method of absolute *laissez-faire* as being ineffective and insist that aggression be staged only in the symbolic sphere.

Children who come from an especially adverse family environment are the ones who benefit the most from the group experience.

Every child needs to feel protected. The feeling of protection is based on the affection of parents and of the other individuals who play an important part in his life. The psychiatrist, social workers, and the group therapist – in the capacity of substitute affective persons – must create a compensatory affective climate that helps the child feel protected.

Therapy group and family constellation

According to Moreno, the therapy group may be constituted in two ways. It can function as a miniature family or as a miniature society. Moreno ascribes great importance to the family constellation, even in adult contexts, because in these groups, maternal, paternal, and fraternal roles can take on new clarity.

With respect to the mini society or the mini universe, the family is clearly included, even if it is exceeded. The structural form of the mini society provides an ideal frame for adult therapy groups because it can be adapted to any culture.

Adlerian psychology emphasizes the system of human relationships. Adler rejected the idea that it was possible to treat the individual in isolation. According to his theory of individual comparative psychology, the principal problem that the difficult child must resolve is the social dimension of his life. It is in this context that the question of the role of group therapy or the small group arises. Children at risk or those who have adapted to parents with sadistic or violent tendencies try to initiate provocations that result in punishment. One has to learn to ignore such provocations, and to try to help these children avoid reproducing the pathological relationship between parent and child. One has to protect them from transferences of this kind.

Other children who, at the outset, were timorous and lack initiative, children who were poorly loved, also become a part of this substitute family, and yet . . . In groups where they were at first hardly capable of paying attention to the others, an empathic climate of mutual assistance developed over time.

Fantasies of group

The French analytic psychodramatists made great efforts at first to unify the frame for psychodrama with that of individual psychoanalysis. There have rarely been such intensive discussions about the frame as those that took place during the 1990s. The frame is a force field, especially a force field for transference:

> One cannot overestimate the importance of the frame, it defines the terrain where the forces and vectors representing the body, language, the other, thought and abstraction all come into play.
>
> (*Privat & Sacco, 1991, p. 5*)

Bleger, Winnicott, Donner, and Baranger are the writers who contributed most to a theoretical shift in the concept of the frame. Their discussions about the frame reawakened the old controversy about individual psychoanalytic treatment, with particular emphasis on the psychoanalytic approach to the treatment of children. The efforts of these authors aimed toward utilizing the classical psychoanalytic method for analytic treatment of children and for analytic group therapy for children without the slightest modification. The discussion recalled the controversy that put Anna Freud up against Melanie Klein (Privat & Sacco, 1995).[1] We will also cite *The Group and the Unconscious*, and *The Group Imaginary*, Anzieu, 1984). The author starts from the idea that in any coherent group, a particular shared group experience or a group fantasy is born and attributes a kind of corporeal reality to the group. He designates the group process as *the illusion of group*, as group fantasies (the mechanical mouth), as fantasies of group rupture (or group castration) that are surrounded in unconscious psychic elements (archaic fantasy, group body, psychic envelope).

Referring to Freud and sometimes to Winnicott, psychoanalytic interpretation during the 1980s and 1990s attributed a maternal function to the group. "The group behaves as a maternal object, even as a primary, narcissistic and undifferentiated maternal object" (Sacco, 1991). From this it follows that "The psychodramatic group constitutes an entity that is capable of providing everything and encloses the child like a mother" (Ibid.). Moreover, he interprets the group enactment, analogous to Freud's *Totem and Taboo*, as the bearer of the fantasy of the murder of the father by the primitive horde. Thus, the group is considered to be the bearer of a cannibalistic instinct. Our author states, in conclusion, "The oral cannibalistic genealogy of identification occupies a strategic position in research on the origins of sexuality. Incorporation of the model cannot mean anything other than the cannibalistic incorporation of the father, onto whom the child projects his cannibalistic orality" (Sacco, 1999).

Another theoretical formulation that references Freud is the "discovery" of an archi-archaic and pre-archaic world when he asks, apropos of the shared group experience: "Is this not an archaic unconscious that is even more archaic than the individual unconscious?" (Ibid.).

Sacco does not explain what he means by a "personal prehistory," which he also calls "archaicity." Perhaps he is alluding to the group existence that precedes individualization, since he also makes reference to what Ophélie Avron calls "interpulsivity" and "innate" social need, a formulation of Bion's. We would state that this theoretical genre of group theory that situates itself in fantasy rejects all reference to any kind of reality, and the actuality of the group only appears peripherally. Yet, in one of his earliest writings, D. Anzieu, the classic writer on psychoanalytic psychodrama for children, attributed the transformation of the child's behavior and personality to the group milieu.

Another group of psychoanalysts, while also calling themselves Freudian, does not believe that the children's group has to regress to the point of throwing the therapists and the children into a state of pre-archaic fusion, but states that it is the latency period that is most favorable for the creation of groups. "The organization of children's groups in the post-Oedipal period signifies the structuring of a common superego which can also be generalized in all of society as well as the group" (Roussillon, 1999, p. 9–26). The superego is formed during the latency period and modulates the relationships of adolescents to the group.

The group as transitional space

The originators of fantastic theories about groups could not avoid making reference to Winnicott and attempted to reconcile their interpretative model based onthe profundities of depth psychology with the Winnicottian perspective (see, for example, René Kaës, who explicitly cites Winnicott before going on to exclude the real world in favor of exclusive attention to the unconscious, *Psychoanalytic Group Psychodrama*, 1999). A number of studies were published to point out the errors of some theoreticians who had made use of Winnicott's ideas. In the volume (*The Paradox of Winnicott*) Diatkine, Green, Kestenberg, Lebovici, Pontalis, and Widlöcher each presented their position. We would like to cite René Roussillon, who observed that Winnicott's major redeeming originality was his introduction of the dimension of reality. At a time when this was still considered unorthodox, he dared to say that "the baby does not exist without the environment that supports him or outside an exterior reality, an external object that is the essential condition of life for his subjective existence" (Diatkine, 1999, pp. 167–170.

One could interpret group play in a Winnicottian sense that would locate it between internal and external reality. Barbara Steck (1999) defined this structure as forming a bridge between everyday social experience and the unconscious. In this transitional space, one can stage fantasies or even myths that, at the same time, are the transposed images of the preoccupations and dynamics of the group. The atmosphere of continuity and trust that is achieved in the space of the group does not solely depend on shared experience; it also resonates with an external reality. This is how the "acting as if" of play (Winnicott's *illusion*) provides access to real-life being and doing in real activity.

On the diversity of groups

Moreno warns us against trying to reduce psychodrama to strictly defined rules and emphasizes that every group has its own structure, coherence, and depth. For him, no two groups are the same, and this is why, from the very beginning, he refrained from defining his theory according to rigid categories. This prudence and Moreno's permissive, non-reductive approach went on to become an important factor to allow the development of varied methods and different schools within the field of psychodrama. Moreno was very open and accepted a great variety of methodologies and practices. As a result, over time, quite dissimilar concepts and methods came into being. Other forms of dramatic therapy practiced according to variations or original adaptations that were very different from Morenian psychodrama, as for example, Perls's therapeutic method or Kelly's fixed role therapy. There are other methods called theatrical therapies, pantomime games, etc., which are employed in the treatment of psychiatric patients. One particular form of psychodrama was developed in France and later expanded remarkably in the United States; this was individual analytic psychodrama, a practice we will have occasion to speak about more later, as well as experimental psychodrama, triadic and tetradic psychodrama, etc. Moreover, Moreno refers to many other psychodramatic techniques: hypnodrama, sociodrama, role playing, ethnodrama, action-drama, psycho-dance, psycho-music, etc. Many psychodramatists apply the psychodramatic technique in different settings. Psycho-educational workers, social workers, and psychologists who work with the mentally handicapped have transformed the structure of psychodrama in original ways to respond to these children's problems. With mentally handicapped children, one utilizes a completely different technique. In nursery schools as well, psychodramatic play has to be more strictly framed in consideration of the limited attention span of the young child. For very young children around four years of age, the use of puppets facilitates the necessary distance and modulates the intensity of the play. The advantage of psychodrama groups organized in alternative schools is that the members of the group have known each other for some time, and thus, a favorable group climate is already established; the inconvenient aspect is the difficulty of reconciling two different contexts. Some colleagues have tried playing in an extended family setting, but although such play may be enjoyable for the participants, it cannot be considered as psychodrama. Many colleagues working with children with behavioral problems, especially if there are many of them in the group, run into the same difficulty at the beginning, that of defusing aggression. They have tried to put the brakes on aggressive impulses by means of relaxation exercises just prior to the psychodrama. For other colleagues, speech therapists who are playing with children with speech and language problems, the play activity sometimes stops the stuttering; however, we believe that it is preferable to form mixed groups that include children with and without articulation problems. We will return to this question as we present specific case examples from our colleagues' psychodramatic practice.

The holding function of the group

The conception of the group apparently shared by French analysts resembles Anzieu's notion of *group illusion*. In this conception, the group takes on the role of a substitute mother in a quasi-concrete sense of the term.

In the 1980s, French psychoanalytic child psychodramatists tended to interpret the group either explicitly or more subtly or by allusion as a maternal substitute. Rodriguez states,

> One might speak of a didactic backdrop formed by the cohesion of the group and which manifests itself in a maintenance role. This flexible relationship, which resembles that of the baby and the parent, creates a protective frame around the Oedipal and pre-Oedipal material present in the child.
>
> (*1995, p. 187*)

(Later, Anzieu called this an "envelope"). He had a very original conception of the therapist-couple as being experienced as an indivisible as well as complementary unit (if we understand it correctly, in a maternal role), and the children integrated in the group fabric representing the baby (Rodriguez, 1995). The author calls this phenomenon, with reference to Pierre Fedida, the "psychoanalytic mother-child paradigm."

Along these lines, we could cite Nicolas Abraham (1987) on the *paido-mater* dyad. According to his conception, the desire for this dyadic union forms the backdrop for all separation anxiety, in both children and adults – which can be traced back to a nostalgic sense of lack. The object of desire, according to him (this allusion is certainly in agreement with Ferenczi) is the original oneness, that unique lost paradise of the mother–child pair, nostalgia for the maternal uterus or for the *thalassa*.

The dyadic mother–child relationship inevitable arises in any children's group run by a single leader. Leadership by two people (a couple of psychodramatists composed of one woman and one man) may specifically allow the group to overcome this, except in the case (as cited earlier) of the male therapy with such maternal nostalgia that he, in the context of his fantasy, and to reinforce his own maternal role, even accepts his dyadic fusion with the female therapist. No interpretation or fantasy can change the fact that a syncretic kind of socialization takes place in the group (José Bleger), which essentially means that beyond the real relationships, there is an element of undifferentiated cohesion that stabilizes the group.

According to some French psychoanalytic writers, this cohesion is attributable to the fantasy of the psychotherapist, who experiences him/herself as an all-powerful goddess-mother, creator of a mini world composed of similar fellow-creatures, as B. Chapelier (1995) put it, not without an element of irony. Chapelier interprets this as the creation of the *myth of the psychotherapist*.

According to the child psychoanalyst and psychodramatist Pierre Privat, who also refers to the "group illusion," the group, as a good object, becomes the instrument for a narcissistic revalidation. The group's reinforcement of the narcissistic self stems from the fact that the child transfers his own illusion of omnipotence onto the group. The belief in the omnipotence of the group, according to Privat, mobilizes a kind of primordial illusion. The illusion of maternal omnipotence is overdetermined, in fact, according to this psychoanalyst-author, because according to his interpretation, the group is also regarded as an all-powerful and fair mother (in the sense that she takes care of each member in an equitable fashion).

> To some extent, the group recreates the maternal symbolic relationship called upon to ward off the state of exaggerated excitement, to assuage castration

> anxiety, and depression evoked by separation anxiety and fantasies of disintegration.
>
> (*Privat-Sacco, 1995, p. 83*)

The group, a network of relationships

> The reality of an illusion is worth at least as much as the illusion of a reality.
>
> (*Moreno*)

Contrary to the symbolic interpretations referred to earlier, which classify the group experience not in the real but in a symbolic dimension, we would tend to accept Moreno's definition as cited above. The group is a network of real relationships where the child can learn the rules of human collaboration.

Slavson (1950) thought that group therapy helped transmute the childish superego, created by the internalization of adult proscriptions, into a group superego. The child wishes to be accepted by the group and modulates his behavior in an attempt to obtain acceptance. To the extent that such adaptation is inadequate, it is within the framework of group psychodrama that he should be able to achieve it.

At the outset, the therapeutic group consists of separate individuals, every person for himself. It is only later that group phenomena begin to appear. It is not possible to speak in terms of the group until it is capable of functioning together. This phenomenon, according to Anzieu, has its antecedents in developmental psychology. Children have to move beyond their pre-genital and Oedipal fixations and their regressions, which prevent any real socialization. In this sense, Anzieu's "group illusion" means that the children project their desire for omnipotence onto the group or, as the author puts it in another place, "the group is transformed into a libidinal object possessed of narcissistic omnipotence" (Anzieu, 1994, p. 132).

We believe that children transfer their desire for omnipotence, at least in part, onto the group. The narcissism of the child who is insufficiently loved, who is incapable of loving himself sufficiently, is often inadequate. To develop their own positive image, these children need the group.

The development of self consciousness in the group

In this regard, the question immediately arises of the relationship between the individual and the group, whether the group plays an enlivening role through the occurrence of identification of rivalrous interactions (see the study by Sacco, *Identification in the group space*, 1999). The reciprocal support of the members does not oppose the formation of a sense of self-worth in the individual, but is rather its precondition. Acceptance of his personality by his companions, sharing feelings in common, Moreno's *sharing*, creates a global affective climate that allows the child, commensurate with his development of a sense of security, to develop his own difference; this is what constitutes the richness of the psychodramatic group.

Moreno's *sharing* affirms that the protagonist can count on the understanding and the echo of the group. Sharing is the premise for creating the reciprocal relationships that reinforce group cohesion. "It is not analysis that the Morenian protagonist needs (any more than our child), but the love of self-discovery" (Lutz, 1976, p. 121).

> Through its special efficacy, group therapy lets the child strengthen his personality. In the group, the child can gain two kinds of experiences (. . .). The group provides safety and protection, but this adjustment, at the level of the group, demands a certain restraint upon the needs and possibilities of the individual self. The sense of self worth that can emerge through conflicts raised to a new level, that is to say, that it isn't the self against the group but the self within the group.

Lutz points out that this stabilization of the child's sense of self improves the child's possibilities of creating relationships outside the group as well.

Eugène Enriquez, from Université Paris-VII, who conducted research at the Laboratory of Social Change, regards the concept of group as being, by definition, inseparable from that of community.

> We consider as a community any voluntary assemblage of persons who feel an intense desire to work together so as to realize those aims that define the meaning of their existence. There are no groups without ideals of community being among their (sometimes illusory) stimulating forces.
>
> (*1992, p. 22*)

The group constitutes the territory for assimilating new lived experiences that can change behavior. Just as the lion's share of the cure in the treatment of illnesses may lie beyond the effects of medication, in the resistance of the living organism, the critical factor for overcoming psychological problems is self-healing. This process is part of the child's marvelous capacity for recreating the self, a process in which the group can assure a supportive frame.

Notes

1 During the past thirty years, we have encountered fantastic interpretive constructs from depth psychology. They include the CEEFRAP group and its illustrious representatives such as Didier Anzieu and René Kaës, and from other groups such as CIRPPA (Center for Information and Research in Psychology and Applied Psychoanalysis) and IRFAPG (Research and Training Institute for the Psychoanalytic Approach to Groups) along with a number of psychodramatists who run groups for adults and children. In 1993 CIRPPA and IRFAPG organized a conference on the frame (*Children's Groups and the Psychoanalytic Frame*) (*Fanciful Notions of Psychoanalytic Training*, 1984, *The Ego-Skin* Dunod, 1985, 1995, Anzieu, 1984, 1995).

11

FAIRY TALE AND THERAPY

Functions of the fairy tale

For millennia, the fairy tale has occupied a privileged place in the imagination of peoples of the East, the South, the North, and the West. It appears in diverse forms in all countries throughout time. The fairy tale introduces its audience to a magic world, where the laws of the real world are noticeably altered, where everything is different, and all wishes and desires may be intensified, where the laws of gravity may be altered, distances mastered (by magical intervention or the intervention of objects such as the seven-league boots or by magical formulas). Nothing is impossible – here, as Philippe Soupault said, people speak that unique language common to all times and all civilizations, the language of symbols (Soupault, 1985). Some experts on fairy tales believe that the fairy tale represents a universal human language, the only language that we can understand retroactively across the ages. Hindu peoples attribute a curative function to fairy tales, because they make it possible to cure people in distress who have lost their sense of life. But to understand the beneficial effects of the fairy tale, we don't need to go quite so far or to ramble through exotic lands, for many professionals and researchers are similarly persuaded. Colette Estin, from INECAT (National Institute of Artistic Creation and Therapy), also associates fairy tales with curative power.

> Far from being a nostalgic reflection of the past, the fairy tale asserts a double-edged resistance against a kind of modernity that juggles us between terror and enchantment, since it opens up the possibility of metaphorically expressing our anxieties, our wishes, our secret gardens, our explorations, and our audacities to come. Let us take the chance: we have to believe in them, in calming, reconciliation, transformation, and healing.
>
> (*Estin, 1990, p. 97*)

We are touching upon the functional therapeutic effect of the fairy tale principally as a psychodramatic tool, because we think that the fairy tale shares in common with psychodrama the fact that it introduces the child to a magical world where, for example, the weak may vanquish the powerful and the forces of evil may succumb. We can discover a number of similarities between the structure of the fairy tale and that of psychodrama. These include atemporality, change of dimension, the reversed role of the small and the large, and metamorphosis: animals turn into humans, humans are transformed into animals, and ferocious animals, even dragons, can become our allies, etc.

In his studies of applied psychoanalysis, Freud was not especially sensitive to the magical element – he rather tended to avoid it. Apropos of the impact of artistic works in general, he states, "I do not really fully enjoy contemplating them until after I have interpreted them" (Freud, 1939: *Moses and Monotheism*).

He did not truly appreciate fairy tales: "Below a certain age, children generally make up fairy tales. Fairy tales are clearly situated in the territory of animism, of omnipotence of ideas and wishes."

Marthe Robert comes to a similar conclusion, "The magical apparatus of fairy tales is essentially in the service of wish fulfillment. Magical means, enchantment, hexes, and metamorphoses only delay the happy dénouement, to the great joy of the story-teller" (Robert, 1967, p. 139).

Fairy tale and familial structure

Marthe Robert, a psychoanalyst and interpreter of fairy tales and the author of a biography of Freud, states, "The fairy tale contains a complete and concentrated romance whose exclusive subject is the family" (1967, p. 139). Elsewhere, on the subject of the younger son, she says, "He goes off to the great world in search of his fortune in order to escape the family fate that gravely threatens his life" (1967, p. 139). As Freud as well as Adler had noted earlier, the development of conflict operates by means of the construction of a family romance in which the child creates, instead of his real family, the idealized image of an imaginary family. When the idealized and perfect image of his parents he created for himself in early childhood is placed in question, he responds by recreating, in his own imagination, the original family constellation. In this confrontation, Marthe Robert tells us, the storyteller achieves a negation of his real family and replaces it with an illustrious family. The child who is frustrated affectively or in his illusions disparages his real parents and erases them from his family story.

The author believes that the family romance that appears in the fairy tale expresses unsatisfied desires, especially claims in the realm of love and power. The fairy tale provides possibilities of transposition, and gives the child the option of projecting into it everything that preoccupies him. He finds solutions for his conflicts. In the fairy tale, he can find ridiculous exaggerations of his parents' negative traits, and can do battle against some terrible parental images that are menacing and even deadly. The family romance of fairy tales may also facilitate separation and stimulate the maturational process. According to the Adlerian psychoanalyst, Philippe Fuguet, the familial fantasy plays a structuring role in the child's development, allowing him to detach from the parental image and to replace it with an idealized counter-image.

> In the fantasy of an illustrious origin, the child takes revenge vis-à-vis his real parents. This may play a narcissistic role, allowing the child to define himself as a subject. The family romance reinforces his megalomaniacal feelings and may have a protective effect against incest; through the familial fantasy the child puts his parents back in their place so as to get ready, with the invocation of a different set of parents, for the process of detachment.
>
> (*Fuguet, 2000*)

Thus, Marthe Robert thinks that the secret explanation for the persistence of the fairy tale is that its action is confined to the family and to its narrow circle. She believes that the kingdom of the fairy tale is only a familial universe, well bounded and closed, where the primary drama of human life is staged. The king represents the head of the family, the witch is the bad mother, and the devil is the image of the negative father. Even though this conception restricts the scope of the fairy tale, it may explain to some degree the stories that are invented in the context of psychodrama. For the most part, these symbolic scenes use the subterfuge of staging the royal couple or the world of animals to depict familial conflicts or the fantasy of an ideal family.

Erikson shares this opinion, but he emphasizes, in relation to the story that is centered on a problem, that the range of problems addressed by the fairy tale is a much broader one. He believes that, in effect, the fairy tale makes it possible to raise the question of the harmonious family, that it represents an ideal family constellation. But in terms of its function, far from being limited to the Oedipus complex or castration anxiety, Erikson confers to it the role of allowing the dual mother-child relationship to open up in the direction of successful triangulation, a prerequisite that makes it possible for the child to acquire his identity.

The symbolic universe of the fairy tale is the carrier of a particular code.

But there is another dimension that extends beyond conflicts, which is the passionate search for meaning. The child seeks to understand why. The Swiss child psychologist Ursula Tapolet emphasizes that the fairy tale is the bearer of the essence of human consciousness; it transmits concentrated knowledge. The symbols of its secret language are located beyond the narrow limits of reality in order that the unsayable can become expressed. "The significant uniqueness of the story, of the fairy tale, of the folk tale, is to permit moving ahead without explanation, along the stages in human development" (Tapolet, 1990).

In his much-appreciated book on the fairy tale, Bettelheim analyzes the question from many angles. He does not limit his interpretation to the narrow range of conflicts and anxieties in classical psychoanalysis (the Oedipus complex, castration complex, and the primal scene), whose reductionism also astonished the arts psychologist, Jacques Weber. Weber does not think that it makes sense to limit one's view to these interpretive principles in trying to understand the problematics facing the child. He believes that the context of interpretation needs to be expanded, because the questions addressed by the fairy tale are infinitely more complex.

Bettelheim, for his part, takes into consideration the interpretive principles developed by classical psychoanalysis as just cited (for example, in his analysis of *Little Red Riding Hood*), along with distinctly different elements taken from developmental psychology (Bettelheim, 1988).

When defining the functions of the fairy tale, Bettelheim approximates Ursula Tapolet's point of view as well as the fundamental principles of Alfred Adler, titling the introduction to his book "The Struggle for Meaning in Life." "Today, as in times past, the most important and also the most difficult task in raising a child is helping him to find meaning in life" (Bettelheim, *The Uses of Enchantment*, 1988).

In the story where the smallest or the weakest one emerges as the victor (such as Tom Thumb, or Johnny Barleycorn), the little one is capable of vanquishing the ogre. All forms of psychotherapy have the goal of liberating the child from his underestimation of his powers, from his negative self-image, something that we individual psychologists call his inferiority complex. According to Bettelheim, strengthening the child's sense of his own value is one of the principal roles of psychotherapy.

Strengthening the personality

Thus, Bettelheim considers it one of the important functions of the fairy tale to stimulate the child – to strengthen his sense that he can overcome his difficulties. The definition of the role of the fairy tale proposed by the Jungian psychoanalyst and fairy-tale scholar, Marie-Louise von Franz (1986), comes very close to the Adlerian conception.

> When children listen to a fairy tale, they naively identify with the hero and internalize the feelings evoked by the story. Any child suffering from an inferiority complex who listens to the story of the ugly duckling hopes he will end up becoming transformed into a swan. In an unconscious way, the fairy tale exercises an encouraging effect on the child, evoking the positive side of life.
>
> (*p. 18*)

Bettelheim supports the idea that fairy tales teach about human nature and strengthen the child's personality so as to let him project himself into the future and become an accomplished being. "The principal feature of the fairy tale is that even the child who starts out as the youngest, most mocked and disdained can become victorious."

"Cinderella teaches us the same thing as the Magnificat: excaltavit humiles (He hath exalted the humble)," says Bettelheim, quoting Chesterton's *Orthodoxy*.

Symbolic transposition of frustrations

Soriano, who studied the magical elements in fairy tales from a philosophical perspective, compared the magical thinking of cave men with the rationality of men in the twentieth century. He emphasized the relative permanence and the appeal of the magical, the kind of irrationalism that has remained unaltered since ancient times and that can still be found in primitive men and in children. Once the magical has been repressed and placed under control, it only returns to adult thinking in dreams and in the arts, and especially in the fairy tale.

For Bettelheim: "Fairy tales and myths speak to us in a symbolic language that at once engages conscious and unconscious layers of our ego." The symbolic mode provides the best means for it to communicate the way to deal with problems, and learn how to safely reach adulthood.

> The child can express himself in images, in movement, in theater, through voice and drawing. One might say that the child learns to express the inexpressible, even including all that has remained hidden because of a pain that was too intense, fear, taboo, disorder, or through ignorance. We have to cope with diverse problems that afflict us without being able to approach them rationally. We can come close to them with the help of our creations and our images. But what is most important is that what is most essential is inaccessible through reason.
>
> (*Bettelheim, 1992*)

> The fairy tale is a source of happiness – its magical power is not only transmitted by its meaning but also by its form, for the fairy tale is an artistic creation. Those who would wish to explain to the child the reasons he is so intensely interested in the fairy tale would only destroy the magical power of the fairy tale, which stems in large part from the fact that the child does not know what triggers his happiness. An important element of the child's experience is unconscious and needs to remain so. This is why you should never explain the meaning of a fairy tale to a child.
>
> (*Ibid.*)

Telling stories, reading, and staging a fairy tale provide new experiences and offer new therapeutic possibilities.

Beyond the pleasure we get from reading or listening to a story, we also feel that the story makes some secret strings hidden inside us begin to vibrate . . . sometimes, it seems as if we have lost our poetical and symbolic sensibility for understanding these stories handed down from the distant past. We need to rediscover how fairy tales describe the adventures of the human soul and how they set in motion the process of transformation.

The role of a fairy tale (performed) in the process of transformation

The child chooses and creates his stories and psychodramatic plays according to his needs, to overcome those factors that during a certain period have come in the way of his development. Through their mediation, he becomes able to master his threatening fantasies, which sometimes have a primitive character, such as the combination of aggression and sexuality one finds during the latency period. Some authors, such as Petzold, have developed stories focused on various phobias. But this author emphasizes that it is the work of therapy that determines the utility and the proper time to make use of this technique for a particular symptom (for example, for enuresis).

In this context, I would like to cite a symbolic story played out in a mental health services facility in the small Hungarian city of Eger.

Led by two psychodramatists, this was the fifth session of a group of five children who presented with a range of different problems – alcoholic father and parental conflicts, academic delay, and problems with relationships and verbalization. Emmi was a ten-year-old girl whose movements, verbal output, and thinking operated in slow motion – she lacked vivacity. She did make efforts to adapt to the group, but in her gloomy way, she remained aloof and never smiled. The child suffered from school phobia and psychosomatic problems – she was fatigued, and had episodic headaches and vomiting. When she was feeling sick in school, her mother would be called by telephone to come and fetch her and bring her back home.

Her classmates made fun of her. "Why did you bother coming back today, just to make more trouble?" She was often ill, stayed home from school more and more and her grades fell. And yet, she used to be a happy child, open and inventive at her kindergarten, and was lively and endearing. Feeling devalued due to her academic failures, she was suffering from a strong sense of inferiority. Dissatisfied by her appearance and her work, she found in somatization a way of escaping humiliation and avoiding the school situation that she could scarcely bear.

Here is the story the group made up and played during the group's second meeting.

The magic pearl

Three poor fishermen who were brothers lived by the seashore. The two older ones were wicked but the youngest one had a pure heart. They heard that at the bottom of the sea there was an oyster containing three magic pearls. They decided to bring it to the surface. The young fishermen dove and tried to open the oyster, but they could not find a way to do it. The three brothers then decided to bring it to the surface in a net so they could remove the pearls. Once they brought it up, they no longer needed to use any force, the oyster opened all by itself as soon as it made contact with the warmth, the sunshine, and the air. It contained two magnificent pearls and one small, pale pearl without any luster.

The two older fishermen grabbed the two magnificent pearls for themselves. They carried them off and begged them to bring them treasures and enormous wealth. But, these pearls did not provide them with gifts. Quite the contrary, they instead devoured all of their meager possessions, their cabin, and the dilapidated furniture it contained. The youngest of the fishermen chose the pearl without any luster or brilliance because he thought that this was the real pearl. And he was right, for this little insignificant pearl turned out to be a precious stone that transformed itself into a magnificent young girl. The fisherman with the pure heart took her as his bride and asked her to turn his wicked brothers into good boys and return to them their vanished possessions.

During the time the group was developing the story to be played, Emmi suggested some elements that changed the course of the story, introducing motifs that symbolically expressed her worries. She was the one who had the idea that the precious stone was small, ugly, and without brilliance, because "there can be good inside of something that appears ugly." Even though at the beginning, the group suggested that the precious stone was the biggest and most brilliant one, the children accepted the changes proposed by Emmi. Her other idea was "to recognize that the real pearl wasn't given to just anybody – the person had to have a pure heart." And when it was time to choose roles, she suggested that she would play the part of the magical pearl enclosed in a seashell. Her capabilities (her creativity, her gaiety, her spontaneity) were, in fact, blocked. At the bottom of the sea, trapped inside a seashell – how lonely and how hard it was to get out. This was the way she dramatized her terrible imprisonment from which it was so hard to liberate herself (she resisted letting herself be brought back up and opened). She was shut in – and deprived of all brilliance. Even though her return to the surface could not be achieved without difficulty, she found a way to express her wish to be found, to resurface, to be liberated from her isolation, so her inner value could blossom and be recognized. Besides being the symbolic expression of Emmi's personal problems, the story also contained a message to the group. It was as if the children's request – analogous to Emmi's – addressed to the therapists was nothing less than to allow potentially existing values that had not become manifest to see the light of day, as if they were saying to us: discover us so we have a chance to discover ourselves. At the end of the story, the metamorphosis takes place – Emmi's transformation. From insignificance to resplendency – the little pearl turns into a magnificent girl.

And, as if by magic, the metamorphosis not only took place in the story, but also in reality. One week after the play in the group, *Emmi's mother came to tell us the news*: the schoolteacher had told her, quite astonished, that Emmi was scarcely recognizable as the same child. She was no longer getting sick, was in a good mood, and was ready to answer questions in class. The psychodrama had brought a turn-around in this child's life. Her psychosomatic symptoms and her school phobia had vanished. The group continued to meet for three more months until school vacation and Emmi did not relapse, and her grades at school continued to improve. In addition to revealing the impact of the potential space provided by the symbolic play, this story indicates the importance of a climate of empathy and welcoming that allows children to dare to emerge from their solitary universe. For children to be able to reveal themselves without fear, they need to have a mirror in which they are reflected as beautiful, valorous, and even magical.

Stories and initiation rites

The fairy tale also recalls initiation rites. They can be found in Hungarian folk tales and continue to be active in the initiation rites practiced by African and Islamic cultures. We find, for example, the motif of the boy who goes off to discover the world and must undergo the sorcerer's trials, serve her for three years, battle the dragon, etc. Mircea Eliade thinks that the trials found in fairy tales should be considered as recollections of initiation rites.

> The fairy tale is multivalent, and its interpretations overlap different networks. The voyage of initiation that precedes the hero's rebirth stimulates and completes the development of the child, prepares him for adult love and life . . . and even refers at times to a mystical rebirth.
>
> (*M.C. Loyer-Dolghin, 1992*)

In most cases, the fairy tale invokes a dramatic situation that appears to be insoluble but that must nevertheless be mastered. Only a heroic act can offer a solution and the role of the main hero is to save the family living in misery or the imperiled kingdom and liberate it from disease or imminent death.

To succeed, our heroine or hero has to demonstrate honesty, simplicity, and devotion in his actions and sentiments. His journey will be successful on the condition that he comes to respect a kind of naïve morality. The youth who is still innocent and ignorant at the time of his departure returns from his voyage matured and experienced.

The fairy tale and the meaning of life

People have attributed many other functions to the fairy tale . . . In conclusion, we will only cite one of these, as proposed by Bettelheim (1976) – the story makes it possible to find the meaning of life.

> One of the most important tasks in raising children is helping them find the meaning of life . . . If we hope to live not just from moment to moment, but in true consciousness of our existence, then our greatest need and most difficult achievement is to find meaning in our lives.
>
> (*p. 3*)

This is how Bettelheim summarized the role of the fairy tale in children's psychological development: to relieve the weight of uncertainty about his future, to help him overcome the difficult twists and turns of his existence, and to discover a sense of meaning in his own life.

12

METHODS FOR DRAMATIZING THE FAIRY TALE

Staging an existing fairy tale

Little Red Riding Hood in the crossfire of learned and childish interpretations

We ask the children to tell us their favorite fairy tale. Their choice is already full of meaning. Similar to asking for someone's earliest childhood memories, every child's (or adult's) favorite story reflects their style of life, their nature, and their imagination. The favorite story is a kind of condensation of vital feeling – any given story may be capable of mobilizing quite divergent sentiments. The function of a story such as *Little Red Riding Hood*, among the most frequently cited favorite stories, may be subject to a whole gamut of different interpretations. The most commonly cited interpretation, shared for that matter by Bettelheim, is Oedipal – the story is about sexual temptation by paternal seduction as represented by the wolf. Sometimes, the redness of the riding hood is further interpreted as representing the color of the first menstrual blood. In Perrault's version, which is earlier than that of the Brothers Grimm, the wolf did not swallow up the little girl at the time of their encounter, but instead, enticed her into the grandmother's bed.

Among many interpretations, I would cite the one offered by Erich Fromm (1951), who devotes an entire chapter to Little Red Riding Hood in *The Forgotten Language*. He agrees that at first reading, this story would sound like a moralizing tale on the dangers of sexual temptation. But he goes on to discover that the story also presents some other aspects.

It alludes to the nostalgic desire of the male to have a baby (see the study by Devereux (1999) on pregnancies among male gods), which is also evidenced by the recurrent motif found in diverse mythologies of children being replaced by stones (cf. the myth of Chronos in Hesiod and elsewhere). Fromm finds the image of a wolf behaving like a pregnant woman ridiculous. The wolf's belly full of stones also symbolizes the male's incapacity to bear children. Crushed, the wolf dies of the stones in his belly.

Similar to any association, the one presented by Fromm is also reflective of the author's interpretive system. The author alludes, in this respect, to the Babylonian myth of Tiamat.

As their favorite fairy tale, the children employed the story of Little Red Riding Hood in a very different way from that suggested by Fromm. One little girl liked the fairy tale because the end of the story evoked the fantasy of her own birth (by Caesarian section . . .). It often happens that in referring to this story, the children are nonplussed by the ending, that is, by the fact that the wolf eats the grandmother. Sometimes the wolf just locks her in a closet, or finds a hiding place for her, similar to his having hid under the bed before Little Red Riding Hood's arrival. We all know how children's anxious imagination can populate the secret, mysterious, and dangerous place that is located under the child's bed. Wolves and bandits hide there to emerge the moment one turns off the light. Other children, especially those in pre-latency who haven't overcome their fear of the wolf, defend themselves by evoking the not entirely reassuring paternal image of the hunter. I had a little patient who, as part of an improvised story, resolved to put the wolf to death in a very original way by way of the primitive feminine image represented by the grandmother. In her story, the grandmother destroyed the wolf when she put her head in its mouth. Since she was suffering from a terrible cold, she contaminated the wolf, who died of his disease.

We have seen that, even when the starting point is an established fairy tale, children make use of it by transforming it so as to express their own problematic or even to allow them to overcome their phobias. To each his own way of using stories.

Stories without an ending[1]

In children's groups that are too inhibited to suggest their own story or make one up, the therapists suggest a beginning or some elements of an unfamiliar story to spark their inventiveness. This is called the technique of the open-ended story. The dramatists tell half of the story, or simply set the frame of the action, and leave the children the task of developing the plot and devising an ending. In some larger groups (a dozen children or more) we sometimes divide the children into two sub-groups once the elements of the story have been told, so each group can further develop the story and perform it as they wish.

Then, the two sub-groups stage their versions alternately while the other half watches as the audience. The confrontation of the two different stories can be interesting and is very entertaining for the children.

Group invention

Group invention is one of the forms of an introductory warm-up. We employ this technique when the group has not yet developed its own technique for spontaneous elaboration. The two principal methods for group invention are:

The chain-story

The children are seated in a circle, and the dramatist goes around the circle enunciating ritual words such as: "once upon a time far away across the ocean, there was once a . . ." and takes a child by the hand. The child who is chosen says a first sentence and touches the next child who will continue the story. The next child joins in the chain and continues the story, and in turn designates another child who will take his turn and add some sentences, and this continues until all the children have participated in developing the narrative. A story will take shape as long as the children can follow the unfolding narrative and are able to keep it going. This technique can reinforce group cohesion because it is based on shared inspiration, and the condition of its formation is reciprocal listening. It is not a given that a story constructed in this way can be staged in a play, for the added episodes do not necessarily result in a coherent narrative. In this case, the therapists can suggest extracting a few motifs from the story to serve as the start of a story that can be staged.

A variant of this method, which helps stimulate the attention and memory of the group, is to ask the children to repeat the words proposed by the previous children before adding their own contribution. This is how the chain-story is assembled from a mosaic of fragments, a technique that allows for a degree of competition, not only because it cuts short the words of a big talker but also because, if he isn't stopped, the narrator has to continue forever. Sometimes, the narrator looks around desperately at the members of the group to get their permission to stop.

The halted story

Another version, the "halted story," can be used to discharge the emotions of group members when there are major conflicts or tensions. This method differs from the chain-story because here, it is not the story-teller who decides the moment to pass on the next narrator, but instead, another child stops her and continues. This method consists of asking the first narrator to tell a fragment of the story. The next narrator follows by negating something of significance that was said just before. This method lets the children express their opposition to another child or to some affirmation by the psychodramatist, if he is the one who had the floor. In this play of words, it is not content that is primary but the desire to contradict! Here is an example of how things can turn around in the "halted story."

First narrator: There was a family of fairies living on a high mountain; the three little fairies were very happy in their garden and fluttered through the flowers.

Second narrator: STOP! Jean who was passing by called out: but those aren't fairies, they're butterflies. And he caught them in his net to add them to his collection.

It is hard to imagine how fragments in such conflict could possibly turn into a story. Most of the time, they actually do not. This technique is used to help children deal with their conflicts with each other or to express their reservations or resistance with respect to the therapists.

Once the chain-story is finished, the staging follows. This is the moment for distributing or choosing the parts. In the case of groups that have difficulty structuring themselves, for example, groups of very young children or a group of hyperactive or very unruly children, one of the adults or one of the "old members" takes on the role of narrator to help frame the play.

These two kinds of intervention in the group may be introduced by the psychodramatist if the group lacks ideas or is not sufficiently calm. It can also be used when a blocked situation arises; this is a phenomenon that people often regard as a form of group resistance, but sometimes takes place simply because of the psychodramatist's lack of skill. One rarely needs this type of intervention, for in any well-developed group, once you ask the question, "Who wants to begin?" the children's ideas start tumbling out, and they bump into each other, every child wanting to be the first.

In some groups, the children begin by putting on their disguises and select a character to play even before the story is articulated, and this is an example of a child-directed (as opposed to leader-directed) approach that is then accepted by the psychodramatists. It is only afterwards, with the actors already in costume, that the story gets constructed (cf. Pirandello: *Six Characters in Search of an Author*).

Targeted stories

We resort to focused stories (about a situation or about a problem) when the group is preoccupied with a current problem that it cannot find a way to put into a story. The therapists choose and propose a story that allows the group to approach the problem in a symbolic mode.

A) Story targeted on a symptom or on the group dynamic

The focused story is an indirect way of responding to the child's problems. It is practiced with marionettes or dolls in integrative therapy or in art therapy, it can be mediated by poems, fairy tales, or folk tales. This type of story stages the patients' underlying problems and relies on the cathartic effect of a dramatic presentation of conflicts. The technique of therapy through stories may involve a full narration of the story with staging of several selected scenes, or sometimes the entire story is played out by the participants (role-playing) or with the help of marionettes.

Child psychologists with an integrated orientation believe that focused stories have their place in cases of phobic symptomatology (fear of the dark, fear of animals), especially in cases of enuresis. They add that it is up to the psychotherapist to sense the right moment in the course of psychotherapy to use a focused story. (Regarding the question of the focused story and therapy using marionettes, see Petzold's article on Little Dick, the story of the little elephant and his wanderings through the desert in Petzold & Ramin, 1995, pp. 356–362.)

In this respect, as in most techniques used in children's psychodrama, the dynamics of the action (the staging of the story) constitute an important means of cathartic experience.

In integrative or Gestalt methodology, the stories are focused on the symptom, but these behaviorist approaches sometimes take into consideration the family dynamics and the affective components of the family.

B) Story targeted on general relational or social problems

The story targeted on problems allows for alternative solutions, and is thus an interactive method, so to speak. The essential feature of the method is that in his narrative, the therapist evokes a situation that affectively involves the children, and then entrusts the children to continue it. The story allows for different elaborations, and many outcomes are imaginable. The focused story may serve to introduce a problem that is preoccupying the group or to touch upon a moral, ecological, or societal question of more general import. Here is an example:

The guenon

An elderly couple finds a baby monkey at the edge of the forest. The monkey was so weak and frail that the old people thought she was going to die. Moved, they took the baby monkey home with them, took care of her, and fed her. After a few days, the little monkey got back her energy and became attached to the people who had found her and cared for her. When the old couple went to visit their neighbors, the little monkey would stay at home.

The years went by and the little monkey turned into a handsome adult guenon.

One day, the people she regarded as her parents went off to visit their friends. But as soon as they set foot outside, the guenon removed her monkey skin and changed into a beautiful girl. She put on an embroidered smock.

When the old couple returned, they looked everywhere for the manioc flour but couldn't find it. They were very puzzled but they didn't suspect the one they thought was a guenon.

Some time later, when the old couple left the house again, the guenon did the same thing again. When they left for the third time, the old couple, suspicious by now, asked a young neighbor to watch what happened while they were away. Then they left the house.

The young man hid in a corner near the house. A little while later, he saw the guenon take off her monkey skin and reappear as a girl. Dressed in an embroidered smock, she was preparing her meal of manioc flour.

The young man immediately fell head over heels in love with the strange girl. He left his hiding place and asked her to become his wife.

"I can't be your wife," says the guenon, "that would only end badly."

"But I really want to," answered the young man. And he started to describe the wonderful life they could have together.

The guenon protested, saying that the young man would not always love her. But he besieged her with such ardor that she could no longer resist and agreed to become his wife. At that very moment, the young man grabbed the monkey-skin and threw it in the fire.

They celebrated their wedding. The couple lived happily together until the day she was about to deliver a baby.

(We tell the story up to this point and ask the participants to complete it. Later, we tell them the rest of the story):

From that day on, the man started to mistreat his wife. He abused her, swore at her, called her a guenon. He became so horrible that the poor woman no longer wanted to live with him.

"I must go back to my own people."

The man would not let her and ordered her to stay with him.

A few days later, the woman told her husband she was going to bathe. But instead of walking to the river she walked off into the forest. Her husband waited and waited for her to come back, but she did not come . . . After several days of waiting, he went off to look for her.

During all this time, the young woman who took refuge in the forest tried to imitate the way the monkeys travel. Her little boy imitated her and they succeeded in jumping from tree to tree the way that monkeys do. The young husband came upon his wife and his son swinging from branch to branch.

"Come back home!" he shouted to her.

His wife pretended not to hear him. The little boy, who felt sorry for his father, threw spiders and insects to him so he would have something to eat. He forgot that only monkeys liked to eat such things, and that people hated insects and spiders. His father was not able to bring himself to eat them.

"Come home," he yelled as loud as he could, "I am begging you."

"No," answered his wife. "I've been punished enough for having married you."

While the father tried to follow them, the mother and son leapt from branch to branch, always going higher, until they reached the very tops of the trees.

Finally, they came to the banks of a great river. The guenon issued loud cries to those who lived on the other side of the river to ask them for help.

"Mother. Father!," she called out, "Help-us, Help, Help."

Echoes made these words resonate from one tree to the other, from one hillside to the next. A great wind came up and became so powerful that it made the crowns of the trees bend toward the other bank of the river, right to the place where the guenon and her little son were waiting for help. When the treetops reached close to them, they climbed the branches, which immediately straightened and deposited the refugees on the other bank.

"Farewell, father," the little boy cries sadly, "you are never going to see me again."

Yet the guenon is silent. The young man had a broken heart and in his despair, he threw himself in the river and tried to swim to the other side. But the current was strong and overpowered him. He was never seen again.

(Story from Guyana, from the collection of Ré and Philippe Soupault "*Magical Tales from Five Continents*" Seghers, Paris 1975)

Note

1 Not to be confused with the novel by Michel Ende, here the issue is about stories to be finished.

13

VIRTUAL WORLD AND PSYCHODRAMA

The paradigm of the zombies[1]

Television burst upon the lives of children over the course of the last century. American statistics estimate that the time children spend watching television is three and a half hours a day (70 percent of children in working class neighborhoods devote three–four hours or more to watching television in Hungary). On television, children can watch a wide range of films, which are fascinating, sometimes primitive, and sometimes full of action. American statisticians who are fans of quantitative approaches have estimated that by the age of 12, a child has watched 244,000 violent acts, among them 14,000 murders. Such violence contributes to arousing children's anxiety and makes violence banal and even legitimizes it. Even the youngest children in kindergartens are not spared from watching it.

The intrusion of the virtual world into children's imagination

By now, the computer and virtual imagery have become a permanent element in the lives of families. According to a recent statistic, the average French family (two parents with at least one child seven years of age or older) has fourteen screens in their home. The virtual world mesmerizes children. Games accessible on the computer, game consoles, tablets, and iPhones are the rage. Children spend several hours of every day playing them. What accounts for their extraordinary appeal? The reasons are multiple, for a start, a global shift in lifestyle that is not limited to Europe and the United States, and which has had an increasing impact upon children and adolescents in many countries throughout the world. Although psychologists and psychiatrists advise against videos for children younger than three years of age, we have seen very small children engaged in watching television before they had even learned to walk or speak, seated in front of the screen and manipulating the images with their fingers in rapt attention.

It is odd to see that such deeply depersonalized parallel universes, where at times, a double known as an avatar takes the place of a real friend, have such primary appeal to the affective needs of adults and of children. Second Life seduced people to become members by claiming that the member could "establish intensive affective contact by means of his avatars." It is by means of similar claims that they recruited children.

The child is invited to project himself into a parallel world that offers virtual friendships to fill a major affective void. However, the psychological impact of this world is far more extensive. It offers adherents the promise of assuaging all of their desires. What is more, it lets them exercise unlimited power. In this way, the desire for absolute personal power is satisfied without any counterbalance, that is, without socialization in the Adlerian sense of the term. The virtual medium introduces the child to a world where some of his deepest psychological needs can find pseudo-satisfaction. "In fact, these virtual worlds are marvelous potential spaces" (Tisseron, 2008, p. 208).

Making reference to Winnicott, psychiatrist-psychoanalyst Serge Tisseron points out that in the potential space of the virtual world, the child cannot clearly distinguish between what is coming from him and what is coming from outside. He tries to satisfy his double need to master and overcome his anxieties. To successfully soothe his psyche and the sources of his pain, he needs a source of support. And as Serge Tisseron puts it, it is the keyboard and the mouse that end up becoming the child's support system along this journey.

The potential space of children's psychodrama is called upon, among other things, to satisfy the same need, that is, to soothe the child's psyche. However, the supports that this space offers the child are of a completely different nature, since these are real beings, adults and children, who participate in his play space, thereby sharing a potential space with him.

Those children whose development has not given them access to the space of shared play find a more primitive form of relationship in the virtual world, that of mirror play. These are the kinds of exchanges that Daniel Stern has called "precocious tonic-postural dialogue" (Stern, 1985). What does this mean? Face to face with the young child, the mother reproduces his gestures and his facial expressions, or better yet, through her own gestures and movements, she reflects what the little one is feeling. In this dyadic resonance, mother and child can thus experience shared emotions. It is this type of primitive twinship relationship, in Serge Tisseron's view, that the Internet voyager joyfully discovers through his avatar. In a similar vein, we have encountered children who, lacking the mirror relationship, invented doubles or imaginary twin brothers for themselves.

The third way of using the computer is the most primitive, and perhaps the most troubling. Once again citing Serge Tisseron (2008), "there are forms of dependency on the computer that are a kind of remake of the original situation." The child is not really interested in the content of the game or its meaning, but only in the state of excitation that the game sets off in him. Wanting to avoid being drowned by his intense internal sensations, the child moves the joystick, strikes the keyboard and casts himself into a "calming" space, although it is anything but calming. The child expects the machine to serve him as a source of excitation and to ward off excitation. Caught in this vicious circle, children become dependent and no longer can do without what Tisseron calls the "mother-computer" (2008, p. 215). We knew of an eleven-year-old child who was riveted by the computer and sat for hours compulsively alternating from site to site. Later, she started to select her favorite programs, such as one that allowed her to construct a living creature (a bird, for example) and to endlessly change its clothing. This little girl, abandoned at birth and adopted at age three and a half, preferred the computer to all exchanges with real people. Faced with this syndrome, some specialists have gone so far as to suggest a form of therapeutic mediation that lets the child use the video game during part of the session. One of my students working in individual therapy with a little boy also decided to try this method as a way to establish contact. The moment the child came into her office, he asked, "But where is the computer?"

The special relationship with the computer would thus appear to offer a way to escape a frustrating reality. Using Adlerian psychodrama for children, we propose creating a virtual world in the original sense of the term. For Aristotle, in effect, the virtual signifies potentiality. In a similar way, we want to revitalize this definition by creating a potential space in which the child is able to develop multiple facets of his personality. The crucial difference is that in psychodrama, support does not take place through the manipulation of objects or a keyboard but is instead given to the child by real persons ready to engage with his solitary world. Along with the therapists, this support includes a group composed of children like him. These potential mirrors are superior to avatars because they are not limited to reflection but allow for real exchange and mutually enhanced awareness, and are bearers of an authentic social dimension.

The group therapy method in individual psychology departs from the idea of the child's need to construct a fictive imaginary world in order to resolve the difficulties (frustration, anxiety) created by his painful life and sense of inferiority. Psychodrama thus offers its participants, who present with different sets of symptoms, a territory for expressing their anxieties and strengthening their sense of self through dynamic activity. In the potential space of play, each child can develop his unique and indivisible individuality that contains multiple facets. By taking on different roles, children can express their potentialities that have not yet become manifest. The potential universe of psychodrama is one in which the child can be together with other children, and it is not prefabricated like those on the Internet, but rather entirely self-invented (with or without the help of the other group members). In this unique space, the child can discover the wealth of his own imagination.

Adlerian children's psychodrama sets for itself the task of letting children stage their conflicts, their anxieties, their desires, and their aggression, so they can locate the means to overcome them in themselves. This is how psychodrama helps to restore self-esteem in children and adolescents, and allows them to give up the symptoms that have become obsolete, recover their equilibrium, and heal. This is a magical space offered to the children to extract them from their habitual world and place them elsewhere, not entirely unlike the virtual universe of the computer, but with the fundamental difference that this is an elsewhere from which they can come back. The emotional discharge that occurs and the story they have made up and enacted together will reverberate in their real lives. Staging their problems in this virtual space is intended to alleviate their conflicts and also to let the children elaborate upon them and resolve them. This takes place not simply by means of wish fulfilment (even if this is a part of the process, since in the play universe, nothing is impossible) but by encouraging the emergence of their creativity. This process entails a transformation of their poor self-image.

From bad self-image to the zombie

Troubled children, especially children who are abused or considered "at risk," are children who are unloved or feel unloved, and they have an odd relationship to the badness they believe they carry within themselves and that endangers the world outside. What becomes manifest is what Ferenczi called identification with the aggressor. Even while still afraid of the monster (external danger? the child's own parent?) the child comes to believe that he is an incarnation of that monster. And as we have just seen, he suffers from a profound sense of devaluation. The flight into the virtual world cannot do very much about this sense of devaluation, even if it provides temporary comfort or momentary overcompensation.

How does this monster manifest itself and how can we successfully tame it?

The troubled child may be the one who has interiorized the distorted and discordant image once reflected back to him by his mother, and this is how "his own creative capacity became atrophied" (Winnicott, 1971a, p. 155).

The frustrated child dreads monsters such as the wolf, the lion, the dragon, or the dinosaur (the latter already evidencing the intrusion of the audio-visual world). One might ask whether the destructive power of these monsters is experienced as an internal force or an external danger. The undifferentiated and terrifying character of the monster seems to stem from primitive imagery that is neither entirely identical to the child nor entirely other – it seems to date back to a state of undifferentiation.

This is particularly telling when it comes to the zombie, whose appearance signals a transformation of the child's imagination that is commensurate with the irruption of the virtual world. In Hungary, we watched the zombie show up in the play of a number of different groups of children who were quite young, and even in preschool children.

The zombie is a monster who differs significantly from the other creatures. Lacking a soul, he can move and speak but has no affective life. He can transform his victims into zombies by simply touching them. Originating in Haitian voodoo, and differing from the philosophical notion of zombie, he shares one thing in common with the aspirations of the child immersed in the virtual world – he is all-powerful. His destructive power is limitless. He is indomitable and invincible, and he knows no rules; he is allowed to do anything. He also lacks any sense of guilt.

In a group led by one of my colleagues, Judit Hajdú, a boy with a history of abuse suggested one day, "Let's play zombies." The beginning of the story he invented was harmless enough – Once upon a time there was a mutant (a zombie). He went to the store to buy a computer and some chips. He came back to his house to play with the computer and to eat the chips. In the ensuing psychodrama, however, this harmless story took a bad turn. The mutant turned all of the children into zombies.

In another Hungarian group, the children played zombies for a whole semester in 2006. In the multiple threads of their story, three different methods emerged of turning people into zombies by means of viruses labeled as A, B, and C. Two scientists worked hard to develop an antidote, but the zombies found out about their efforts, killed them, and ate them.

In a group of marginalized children in Transylvania, one of the participants suggested playing zombies. During the play, the zombie killed six of the characters and turned them into zombies by sprinkling them with a magical powder. The zombies continuously died and were reborn, and this resulted in a chaotic situation, much enjoyed by the children but considerably less so by the therapists. The therapists then suggested a compromise that the group ultimately accepted – a zombie had only three lives and had to decide at the end of the play whether he wanted to come back to life or to die.

In a fourth story, staged in a children's psychiatric hospital, a traveler turns on the television, from which a warrior zombie emerges and transforms him into a barbarian skeleton (see Figure 13.1), and the two of them set off to massacre everyone.

FIGURE 13.1 Death and the Zombie

It is apparent then that the omnipotent and indomitable zombie gives the child the option of staging an excessive level of aggression that can regress back to the most extremely primitive level – cannibalism. This has been a source of concern for us – how do we keep these lawless and faithless beings, immortal and all-powerful, from doing limitless harm? How do we stop the process? In the technique of Adlerian children's psychodrama, the "happy ending" is not obligatory, and we do not feel compelled to keep the children from playing out a story that ends badly. But when it comes to zombies, we felt like we had allowed a "genie" to escape from the bottle (from the computer) that we were unable to successfully overcome. Ultimately, in keeping with Adler's fundamental law, the solution emerged from our patients.

In most of our groups, it was the children, in fact, who found a way to get beyond the impasse of the zombies that they had brought to life. Much less maddened by their zombification and more inventive than the therapists, the children found solutions, some of them quite fantastic. In the first story, for example, they called upon a zombie from the television to bring the dead back to life. In the second story, the series ended by exposing the zombies to laser light, which let them become human again. In the last example, it was the boy who had made up the story who stopped the massacre, declaring that the world of the zombies would end at midnight; they would all be reabsorbed into the television. In this way, the alien force returned to the milieu whence it had come!

To summarize – Adlerian psychotherapy for children finds itself confronted by elements of an imaginary world in the process of transformation, of which the zombies are only one example. It seems to us that it is essential to provide children with a frame (with support, others would say) that allows them to confront their phantoms without being snatched up by them and to find solutions that keep them from taking recourse to the virtual world as their principal way of escaping a too painful reality. Lacking other available means of expression than those provided by the virtual world, the child without recourse, without points of reference, without an anchoring point, will have a hard time escaping that world. Also, lacking other means of expression, he will tend to privilege aggression.

Individual psychology does not believe in stimulating the child's imagination by means of prefabricated elements (whether they are integrated passively or dynamically), but only by means of the child's own creativity. The child is capable of constituting himself as a subject if he feels valued inside a space constructed to have this effect, inside a humanely accessible milieu in which his personality, isolated up to this point, can flourish in the presence of his peers.

Virtual characters in the service of dealing with real problems

The aim of Adlerian children's psychodrama is to encourage the development of a process of self-healing (of resilience) by allowing children who have been traumatized by their lives and psycho-affective difficulties to express their problems in a symbolic language. We create an atmosphere where the therapists' acceptance and the holding capacity of the group allow a child suffering from deep pathological feelings or a full-blown inferiority complex to reestablish his self-image, a phenomenon often called resilience, and to revalorize his own personality.

How should we relate to the virtual world, and with the generation of *digital natives* or the *Internet generation*, who have never known a world without virtual reality? Can we simply ignore them, even though this seems to represent such a generalized phenomenon, or perhaps something akin to a mutation?

It has been about thirty years since we set the rules for children's psychodrama, insisting on the requirement that the stories be original. Nowadays, it is hard to ignore the fact that for large numbers of children, their imagination has been conditioned by television and virtual games. We try to understand the reasons for choosing a virtual character as the one to identify with, and let the child make use of it to express his real problems, frustrations, and anxieties. Here is a story that illustrates how sick children may need to use a virtual hero to help them confront imminent danger.

Examples of individual and group psychotherapy starting from identification with a virtual character

Identification with a virtual character in the fight against cancer

Hannah Montana

When she was five and a half years old, Detti had surgery for a malignant brain tumor. Four years later, she developed the same symptoms she had the first time around, the same kind of headaches – she had relapsed. She underwent a second operation followed by chemotherapy. The dressing was too tight, causing an injury to her forehead. The plastic surgeon repaired the skin defect using a graft taken from her arm, but she was left with an ugly scar on her forehead. In the early psychodrama plays, Detti called her scar an Indian headdress and she chose roles to match. Detti's hair fell out from chemotherapy. Besides chemo, her treatment included steroids, which caused rapid weight gain. Her body image was greatly altered. Her physical state deteriorated, and the team asked the psychologist to prepare Detti's mother for a bad outcome. Detti was admitted several times to an isolation unit in a critical condition. Separated from everyone, she lived in a sterile environment to which only her mother had access. In this lonely situation, she surrounded herself with objects decorated with images of Hannah Montana (Figure 13.2): (portable computer, pillow, covers, pajamas, and pencil-case). These transitional objects gave her great reassurance. A few months later, Detti was able to rejoin the other children. A blonde wig with braids had been made for the little girl, which actually looked very good on her.

FIGURE 13.2 Hannah Montana

Hannah Montana – first play

A monodrama; The child plays alone with two psychologist-psychodramatists.

Detti has invented and directs the scene. She has chosen to transform herself into Hannah Montana, whose exceptional life she has been dreaming about for many months.

Before starting the scene, the girl selected beautiful fabrics and silk scarves to beautify herself and the psychologists. The play begins . . .

Characters:

Detti in the role of Hannah Montana.
The psychodramatists are the accompanying dancers.

Hannah and her two helpers are getting ready for their first concert together, and the dancers are still quite clumsy. Hannah is going to teach them the gestures and movements to perform and the songs to sing.

CLICK: magical gesture – she snaps her fingers and this transforms the characters.

CLICK: Beautiful hair, CLICK: Beautiful nails, CLICK: Presents, Detti, in the role of Hannah Montana: You are going to be beautiful just like me!

CLICK (magical gesture): You can dance and sing.

Let's see if you can do everything that I can do.

The psychodramatists, in their role of two dancers, begin trying to imitate her, and let her know how grateful they are to her.

At a certain moment in the ongoing dance ensemble, Hannah makes the magic gesture CLICK and says, smiling, "I am cured."

At the end of the session, Hannah showers her acolytes with gifts: a telephone, a jeweled box, tape recorder, and beauty products. Next, Hannah (or rather, bynow, Detti) announces: You can have everything you want, you can make a movie, you are going to be my older sisters, while I'm home I'm going to keep messing around. That's what we are going to play the next time.

The dancers: "Why are you giving us all of these gifts?"

Hannah (or rather Detti, whose words now are no longer addressed to the apprentice dancers, but to the psychologists): "Because you, you get the children to laugh."

Detti wanted to continue her story with the psychologists. She eagerly anticipated the time of the next session, and leapt out of bed happily when she learned that this was the moment for the "film shoot."

She makes up stories for the group. Appearing on stage along with Hannah Montana is the star, Miley, the young student who is her double. In one of the later plays, Miley takes on the role of director. Hannah and her group enjoy brilliant success. They are sought after for additional performances.

Detti in her role as Miley: "Do you know what we are going to do? We'll disguise ourselves as belly dancers."

Everything succeeds marvelously and they sign autographs for an enthusiastic audience.

Detti's mother confirmed how important these sessions were for Detti: her daughter would emerge from them as if transformed. For days after the meetings, she would keep talking about the story that had been played, and remembered it down to the smallest details. "It's as if she filled herself up with energy, force and life," said her mother.

In the course of her treatment, Detti had to undergo a painful procedure – a lumbar puncture for analysis of her spinal fluid. This was a procedure without anesthesia. A number of medical students were present for the operation, which did not seem to bother Detti, even though the procedure was quite painful.

Praised by the medical team for her courageous behavior, she pleased her therapist by making the secret gesture, CLICK, saying, "Of course you know that I am an actress."

After several months, Detti was able to leave the hospital, and she rejoined her class at school. However, as a consequence of her treatments and surgical interventions, she was left with sequelae that affected her ability to learn and to remember. She made huge efforts to succeed in the rhythm of the school year. This was all the more difficult because her teachers and fellow students did not know about her illness or the road she had traveled during the period of her absence.

Comments from the psychotherapists

What did the girl play?

As therapists, we thought she was projecting herself into this other life where she could do anything, where she was unique and had beautiful hair. At the hospital, the children could not make any decisions on their own – the doctors or parents made all the decisions. In the play, she was the one who controlled everything – she gave the orders and we followed them. We performed the gestures and movements and did everything she asked us to do. She was in control, and could experience her own agency and magical powers that let her change whatever she wanted and whenever she wanted it. Her recovery of her beauty played an important part in her overall recovery and she also let us enjoy beauty products, jewels, clothing, and accessories in lively colors, and a beautiful long hairdo.

Commentary

The young therapists willingly entered the magical world that was created by this child. The marvelous atmosphere and Detti's rapture touched them to such a deep degree that they felt embellished and their hair felt thicker and shinier.

Detti chose Hannah Montana as a character to identify with, an adolescent whose close relatives could not see her as more than a little high school kid of no importance, did not recognize that she had another life, the life of a beautiful singer and dancer who was admired and adored. Transferred back to Detti, all of this signified: you see me as little, without hair, sickly, diseased, and powerless.

But I am not only those things. She fantasized that she had another face unknown to everyone, the face of a magnificent singer and dancer, beautiful and admired. The therapists entered into her game. They participated in her imaginary world in order to share her "potential space." In the Adlerian spirit, they reversed roles – it was the therapists who were clumsy and dependent and they were asking the great actress to teach them what to do. Through their eyes, she could see herself as beautiful, gifted, and creative. Having partners to share this image, she no longer was left isolated in the compensatory universe that she had created for herself. This *sharing*, or to put it differently, this *regard* allowed her to change her self-image and regain her confidence. These were important factors that contributed to mobilizing her strength to fight against her illness, despite the somber prognosis that she could not ignore.

In the course of the play, the therapists came to understand that Detti's identification with Hannah Montana as an ideal character was not fortuitous; rather, it served the interests of overcoming and overcompensating for her real condition as an emaciated and fragile little girl. Through this ruse, she could fantasize that she had recaptured her former beauty and become an exceptional being, a magnificent star. This is how she viewed herself inside the magical universe that she had created for herself. And this is also how the therapists viewed her, as a magical person. This was not merely an illusion within an illusory world, but an encounter within the same potential universe.

Thanks to this shared experience in the realm of joint play, the child felt that she was omnipotent and capable of rising to every test. In her enchanted universe, she understood the potential use of her magical power. At a moment in the play, she announced in a soft voice (that completely shocked her therapist), "I am cured."

We believe that the enchanted world of Hannah Montana invigorated Detti in her battle against her disease. She was no longer a patient like everyone else, but instead, she had another life where she was the star, an exceptional person. In one magical stroke, everything she wished for could come to pass.

(Battle of the Little Pink Pony and the stone dog) Session of "equestrian therapy"

This session took place at an equestrian center, a large facility with fields and wooded areas. Annamaria Szentes, a psychologist working at the University of Budapest pediatric oncology service, owns a horse called Mirza that is trained to work with children. Together with her colleague, Erös Nikoletta, she launched a program for children who were formerly hospitalized on the oncology service and are now convalescing. For about two years, they have specialized in horse-assisted psychodrama. The groups are composed of four to eight children of different ages (five to eleven years) and they meet on Sunday mornings. Since the facility has no covered riding area, they are only able to ride when the weather is good. I will tell you about the morning I visited.

FIGURE 13.3 The stone dog

Participants: Four children who are seven to ten years of age, two siblings – Miki who is nine years old and his sister Nora, a little girl with a doll face who has been hospitalized on multiple occasions due to inadequacy of her immune system.

The two other children are the offspring of a mixed German-Hungarian couple; the boy, Bélus, is a ten-year-old who had a leg amputated due to cancer, but can walk with a limp. His sister Ildi is three years younger, a pretty little girl who is very inhibited and has difficulty revealing herself or playing.

Thus, the participants:

Nora (7) (the child with the illness) and her brother, Miki (9)
Bélus (10) (the child with the illness) and his sister, Ildi (8)

Nature of their illnesses:

Nora – autoimmune disease
Bélus – bone cancer. Wears a prosthesis because his left leg was amputated below the knee when he was six years old.

The four children have never played together before

There are three of us to set the frame for them, two young therapists and myself as a visitor.

The horse Mirza who was ridden the same morning by Annamaria's husband arrives in a very relaxed state, but he is not able to accommodate the children because of the rainy weather.

The children arrive at 9:30 in their parents' car, and they will be picked up again at 11:30.

We are all crammed into a small cloakroom furnished with a bench and a few chairs. The accessories for disguises are kept in a cupboard on the wall. The psychotherapists were not certain that the children, who hardly knew each other (except, of course for the brothers and sisters), would be willing to improvise a story, and so they had planned to suggest a story they had selected that related to the children's problems. But as soon as we were seated in the narrow cloakroom and the therapists had asked them about any interesting things they had experienced or seen recently, the children started talking about their favorite characters. Miki spoke about Indiana Jones, and Nora about the pink pony, who sometimes had wings. The two of them also mentioned the Holograms. "They are creatures – they said – who look like you but they only respond after a delay" – They regularly played at holograms as a family. Bélus was passionate about the Terminator. His sister, Ildi, said nothing and could not express herself.

Terminator, Indiana Jones, and the pink pony

After listening to the children, the therapists dropped their idea to suggest a story. Confident in the children's own capacity to find the means for symbolic representation of their problems, they asked them instead to choose the character they wanted to play. Miki chose Indiana Jones, an Indiana Jones who could invent all sorts of machines. Nora wanted to be a pink pony with a horn on her forehead. Bélus chose a Terminator that could be programmed in various ways. It could become good or evil. One of his arms could also be transformed into a machine gun. Since Ildi was not really functioning, the therapist, Niki, decided to help her

FIGURE 13.4 Indiana Jones, Terminator, and the pink pony

out by functioning as her double. They would be fairies flying in the air. And what would our role be? (that is, the therapists' role), asked Annamaria. To tell the truth, said Bélus, we could really use a stone dog (Figure 13.3).

What for?
The stone dog turns everything he touches to stone.
The children chose Annamaria to play this role.
As for me, they gave me the role of the Old master-programmer.

So the characters in the psychodrama were:

The little pink pony – Nora
Indiana Jones – Miki
Terminator (programmable to be good and evil) – Bélus
Sky fairies – Ildi and Niki
Stone dog – Annamaria
Old professor-programmer – KH

Even though Mirza the horse was not present, the children gave him the role of a chariot. But there was no lack of animals, since there were several dogs, including two dogs who posted in front of the glass-paned door, to which the children assigned the role of guardians.

The locations

Although consistency of place is a respected feature of group therapy, horse-assisted children's psychodrama has the unique feature of taking place in several locations, both outside and in a closed space (especially when the weather is bad) for the preparatory phase and the drawing activity that concludes the session. This session unfolded in four different spaces.

1 the cloakroom mentioned above
2 a building about 50 meters away that they baptized as the wooden dog's den
3 a kind of veranda with a wooden roof but open on three sides
4 the entire area of land around the equestrian center with its fields and wooded areas, which played a part in the story despite the rain.

Everyone was disguised. To play the stone dog, Annamaria transformed herself into a fearsome monster all wrapped in black. Although Nora, the pink pony, did not have a horn, the usually timid little girl played as if she had been furnished with a formidable weapon. Indiana Jones was recognizable by his handsome chestnut fedora, and the Terminator was wearing a horseman's helmet, while Ildi had a little purse with a shoulder strap containing a powder that could put stone dogs to sleep, and she also had been given a fan that could make the storms come as long as the little girl had the courage to shake it. Annamaria, the therapist in the role of the stone dog, threatened all the children in a loud voice – anyone with the temerity to come close to her would be instantly petrified. The threat frightened the children, who wondered how they were going to render harmless this monstrous dog. Terminator, who didn't know whether he wanted to use his power to be good or evil when the old professor asked him how he wanted to be programmed, chose to fight the stone dog with his hand turned into a machine gun.

After the fierce battle, the stone dog was beaten back to retreat across the meadow and he hid in a neighboring outbuilding, a kind of barn covered with a layer of hay that, according to the children, must have been "his den." The troupe followed him at a gallop, but once they entered the outbuilding with its dim light, they couldn't see anyone. Still, Nora, the little pink pony, could see that something was moving in the hay. In fact, this was the stone dog, which was stirring again. The battle with Terminator and Indiana Jones restarted in full swing. Encouraged by the therapist, who doubled to help her spread the magical powder that made the winds blow with her fan, Ildi, the fairy of the air, ended up making only a timid gesture but it nevertheless unleashed an enormous tempest. Annamaria, the stone dog, was wounded but one learned that it had a magical device (which was none other than a little car belonging to Miki) that could immediately heal his wounds.[2] Recovering his forces, the stone dog proclaimed to all that he was going to find a good hiding place for his magical device that nobody would be able to detect (Annamaria lifts up a corner of the bed of straw and stuffs in the device). The old scientist asks Indiana Jones if he could make an instrument that would be able to detect the hiding place of the magical device. Indiana Jones moves back to the entryway, where, flanked by the excited "guardian" dogs, he constructs his detection machine.

With his machine, Indiana Jones uncovers the hiding place of the stone dog's restorative device and takes it back. Meanwhile, the Terminator wonders whether he shouldn't get reprogrammed to be evil but he responds affirmatively to the Old Programmer's question whether he wouldn't prefer to continue his battle against the stone dog. The old one now finds a khaki cap with a visor "which transforms anyone who wears it into a benefactor of people and humanity" and puts it on the Terminator's head (as it turned out later this "found object" was actually Bélus's own hat). The children wonder what to do with the stone dog, which is lying dead on the straw, but Terminator lets them know that he only appears to be dead and could wake up again at the end of five years. Indiana Jones points out that in a different universe, let's say in a rainy universe, five years might not last as long, maybe only for five days. So it was important to hurry. How could they keep him from starting to petrify people again? They had to change him somehow, but how? Maybe they needed to find him a heart.

Miki, alias Indiana Jones: To find a heart you have to travel a long way, all the way to the fire-spewing volcano – and accompanied by Briard, the guard dog, he immediately begins running toward the woods.

The dramatist, Niki, tries to catch up with him (since the terrain was rough, the little boy was at risk of falling) but by the time she gets to him, he is already on his way back with a sling-shot, a piece of tree root in the shape of a Y that he brought back from the volcano. He would use this to thrust the heart (which was none other than a blueberry) toward the stone dog.

The stone dog starts to come back to life. "What happened? Where am I?"

Annamaria removes her monster disguise. The happy troupe leaves the den in a downpour and goes outside in the rain; Indiana Jones circles around a grassy patch of ground and exclaims, "Careful, the ground is mined; it's going to explode!" Everyone runs off and to escape, they all climb into a boat – and the sound of a terrible explosion is heard (!). But they have already reached safety. This is the end; the players take off their disguises and leave their roles (as they remove their disguise, they each announce, "I was a such and a such, for example, the pink pony, and I am Nora, etc.").

Further development:

Questions we asked the children: "What did you like the best? What did you dislike the most?" Here are some of their responses:

The best:

> Ildi: "It was the wind."
> Nora: "When I vanquished the stone dog."

The worst:

> KH: "I couldn't catch Miki, he ran so fast."
> (Miki says: "But I'm the best runner in my class.")

As planned, the parents show up in their cars at 11:30 to pick up the children, who tell them with a great deal of enthusiasm that they played really well. (Nobody complained about the fact they couldn't ride horses); Miki, to his parents, "I almost had the main part."

The characteristic features of the play:

The extension of space, not only in the imagination, as Annamaria suggested, but also in reality. This seemed to replace the sensation of freedom provided by horseback riding. The presence of animals – given the absence of horses because of weather conditions, the children called upon the dogs they appointed as guard dogs, which ran alongside the stone dog in one of the scenes, and in another, joined Miki in his quest, etc.).

The children's choice of roles: the Terminator, who typically played a mean and aggressive character, succeeded almost until the end to hold on to the role of combatting the stone dog. This time, Nora, who was in the habit of selecting the role of a passive, timorous animal (a little bunny), took on the role of a courageous warrior. She often (when Terminator and Indiana Jones were not in the scene) assumed the role of solitary combatant who, with the help of her imaginary horn, valiantly stood up to the stone dog with his mortifying powers.

Miki's original inventions contributed substantially to the marvelous course of the story. He was the one who had the idea of the fire-spewing volcano that needed to be called upon to transform the heart of the stone dog. And as soon as the idea germinated in his mind, he set off, since he also knew exactly where the volcano was located (!?). It was also this nine-year-old boy who introduced the notion of the relativity of time into the game (as a function of space). And also, the idea of the explosion. It is equally remarkable that despite his many discoveries, he did not regard himself as the sole hero of the piece. It should be noted that, contrary to the usual dynamics of children's psychodrama, the children did not face the enemy as a group, but instead, each one fought alone using his own means.

What were the children trying to express with their stereotyped and mismatched characters? We asked ourselves this question. When we asked the children about the title of the piece they were about to play, they were self-conscious at first and ended up saying: "Meeting between different characters." The difference may have related to the two sets of siblings who did not really know each other beforehand, or from the fact that each pair was composed of one sick child and one who was well, but above all, the diversity of the roles they selected. What does Indiana Jones have in common with a little pink pony or with the Terminator? Not to speak of the fairy of the skies, the role that Ildi was determined to take on. (In the end, the little girl was convinced that by making the wind blow she had taken part in the battle against the villain.)

But let us come back to the essentials:

What did the children accomplish by staging this play using these disparate characters and heroes they had seen on television?

They succeeded in broaching the most anxiety-making aspect of the sick child's fate; they fought against the pitiless, menacing, heartless stone dog, which was none other than the disease – the fatal disease.

How touching it was to see the little girl with the cherubic face summon her forces to confront the terrible stone dog. With intrepid courage, her smooth and rounded face armed with her invisible horn, she stood up bravely to the black, deformed monster whose touch she knew was fatal. Regardless, she went after him multiple times.

The other patient, the one-legged little boy who had been brutally marked by his illness chose, out of habit, to express in the role of the Terminator his aggression and desire for vengeance against the whole world. However, this time, his aggression was not directed at just anybody, as before, when the identity of the victim was irrelevant. This time, it was directed against the real enemy, the disease, as represented by the stone dog. With the super-human power of his machine-gun hand, he no longer allied with the destructive force, but instead, asked to be programmed to destroy it. Troubled when the possibility of the positive transformation of the stone dog was suggested, he seemed to be thinking: if it is possible for the stone dog to be positively transformed, doesn't that mean that I'll be the bad one? But the idea of becoming a positive hero, the one who saves people, a benefactor of humanity, offered a perspective that motivated the right choice. Miki, this healthy, astute, original, quick, and fidgety boy, a truly magical child, was also among us. Not living directly under the threat of death, he had less trouble acknowledging the possibility of the transformation of the stone dog than the two others.

He had certainly been affected by his family situation, with a little sister who had absorbed all of his parents' attention for years by now. Less heard, he felt that he was less loved. In his role, it was not simply his need to keep moving that launched him. He had found a goal, that of calling upon the forces of nature to replace the stone heart. In addition to his heart-thrower, he had also gathered a blueberry from near the volcano. This was a gesture truly filled with poetry. In fact, it was almost too much for him, and once the play was over, he asked to continue in the role of the super bad guy.

Considering that the major therapeutic agent in the psychodrama was the mobilization of the children's imagination, the dramatists had opted for putting characters on stage that the children had suggested. However, we had asked ourselves how identification with these television characters who, moreover, had such dissimilar personalities, could satisfy their need to see themselves as heroes. The psychodramatists did not fall back on Aichinger's method (calling upon an outside enemy to allow different heroes to unite in opposition), because this enemy was already unconsciously present in the group. It had been named by the most affected child, Bélus, the boy with one leg: "a stone dog that turns everyone it touches to stone."

In psychodrama, psychotherapists are called upon to play negative parts at the children's request or those parts that nobody wants. The therapists working in the oncology service, often confronted by death, are particularly sensitive (sometimes unconsciously) to the symbolic content of the stories that are invented. In her role, Annamaria played out the repeated disappearance and reappearance of the horrifying monster with remarkable presence, howling with the dogs. But even in the heat of combat, she never petrified anyone, and with her successive deaths, she always signaled the victory of the combatant. However, she did let them know that once she was deprived of her regenerative device, she could disappear definitively. This is what actually happened. The stone dog was lying dead in the hay when Bélus remembered the critical five-year period that reminded him of the risk of relapse.

Toward the end, when the question came up of how the play would end, the issue of the stone dog's fate left the therapists (myself included) hesitating. Should he be allowed to die or be transformed? In other words, should we make the illness disappear or make it harmless? The second option seemed a bit better, given that for those individuals (children) suffering from cancer, the affected tissue and even the tumor itself were in some way a part of their own bodies (in the sense that Didier Anzieu calls the "me-skin"). This certainly motivated us to opt for the transformation of the stone dog by means of implanting a new heart.

The emotional presence, flexibility, and the improvisational capacity of the therapists despite the adverse meteorological conditions (bad weather, rain, wind) and the cancellation of the equestrian program made it possible to unleash the children's passion for playing. Their intense desire to identify with the television heroes, with the Terminator and Indiana Jones for the young boys and with the pink pony for the girl, allowed them to move into a magical world where they could express their will to live. In this magical world they created themselves through their own imagination, they could externalize their fears and anxieties in a play that was their own invention in which they were the heroes. One can confirm that through their empathy and their stimulating play, the dramatists helped the children (directly and indirectly affected by the illness) to take the devil by the tail, and to battle against an enemy that permanently haunted them: death.

The reference to television personalities did not constitute an obstacle to the invention of an original play. The same was true about the framework provided earlier by the fairy tale when the boys imagined they were fighting dragons with three, six, and nine and even more heads. We might even think that the fairy tale, like the televised story, served to prepare the affective atmosphere. (Before beginning the play, the children, especially Miki and Nora, related their experience of the television program with great excitement, and this had given the Terminator the idea, for example, to compensate for his lack of a limb through programming that changed his arm into a machine gun.)

The children were very involved in the play; just see the lovely little pony with her single imaginary horn, the Terminator who succeeded this time in making a good choice of victim. The monster staged by the therapist linked monstrosity to the dangerousness of the character (even an outside observer, such as the groom, found her monstrous and frightening in her accoutrement). My interventions as the old programmer-professor (dissuading the Terminator from turning himself back into villain, suggesting that Indiana Jones capture the repair device, signaling the impact of her gesture to the sky fairy) served to facilitate the expression of latent content, to aid in the expression of the inexpressible, and to vanquish the invincible. These elements conjured up the illness or, if you will, the anxiety of an imminent death.

The elements borrowed from television simply served us as accessories, and I believe that together, we made a step in this direction.

Once the play was finished, we asked the children to draw what seemed to them most important about the piece they had just played. We will show you two drawings.

Nora's drawing of the little pink pony with her horn (here, the larger figure, crossed out) next to the other children-actors (Figure 13.5).

Miki's drawing, which we found especially meaningful; paying no attention to his own performance, the boy chose to depict his sister's battles. Above, one sees the little pink pony in combat against the stone dog (Figure 13.6).

FIGURE 13.5 The marvelous little pink pony

FIGURE 13.6 The little pony battles the stone dog

Virtual world to express a core problem

Michel Stora adopted an original method, which was to play video games with the children. In his 2003–2004 Workshop for a group of seven to nine-year-old children with "failing" mothers, he selected the game Ico. Each child played by taking turns manipulating the joystick for 15 minutes, and the next child would continue the story begun by the previous child.

The Ico in the virtual game was a child born with horns. The children chose him as an avatar, while Yorda is the persecuted daughter of an Evil Queen, a character with a pale complexion and a frail character. Ico is supposed to save the frail Yorda who is menaced by her wicked mother, from falling into the void and becoming "wicked" like her.

In this way, Michel Stora made use of an existing video game to allow the children to express a shared core problem – their relationship with a mother who is not good enough, or even "failing." (See Michel Stora: *The video game, a new therapeutic intervention*, in *The child at risk in the virtual world*, 2006.)

FIGURE 13.7 Superman

Self-healing with Superman

Blaise is a ten-year-old boy. He lost his mother to cancer on the day before his seventh birthday, following a long illness. His little brother was only two years old. Their father remarried a young woman with two adolescent sons, one of whom was also called Blaise, something he accepted fairly well; there was Little Blaise and Big Blaise. Intelligent and successful in school, he had no behavioral problems. The family lived in harmony. Blaise was rather introverted and withdrew when faced with an unfamiliar situation. It was his adoptive mother who brought him to the Consultation, fearing that this boy had not been fully able to grieve for his mother.

Blaise arrived in the group at the time of its second meeting and announced that he did not want to play. At the insistence of the others, he chose the part of a zombie who lived in a cave and did nothing. Asked about the habitual activities of the zombie, he specified that when he was annoyed, he would catch people and gnaw at their flesh. This was a zombie cannibal. Moreover, it was impossible to kill him, for he was one of the living dead.

Having stated this, he installed himself at a remove in his "den."

During this time, a fairy-tale type story was unfolding on stage, in which the hero had gone off to save the king's daughter by killing the evil sorcerer. Now, contrary to the agreed-upon story, the bad sorcerer was disinclined to let himself be beaten by mere mortals.

How would the psychodramatist resolve this situation? She called upon the zombie, the only one who could overpower the evil sorcerer and save the princess. Taking aggressive impulses and transforming them into a form of energy capable of saving others is one of Adler's key concepts, a movement from the will to power to *Gemeinschaftsgefühl.*

This invitation to come to the rescue in a desperate situation that the psychodramatist extended to Blaise bore fruit eleven weeks later. Through psychodrama, this exceptional little boy developed and resolved a story that represented a much more complicated internal struggle, whose stake was nothing less than the battle of good and evil and the rescue of mankind.

He once again resorted to television, as with the Zombie, we might say "under the pretext of television" because he decided to make use of Superman. Blaise, while having promised to suggest stories, kept postponing doing so, saying that he wasn't ready yet, and instead, started cutting out paper figures. He had the habit of playing alone with the characters he had drawn. He even spoke about his favorite character, a ghost who was sometimes nice, sometimes funny, sometimes bad. His first idea was to have the characters he had drawn perform in the play but he changed his mind, and suggested to the member of the group that they play a real psychodrama in which he would assign the roles. He called them, "Can't-stand-on-his-legs, The one-legged chief, the Evil spirit, the Preacher, and Superman," and presented them one by one:

- Can't-stand-on-his-legs is very sick, which explains his name. He's a positive character but he can't do anything, and spends his day in bed under covers and pillows.
- Superman, good character, he saves the world many times over.
- Evil spirit, this is an evil being. He has great power but no brain, so he needs the chief to tell him what to do.
- The one-legged chief is evil, and that is why he is missing a leg.
- The Preacher is a positive character, an ally of Superman. He can feel the presence of the evil ones. He can communicate with Superman by telepathy.

The story told by Blaise

> The one-legged chief decides to conquer the world. He sends his favorite ally, the Evil spirit, to assemble all the wicked beings in the whole world. They meet at the top of a tower and the Chief tells them what they have to do. These evil ones then decide to exterminate the inhabitants of New York and to seize power. While they are meeting, the Preacher senses the presence of the Evil spirit who is getting ready for something terrible. He warns Superman by telepathy and asks him to come urgently to save the city.
>
> Superman arrives with his allies Can't-stand-on-his-legs and the Dwarf. However, the Evil spirit intercepts the message and takes possession of Superman, who thus turns evil. The Preacher chases him away, so everything comes back in order: Superman destroys all the evil ones and he saves the world.

Blaise selects the role of Superman (Figure 13.7), and assigns the role of Can't-stand-on-his-legs to one of the Facilitators, the other one will be the Evil spirit and the one-legged chief. Blaise wants to give Rebekka (whose father is a pastor) the role of the Preacher, but she objects vehemently and chooses to be the Dwarf, while Stéphanie is happy to be the Preacher.

The story staged

In the course of the play, the story undergoes many changes. Superman is possessed by the Evil spirit and the Preacher is unable to exorcise him. This threatens the world with destruction, for the Evil spirit multiplies Superman's powers, and Superman turns into an evil force provided with enormous destructive power. This super force, called upon to save the world, now prepares to destroy it. "Every good thing has its other side," Blaise's favorite expression that he chose as the title of his piece, is fulfilled; even the great Superman cannot seem to escape this ambivalence.

The first thing that happens is that he attacks his own friends. And the first one he goes after is the weakest: Can't-stand-on-his-legs. Or to put it more precisely, he could have been the one, but just at this moment, the story takes an odd turn. Superman turns against his own evil side. And the group helps him in a breathtaking scene: the battle between Superman and the Evil spirit who inhabits him. The battle is long and hard. But it is worth the effort: the forces of good emerge as the victors and the city is saved. Superman is very tired and he is sad as well. The city, however, is overjoyed and celebrates its hero.

For Blaise, this play was a cathartic event. His battle was astonishing, and the other players gathered around him, encouraged him, and supported him. At one moment, the outcome of the battle became uncertain, and it seemed that the evil forces would come out on top; but by mobilizing all of his forces, Superman succeeded in emerging victorious.

Can't-stand-on-his-legs, who, according to Blaise, didn't do anything, finally took on a key role, despite or because of the fact that he didn't do anything but instead, contented himself with just being present. The evil spirit of Superman turned against his weakness, even though Can't-stand-on-his-legs posed no threat to the evil ones. But Superman's love proved to be greater and stronger than the power of the Evil spirit. This made it possible for Superman to battle against the evil that dwelled within him and to conquer it.

Blaise had accomplished an admirable feat – he had succeeded in staging his repressed feelings, his anger at his bedridden and powerless mother along with his love that proved stronger than his rage. This magical power that already had saved so many heroes ended up presiding over the positive outcome of his battle.

Blaise insisted on specifying that this had only been a puppet show.

In this boy's grief work, the drawing of a ghost that he always carries with him bears an important part. This is his transitional object, his double, his remedy, and his friend. It is a symbolic representation of the presence of the lost mother. One day, when visiting friends, he almost lost the drawing, and he panicked when he came home and feared he would never find it again. But the little crumpled drawing was finally found in the garden. Since that time, he has held on to it jealously.

Blaise selected a television character, the main figure in numerous films, an omnipotent crusader with exceptional gifts, superhuman power, the ability to fly, etc. Only the Superman of television and film is an incarnation of a character that is the custodian of dehumanized values . . .

With all of these qualities, he was able to turn into an ego ideal, an ideal of overcompensation and escape for a tormented boy. However, when, after quite a long period of solitary rumination, Blaise found the courage to stage this story, it was not the omnipotent and assured characterization of himself but the boy's double – the bearer of his doubts and his ambivalence towards a mother who disappeared but who during her lifetime, could not stand on her own two feet to offer him security and support. In this sense, being not good enough, she could barely be present in her young son's life. Deeply frustrated, Blaise was still unable to face up to his own resentment, and his guilty ambivalence constituted a major obstacle that prevented him from grieving. Blaise fled from his anxieties and constructed lively stories, with the characters he drew and animated becoming the actors and interlocutors in his monologues, and some of which bore some resemblance to his virtual heroes. Once he was able to step across the barriers of his solitude and stop languishing all by himself, he succeeded in utilizing the potential space of psychodrama to share his questions with the members of the group. His Superman was different from the one on television, because he was not the all-powerful avenger of all misdeeds, the possessor of absolute truth, but rather, by way of the subterfuge, he was a double for Blaise that allowed him to externalize his own internal struggle. He conquered the evil that ate at him from the inside to become a real hero, engaging in combat to save the others, and indeed, to save "endangered humanity." In bitter combat against what he termed the evil that was eating at him, his own desire for vengeance, he found the means to accomplish his own rehabilitation.

Notes

1 Text taken in part from Hanna Kende's lecture at the XXIst International Congress of Individual Psychology.
2 What a lovely discovery, curing by rubbing, the opposite of killing by touching.

14

FINAL WORD ON THE FUNCTION OF PSYCHODRAMA WITH CHILDREN

Many schools of philosophy have characterized human beings as *Homo sapiens (Linnaeus)*. For Benjamin Franklin and Henri Bergson, man is primarily a toolmaker – *Homo faber (a tool-making animal)* – and "intelligence, considered in what seems to be its original feature, is the faculty of manufacturing artificial objects" (Bergson, 1907). Somewhat compromised by the fact that some other animals are also capable of using tools, this formula has since been extended as "endowed with an intelligence capable of transforming the world around him." Huizinga's work *Homo ludens, a Study on the Play Element in Culture* ([1951] 1988) defines man's essence by his capacity for play. Huizinga defines play as being "a voluntary action or activity, completed within certain fixed limits of time and place [. . .] following rules that are freely agreed upon, and outside the sphere of utility or material necessities." And he adds, "The ambience of play is one of delight and enthusiasm [. . .]. The action is accompanied by feelings of transport and tension, and brings about joy and relaxation." Huizinga also says that play is, "an accord that tends to realize, in a given time and space, following certain rules and in a given form, something that resolves a tension, and which is a stranger to the ordinary course of life" (1988, pp. 176–177).

It seems to us that these words also capture the essential characteristics of psychodrama with children.

Moreno said, "*Das Spiel ist der Königsweg der Kinder*" (play is the royal road of children). Winnicott regarded play as a criterion for mental health and defined the task of psychotherapy as "restoring the capacity of play to those who have lost it" (Winnicott, 1971a).

Piaget noted that play, which takes up 70 percent of children's active time, constitutes an essential activity and is a principal way of satisfying the child's need to ease tension.

Video games play a major and growing part in the life of children who are digital natives in generation Z, and all of those who were born in the age of the computer. A recent study suggested that it is the French who are the prime consumers of video games in Europe. Those who control the media and the manufacturers of video games, consoles, and shared virtual spaces have long since discovered that the key to selling their wares is to offer the solitary, devalued adolescent heroic exploits in a different world, a marvelous world where, by means of auxiliary selves, he can redeem his failures, go beyond himself, and become different. The virtual world can turn into a true passion.

It is an alienating passion, we would say.

By contrast, we regard children's psychodrama as an important means to restore the genuine function of play.

No less passionate, the original psychodramatic plays children create to help resolve their own problems that they stage together with real other children are of an entirely different nature. This magical world is constructed by the child's own creativity, where a succession of different characters give him access to his authentic personality, which, through the play, can rediscover a way to manifest itself. It is such discovery that feeds the child's passion for play. Alfred Adler, similar to modern researchers on infant behavior, emphasizes the child's natural tendency to seek accomplishment and self-perfection. We would regard this as the true function of play; this passion for play revalorizes, reconstructs, and heals the self.

We would like to focus on another aspect of psychodrama with children, which is no less important. We regard this method as an important means of *prevention* and have developed it accordingly. We encountered children who were lost, isolated, marginalized, some of them having suffered from abuse. These were children who were considered "at risk," who came from marginalized or poorly integrated immigrant families, and we organized the workshops in an attempt to spare them the fate of their older siblings, some of whom had found no other response to material, nutritional, social, and affective deprivation than to become mistrustful, aggressive, and cultivate the desire for vengeance. We wanted to offer the children who came to the workshop a new means of expression, but how does one comfort these children in their misery? How do we keep "difficult" children from turning into delinquents? Some of our children came from families of migrant backgrounds. As a mother of a Maghrebi family put it, "Before, I was afraid that my children would turn into delinquents, but now I am afraid they will become terrorists." If we trace the histories of the Jihadi terrorists who perpetrated the terrible brutalities in France on November 13, 2015, we find that many of them grew up in the Parisian *banlieues* and started out as juvenile delinquents. By the time these young people are twenty or thirty years old and they are launched on this path, we believe it is already too late to "defundamentalize" them.

However, when we encounter similar children at an earlier stage, it is possible to save them from this fate. Psychodrama with children is directed at supporting their self esteem, their self respect, and their respect for others like them. Later on, these qualities will help them to avoid falling prey to the siren calls, which invite them to false heroism, to become heroes not by sacrificing themselves to save or help others, but instead, by murdering other children, women, and adults, no matter whom, anyone who gets in their way.

Psychodrama with children is a method that encourages every child to feel a sense of solidarity with others, in the sense of Adler's *Gemeinschaftsgefühl*, and today, it is being called upon to help prevent children in every country and from every background from succumbing to religious extremism or violent dehumanization!

BIBLIOGRAPHY

Abraham, N. 1987. *L'écorce et le noyau*, Paris, Flammarion.

Adler, A. 1928. *The Neuroses and Understanding Human Nature*, George Allen & Unwin.

Adler, A. 1973 (1928). *Der Sinn des Lebens*, Frankfurt, Fischer.

Adler, A. 1977 (1930). *Praxis und Theorie der Individualpsychologie*, Frankfurt, Fischer.

Adler, A. 1978 (1928). *Über den nervösen Charakter*, Frankfurt, Fischer.

Adler, A. and Jahn, E. 1958. *Religion et psychologie individuelle comparée suivi de la névrose obsessionnelle et les enfants difficiles*, Paris, Payot.

Aichinger, A. and Holl, W. 1997. *Psychodrama Gruppentherapie mit Kindern*, Mainz, Grünewald.

Ancelin-Schützenberger, A. 1966. *Précis de psychodrame*, Paris, Éditions Universitaires.

Anders M. 1976. *Guppenarbeit mit auffälligen Jugendlichen*, Thübingen, Katzmann.

Ansbacher, R. 1956. *The Individual Psychology of Alfred Adler*, New York, Basic Books.

Anzieu, A. 1996. *Le Travail du dessin en psychothérapie de l'enfant*, Paris, Dunod.

Anzieu, D. 1972. *Le Travail psychanalytique dans les groupes*, Paris, Dunod.

Anzieu, D. 1994. *Le Psychodrame analytique chez l'enfant et l'adolescent*, Paris, PUF.

Anzieu, D. 1995. *Le Moi-Peau*, Paris, Dunod.

Anzieu, D. and Martin, J.-Y. 1976. *La Dynamique des groupes restreints*, Paris, PUF.

Anzieu, D. and Kaës, R. 1979. *Crise, rupture et dépassement*, Paris, Dunod.

Anzieu, D., Béjarano, A., Kaës, R., Missenard, A. and Pontalis, J.B. 1995. *Le Travail psychanalytique dans les groupes*, Paris, Dunod.

Artaud, A. 1938. *Le Théâtre et son double*, Paris, Gallimard.

Axline, V. 1981. *Play Therapy*, MMP.

Babits, M. 1984. *Halálfiai,* Budapest, Szépirodalmi.

Bálint, M. 1968. *The basic fault Therapeutic aspects of regression*, Northwestern University Press.

Bandura, A. 1973. *Aggression: a social learning analysis*, Englewood Cliffs, N. J., Prentice Hall.

Barrucand, D. 1970. *La Catharsis dans le théâtre, la psychanalyse et la pychothérapie de groupe*, Paris, Epi.

Basquin, M., Dubusson, P., Samuel-Lajeunesse, B. and Testemale-Monod, G. 1972. *Le Psychodrame: une approche psychanalytique*, Paris, Dunod.

Beaudouin, Ch. 1929. *Psychanalyse de l'art*, Paris, Alcan.

Berge, A. 1968. *Les Psychothérapies*, Paris, PUF.

Bergson, H. 1907. *L'évolution créatrice*, Paris, Alcan.
Berkovitz, I.H. 1972. *Adolescents Grow in Groups*, New York, Brunner/Mazel.
Bettelheim, B. 1954. *Symbolic Wounds*, New York, Glencoe.
Bettelheim, B. 1971. *The Informed Heart, Autonomy in a Mass Age,* New York, Avon.
Bettelheim, B. 1971. *Love is Not Enough, the Treatment of Emotionally Disturbed Children*, New York and Chicago, Avon.
Bettelheim, B. 1976. *The Uses of Enchantment. The Meaning and Importance of Fairy Tales*, New York, Knopf.
Biermann, C. 1981. *Handbuch der Kinderpsychotherapie*. I-IV, Munich.
Biner, P. 1968. *Le living théâtre*, Lausanne, La Cité.
Bion, W.R. 1961. *Experiences in Groups and Other Papers*, London, Tavistock.
Blatner, H.A. 1973. *Acting-in, Practical Applications of Psychodramatic Methods*, New York, Springer.
Blomberg, S. 1980. Influence of maternal distress during pregnancy on postnatal development in *Acta Psychiatrica Scandinavica*, 62, 405–417.
Bosselmann, R. and Cellert *et al.* 1993. *Variationen des Psychodramas*, Meezen.
Breton, A. and Soupault P. 1985. *The magnetic fields*, London, Allas Press.
Brezinka *et al.* 1994. Denial of pregnancy, in *J. Psychosom. Obstetr, Gynecol.* March 15 (1) 1–8.
Bustan, M. N. and Coker, A. L. 1994. Maternal attitude toward pregnancy and the risk of neonatal death in *Am. J. Public Health*, March 84 (3) 411–414.
Caillois, R. 1958. *Les Jeux et les hommes*, Paris, Gallimard.
Clancier, A. and Kalmanovitch, J. (ed). 1999. *Le paradoxe de Winnicott*, Paris, In press edition.
Clauser, G. 1959. Märchen als Rollenspiel. In *Arzt im Raum des Erlebens*, Munich, Lehmann.
Conchon G. 1964. *L'État sauvage*, Paris, Albin Michel.
Cooley, C.H. 1909. *Social organisation: A study of the larger mind*, New York, Charles Scribner's.
Darrault, J. and Klein, J.P. 1990. La thérapie comme constitution de son mythe original. In *Art et Thérapie*, 36/37.
Dars, E. and Benoit, J.C. 1972. *L'Expression scénique. Art dramatique et psychothérapie*, Paris, Éditions ESF.
Delaroche, P. 1996. *Le Psychodrame psychanalytique individuel*, Paris, Payot.
De Neuter, P. 1978. *Les entretiens préliminaires: évaluation d'une indication d'une demande*, in Matisson-Rouye, 245–262.
Diatkine, R. 1954. Fantasme et réalité en thérapeutique dramatique. *Evol. Psychiat.*, XIX. 4, 59–683.
Diatkine R. 1999. Une grande liberté d'espriz in *Le paradoxe de Winnicott*, 167–170.
Diatkine, R., Kestemberg, E. and Lebovici, S. 1952. Applications de la psychanalyse à la psychothérapie de groupe et à la psychothérapie dramatique en France. *Evol. Psychiat.*, XVIII, 3.397–412.
Diatkine, R., Soccaras, F. and Kestemberg, E. 1950. Le transfert en psychothérapie collective. *Encéphale*, 39, no. 3, 248–274.
Drabkova, H. 1966. Experience resulting from clinical use of psychodrama with children. *Group Psychother.*, XIX.
Dreyfus, C. 1975. *Les Groupes de rencontre*, Paris, Epi.
Dreyfus-Moreau J. 1950. A propos du transfert en psychothérapie collective, *Revue fr. Psychanal.*, no. 2, 244–257.
Dreyfus-Moreau, J. 1955. Bilan d'une expérience de psychanalyse collective. *Revue fr. psychanal.*, 19, no. 3, 333–356.
Duflot, C. 1992. *Des Marionnettes pour le dire. Entre jeu et thérapie*, Paris. Éd, J. des Psychologues.
Durand-Dassier, J. 1973. *Groupes de renconte Marathon*, Paris, Epi.

Enriquez, V. G. 1992. *From colonial to liberation psychology*, Quezon City, University of the Philippines Press.

Erikson, E.H. 1963. *Childhood and Society*, New York, W.W. Norton.

Estin, C. 1990. Vous croyez au conte, vous? *Art et Thérapie*, no. 36.

Fain, M. 1968. Réflexions sur l'acting out. *Rev. fr. psychan.*, 32. 5–6.

Fanchette, J. 1971. *Psychodrame et théâtre moderne*, Paris, Buchet-Chastel.

Ferenczi S. 1927-1933. *Oeuvres Complètes,* IV, Confusion de langue entre les adultes et l'enfant, 125–135.

Ferenczi S. 1933. *Sprachverwirrung zwischen Erwachsenen und dem Kind.* Die Sprache von Zärtlichkeit und der Leidenschaft. In. Zeitsch. für *Psychoanalyse Heft* 1–2.

Ferenczi, S. 1968–1982. *Oeuvres complètes,* I-IV, Paris, Payot.

Ferenczi, S. 1968. *Thalassa: A Theory of Genitality*, New York, W.W. Norton.

Fesbach, S. 1956. The catharsis hypothesis and some consequences of interaction with aggressive and neutral play objects. *J. Pers*, 24.

Fonagy, P. and Target, M. 1996. Playing with reality, in *Internat. Journal of Psychoanal.* 77 (2) 217–238.

Foulkes, S.H. 1957. *Group Psychotherapy. The Psychoanalytic Approach*, London, Penguin.

Franz, von M.-L. 1986. *Psychologische Märcheninterpretation.* Kösel.

Freud, A. 1965. *Normality and Pathology in Childhood*, Karnac Books.

Freud, S. 1940–1952. *Die Traumdeutung* Ges. Werke II. III, London, *Imago.*

Freud, S. 1949. Der Untergang des Oedipuskomplexes. In *Ges. Werke.* XIII, Fischer.

Freud, S. 1960. Zur Dynamik der Übertragung. In *Ges. Werke.* VIII, Frankfurt, Fischer.

Freud, S. 1967. Das Ich und das Es. In *Ges. Werke.* XIII, S. Frankfurt, Fischer.

Freud, S. and Breuer, J. 1956. *Études sur l'hystérie.* Paris, PUF.

Friedmann, A. 1972. *Vorbereitung von Kindertherapeuten zur Spieltherapie über das Psychodrama* in Petzold, H. (ed) Angewandtes Psychodrama, Paderborn, Junfermann.

Fromm, E. 1951. *The Forgotten Language. An Introduction to the Understanding of Dreams, Fairy Tales and Myths*, New York, Rinehart and Co.

Fuguet, P. 2000. *Les parents, le divorce et l'enfant*, Paris, ESF.

Garnier, Ph. and Bonnot-Matheron, S. 1981. *Le Psychodrame. Une Psychothérapie analytique*, Paris, ESF.

Gillibert, J. 1985. *Le Psychodrame de la psychanalyse*, Champ-Vallon.

Girard, R. 1972. *La Violence et le sacré*, Paris, Grasset.

Graves, R. 1960. *Greek Mythology*, London, Penguin Books revised ed.

Green, A. 2011. *Jouer avec Winnicott*, Paris, PUF.

Green, A. and Kernberg, O. 2000. *L'avenir d'une désillusion*, Paris, PUF.

Heigl-Evers A. 1972. Rolle und Interventionsstil der Gruppenpsychotherapeuten in Gruppenpsychoter. *Gruppendynamik*, no. 5.

Heisterkamp, G. 1985. Progressive und regressive Momente in der Therapie. *Beiträge zur Indivi-dualpsychologie*, 6.

Hermann, I. 1984. *Az ember ősi osztönei*, Magvető, Budapest.

Hetmann, F. 1986. *Die Göttin der Morgenröte, Schöpfungsmythen aus aller Welt*, Frankfurt, Fischer.

Huizinga, J. [1951]. 1988. *Homo ludens*, Routledge.

Itard, J.M.G. [1801, 1806]. 1962. *The Wild Boy of Aveyron.* Trans. G. Humphrey and M. Humphrey. New York: Appleton-Century-Crofts.

Jeammet, P. and Kestemberg, E. 1987. *Le Psychodrame psychanalytique*, Paris, PUF.

Jeanmaire, H. 1951. *Dionysos, histoire du culte de Bacchus*, Paris, Payot.

Jung, C.G. 1952. *Psychologie de l'inconscient*, Geneva, Georg.

Jung, C.G. and Wilhem, R. 1965. *Das Geheimnis der goldenen Blüte*, Zürich-Stuttgart, Raucher.

Kaës, R. 1999. *Les Théories psychanalytiques du groupe*, Paris, PUF.

Kaës, R. and Anzieu, D. 1973. *Fantasme et formation*, Paris, Dunod.

Kalogeras, V. 1956. *Nouveaux points de vue sur la catharsis aristotélicienne*, Thessaloniki.

Kaplan, H. and Sadock, B. 1972. *Sensitivity Through Encounter and Marathon*, New York, Dutton.

Kende, H. 1988. Éros ou l'image de l'enfant gâté dans la mythologie grecque. *Bulletin de la S.F.P.A*, no. 60.

Kende, H. 1989. L'enfant difficile, mythe et réalité, in *Cahiers du Centre de Recherche Interdisciplinaire de Vaucresson*, March.

Kende, H. 1991. Angoisse existentielle et/ou Oedipe. *Actualités Psychiatriques*, no. 465.

Kende, H. 1992. L'Enfant au pays des marionnettes. *Art et Thérapie*, no. 44/45, Dec.

Kende, H. 1992. Jeu, réalité, devenir de l'enfant maltraité, *Revue Jnternationale de criminologie*, Geneva, vol. XLV. no. 1, 29–50.

Kende, H. 1992. Le Bouc émissaire ou la psychologie de la victimisation. *Bulletin de la S.F.P.A*, no. 68.

Kende, H. 1992. Le Diable et son hologramme, l'enfant difficile telqu'en lui-méme. *Revue Internationale de Criminologie*, Geneva, vol. XLV. no. 3, 42–353.

Kende, H. and Lepineux, C. 1986. Enfant marginal et psychodrame. *Journal des Psychologues*, May, no. 37, 34–36.

Kerényi, K. 1957. Le symbolisme dans la religion antique, in *La religion antique*, Geneva, Georg.

Kestenberg, E. and Jeammet, P. 1987. *Le Psychodrame psychanalytique individuel*, Paris, PUF.

Klein, M. 1957. *Envy & Gratitude*, London, Tavistock.

Klein, M. 1961. *Narrative of a Child Analysis*, London, Hogarth Press.

Klein, M. 1982. *The Psychoanalysis of Children*, London, Hogarth Press.

König K. and Lindner, W.-V. 1991. *Psychanalytische Gruppentherapie*, Göttingen, Vandenhoeck.

Kouretas, D. 1962. Aspects modernes des cures psychothérapiques pratiquéesdans les sanctuaires de la Grèce antique. *Revue franç. psychanal.* 5/6.

Lacan, J. 1971. Le Stade du miroir. *Écrits I*, Paris, Seuil.

Lagache, D. 1952. Le problème du transfert. *Revue fr. Psychanal.*, no. 1–2, 5–115.

Lagache, D. 1968. Acting out et action. Difficultés terminologiques. *Revue fr. Psychanal.* 32.

Laing, R.D. 1971. *Le Soi et les autres*, Paris, Gallimard.

Lajeunesse, B.S. and Missenard, A. 1971. Le psychodrame analytique en groupe. *Perspectives Psychiatriques*, no. 33.

Laplanche, J. and Pontalis, J.-B. 1967. *Vocabulaire de la psychanalyse*, Paris, PUF.

Laxenaire, M. 1975. *Les Processus de changement en psychothérapie degroupe*, Nîmes.

Laxenaire, M. 1986. Moreno et la voie psychodramatique, *Journal des Psychologues*, May, 16–28, no. 37, 21–23.

Laxenaire, M. 1984. Aperçu sur l'héritage morenien. *Psychol. méd.*, 16. no. 3, 429–432.

Lebovici, S., Diatkine, R. and Kestemberg, E. 1952. Applications de la psychanalyse à la psychothérapie de groupe et à la psychothérapie dramatique en France. *Evol. Psychiat.*, no. 3, 397–412.

Lebovici, S., Diatkine, R. and Kestemberg, E. 1970. Bilan de dix ans de pratique psychodramatique chez l'enfant et l'adolescent. *Bulletin de Psychologie*, no. 13/16, 63–179.

Lehmkuhl, U. 1993. Verarbeitungsstrategien der Scheidung von Kindern, Jugendlichen und deren Eltern. *Beiträge zur Individualpsychologie*, 20.

Lemoine, G. and P. 1972. *Le Psychodrame*. Paris, Laffont.

Leutz, G.A. 1974. *Psychodrama, Theorie und Praxis*, Berlin-Heidelberg, Springer.

Leutz, G.A. 1985. *Mettre sa vie en scène: le psychodrame*, Paris, EPI.

Lévi-Strauss, C. 1949. L'Efficacité symbolique. *Revue Hist. Relig.*, 135, no. 1., 5–27.

Lorenz K. 1963. *Das sogenannte Böse-Zur Naturgeschichte des Agression*, Munich, DTV.
Lorenz, K. 1966. *On Aggression*, London-New York, Routledge.
Lorin, C. 1989. *Traité de psychodrame d'enfant*, Toulouse, Privat.
Loyer-Dolghin M.-C. 1992. Contes, une école de sagesse in *Art et Thérapie*, no. 40/45.
Lutz, Ch. 1976. *Praxis der Gruppentherapie mit Kindern*, Stuttgart, Thiemen.
McGue, M. *et al.*, Research outputs in *J. of Abnormal Psychology* 106, 3. 439–448.
Maisonneuve, J. 1990. *La Dynamique des groupes*, Paris, PUF.
Masud Khan, M. 1973. *Hidden Selves*, London, Karnac Books.
Mateychek, Z., Dytrych et al., 1988. *Unwanted developmental effects of denied abortion*, New York, Springer.
Matisson, M.D. 1971. *Sociothérapie ou psychothérapies*, Paris, Éditions Universitaires.
Matisson, M.D. 1973. *Le Psychodrame*, Paris, Éditions Universitaires.
Matisson M.D. 1978. Psychodrame et psychodramistes ou? quand? pourquoi? in *CERF-CERI cahier*, no 4, 197-208.
Mead, G. H. 1934. *Mind, self and society*, Chicago, Charles W. Morris.
Mérei, F. [1970]. 1996. *Közösségek rejtertt hálózata*, Budapest, Osisris.
Mérei, F. and Erdélyi I. (ed.) 1987. *A pszichodráma önismereti és terápiás alkalmazása*, Budapest, Akadémia.
Monod, M. 1947. Le Psychodrame de Moreno, *Sauvegarde*, no. 15–16.35–49.
Moreau-Dreyfus, J., Lebovici, S. 1947. La psychothérapie collective chez l'enfant, *Sauvegarde*, 2, no. 15-16.
Moreno, J.-L. 1914. *Einladung zu einer Begegnung*, Vienna.
Moreno, J.-L. 1920. *Das Testament des Vaters*, Berlin-Potsdam, Gustav Kiepenheuer.
Moreno, J.-L. 1923. *Königsroman*, Berlin-Potsdam, Gustav Kiepenheuer.
Moreno, J.-L. 1923. *Rede über die Begegnung*, Berlin-Potsdam, Gustav Kiepenheuer.
Moreno, J.-L. 1925. *Rede vor dem Richter*. Berlin-Potsdam, Gustav Kiepenheuer.
Moreno J.L. 1943. Mental catharsis and psychodrama, *Sociometry*, 3.
Moreno, J.-L. 1946. *Psychodrama* I, New York, Beacon House.
Moreno, J.-L. 1953. *Who Shall Survive? Foundations of Sociometry, Group Psychotherapy and Sociodrama*, New York, Beacon House.
Moreno, J.-L. 1956. *Psychothérapie de groupe et psychodrame*, Paris, PUF.
Moreno, J.-L. 1959. *Psychodrama* II. *Foundations of Psychotherapy*, New York, Beacon House.
Moreno, J.-L. 1969. *Psychodrama III. Action Therapy and Principles of Practice*, New York, Beacon House.
Moreno, Z. 1973. *Psychodrame d'enfant*, Paris, Epi.
Mormin, G. and Viguier, R. 1993. *La Théorie analytique adlérienne*, Paris, Masson.
Nacht, S. 1968. Sur le passage à l'acte, *Revue fr. psychan.*, 32. no. 5–6.
Oppenheim, D. 1996. *L'enfant et le cancer*, Paris, Bayard.
Oppenheim, D. 1999. *Ne jette pas mes dessins à la poubelle. Dialogue avec Daniel, traité pour cancer entre sa 6e et 9e année*, Paris, Seuil.
Ottlik, G. 1953. Iskola a határon, Budapest, Magvető.
Papanoutsos, E.P. 1953. *La Catharsis des passions d'après Aristote*. Athens, Coll. Institut Français d'Athènes.
Pélicier, I. 1986. *Angoisse et tranquillité*, Paris, Dacosta.
Petzold, H. 1975. Masken und Märchenspiel in der Integraviten Therapie. *Integrative Therapie*, I.
Petzold, H. and Schmidt, J. 1995. Psychodrama und Theater. In Petzold, H. (ed.) *Angewandtes Psychodrama*, 1972, Junfermann, Paderborn.
Petzold, H. and Ramin, G. 1995. *Schulen der Kindertherapie*, Junfermann, Paderborn.

Pörtner P. as cited in Ferdinand Buer. 1999. *Morenos therapeutische Philosophie*, Opladen, Leske & Budrich.

Price, J. 1967. Psychodrama with withdrawn patients. *Group Psychother.* XX.

Privat, P. 1997. De la problématique individuelle á la dynamique groupale, in *Revue de psychothérapie psychanalytique de groupe*, no 28.

Privat, P. and Sacco, F. 1995. *Groupes d'enfants et cadre psychanalytique*, Paris, Erès.

Raguenet, G. 1999. *La Psychothérapie par le conte*, Paris, L'Harmattan.

Rank, O. 1924. *Das Trauma der Geburt*, Vienna, Internationaler Psychoanalytischer Verlag.

Rank, O. 1973. *Don Juan et le double*, Paris, Payot.

Reinberg, A. 1979. *L'homme malade du temps*, Pernoud/Stock.

Ringel, E. 1983. Die Übertragung in der I.P. *Zeitschrift für I.P*, 3.

Robert, M. 1967. *Sur le Papier*, Paris, Grasset.

Robert, M. 1974. *D'Oedipe à Moise*, Paris, Calmann-Lévy.

Rodriguez, R. 1995. De l'interprétation oracle aux interpretations scéniques in *Revue de psychodrama psychanalytique de groupe,* no. 25.

Roe V. and Drivas A. 1993. Planned conception and infant functioning in *American J. of Orthopsychiatry*, 63 (1) 120–135.

Rogers, C.R. 1970. *On Encounter Groups*, New York, Harper & Row.

Rosen, J. 1965. Acting-out and acting-in. *Evol. Psychiatr.*, XXX. 11.

Rottmann, W. 1974. Coulter electronic particle counter essay in measurement of cell interactions in *J. Methods Enzynol*, 32, 597–611.

Roussillon, R. 1984. Actualité de Winnicott. In *Le paradoxe de Winnicott*, Paris, In press. 9–30.

Roussillon, R. 1995. Les Fondements de la théorie du cadre et la spécificité du travail de symbolisation groupal à la latence. In Privat P. and Sacco F.

Roussillon, R. 1999. La capacité d'être seul en face du groupe. In *Revue Française de Psychanalyse*. LXIII.

Sacco F. 1991. Psychodrame de groupe á l'adolescence in *Revue de psychothérapie psychanalytique* no. 16, 37–43.

Sacco, F. 1999. De l'agir du jeu pratique du psychodrama de groupe, in *Revue de psychothérape psychanalytique de groupe*, no. 33, 71–90.

Sechehaye, M.A. 1950. *Journal d'une schizophrène*, Paris, PUF.

Segal, H. 1963. Les facteurs de guérison en psychanalyse. *Revue Française de Psychanalyse*, 4–5.

Shearon, E.M. 1980. Psychodrama with children. In *Group Psychotherapy and Psychodrama*, 33.

Sheelen, L. 1983. *Théâtre pour devenir autre*, Paris, Epi.

Slavson, S.R. 1950. *Analytic Group Psychotherapy: Children, adolescents, adults*, New York, Columbia University Press.

Slavson, S.R. 1953. Sources of counter transference and group-inducedanxiety. *Internat. J. Group Psychother.*, no. 4.

Slavson, S.R. 1954. *Introduction to Group Analytic Therapy with Children*, New York, Oxford University Press.

Smilansky, S. 1968. *The Effects of Sociodramatic Play on Disadvantaged Prescool Children*. New York, Wiley.

Solié, P. 1981. *Mythanalyse jungienne*, Paris, ESF.

Soriano, M. 1977. *Les Contes de Perrault*, Paris, Gallimard.

Souriau, E. 1950. *Les Deux cent mille situations dramatiques*, Paris, Flammarion.

Spitz, R.A. & Wolf, K.M. 1946. Anaclitic depression: an inquiry into the genesis of psychiatric conditions in early childhood. *The Psychanalytic study of the child*, 2, 313-342.

Stadler, A.E. & Witte, K.H. 1995. *Individualpsychologische analytische Psychotherapie für Kinder und Jugendliche*. In Petzold, H., Ramin G- (Hrsg) Schulen der Kinderpsychotherapie, Paderborn, Junfermann.

Stanislavski, K. 1950. *Ma Vie dans l'art*. Paris, Edition théâtrale.
Stern, D.N. 1985. *The Interpersonal World of the Infant*, New York, Basic Books Inc.
Straub, H. 1995. Psychodramatische Kindertherapie mittels Puppen, in Petzold H. and Ramin, G. *Schulen der Kinderpsychotherapie*, Junfermann, Paderborn, 202–211.
Straus, P. 1982. *L'Enfant victime*, Toulouse, Erès.
Strauss, R. 1974. Widerstand und Abwehrmechanismus in der Psydhodramatherapie. In *Gruppenpsychotherapie und Gruppendynamik*, 1.
Tappolet, U. 1990. Le conte, la marionnette, l'art du guérisseur. In *Art et thérapie*, 36/37.
Testemale-Monod, G. 1959. Le Psychodrame. In *L'inadaptation scolaireet sociale et ses remèdes*, Paris, Bourrelier.
Tisseron, S. 2008. *Virtuel mon amour*, Paris, Albin Michel.
Tisseron, S. and Stiegler, B. 2009. *Faut-il interdire les écrans aux enfants*, Paris, Mordicus.
Tisseron, S. and Stora, M. 2006. *L'enfant au risque du virtuel*, Paris, Dunod.
Vajda, Z. 1999. *A gyermek pszichológiai fejlődése*, Budapest, Helikon.
Van Damme, P. 1994. *Espace et groupe thérapeutique d'enfants*, Paris, Epi.
Veraldi, B. et G. 1972. *Psychologie de la création*, Paris, Marabout.
Vergoz, C. 1990. D'une théorie de l'imaginaire? une pratique de l'invention du conte: le mythodrame actanciel. *Art et Thérapie*, 36/37.
Veyne, P. 1983. *Les Grecs ont-ils cru? leurs mythes? Essai sur l'imagination constituante*, Paris, Seuil.
Villiers, A. 1951. *La Psychologie de l'Art dramatique*, Paris, Armand Colin.
Voutsinas, D. A propos de la catharsis. *Bull. Psychol.*, 1969–1970 no. 16–17
Weiner M. 1965. *Therapist disclosure. The use of the self in psychotherapy*, Boston, Butterworth.
Well, C.G. 1962. Psychodrama with children in a sociometrically structured setting. *Group Psychother.*, XV.
Widlöcher, D. 1979. *Le Psychodrame chez l'enfant*, Paris, PUF.
Winnicott, D.W. 1969. *The Use of an Object*, London, Tavistock.
Winnicott, D.W. 1971a. *Playing and Reality*, London, Tavistock.
Winnicott, D.W. 1971b. *Therapeutic Consultations in Child Psychiatry*, London, Tavistock.
Yalom, I. 1970 *Theory and Practice of Group Psychotherapy*, New York, Basic Books.
Yalom, I.D. 2007. *The Gift of Therapy*. Piatkus Books.
Zulliger, H. 1952. *Heilende Kräfte im Kindlichen Spiel*, Stuttgart. Klett.

INDEX